Red Blooded

The Alan Quinlan Story

Red Blooded

The Alan Quinlan Story

Alan Quinlan
with Kevin MacDermot

Irish Sports Publishing

Published by Irish Sports Publishing (ISP)
Ballybeg, Kells, Co Meath

First published 2010

Copyright © Alan Quinlan, 2010

The moral right of the author has been asserted.

A CIP record for this book is available from the British Library

ISBN 978-0-9563598-3-4

Printed in Ireland with Print Procedure Ltd
Layout and typesetting: Paul McElheron & Associates
Cover Design: Jessica Maile
Photographs: Inpho Sports Agency Ltd, and Alan Quinlan's personal collection

To Ruth and to AJ, our beautiful son,
thank you both for all your help and support.
To my Mum and Dad, for everything you have given me in life.
To my brothers, Andrew and John, and my sister, Carol,
for all your support and love throughout my life.
I love you all and appreciate everything you have done for me.

ACKNOWLEDGEMENTS

The last ten years have been an incredible journey and one in which I've been given a lot of help along the way.

I've dedicated this book to Ruth, my son, AJ, and to my Mum and Dad, brothers and sister, but that doesn't seem gratitude enough for all the support they have given over the years. So, once again, thank you.

To my friends who've been there for me in the good times and the bad: You know who you are and I will always be appreciative of how you followed me through thick and thin. Not only did you come and support me when I played but, in my darkest moments, you were able to put a smile on my face and help me look on the brighter side of life.

To my coaches and team-mates at both Clanwilliam and Shannon. Clanwilliam is where it all started for me and I owe much to its coaches, players and supporters.

I was lucky to play with a great club like Shannon which, along with Clan, helped mould me, from the raw youth that I was, into the kind of rugby player who might have a shot at breaking into the ranks of professional and International rugby.

To the extraordinary team-mates that I have played with down through the years, both in red and green jerseys: I've been incredibly lucky to have played with some of the greatest rugby players this country has ever produced. I could never have enjoyed such a long, or successful, career without having these men at my shoulder when I went into battle.

No acknowledgements would be complete without mention of the Munster fans. During the amazing Heineken Cup journey of the last decade, and more, the Red Army has been without equal. At home games they are worth an extra man while, away from home, they have outnumbered and out-sung the support of every other team in Europe. They never failed to lift us in a game and have borne the disappointments with the same grace and good nature that they enjoyed the victories.

I'd like to thank my agent, John Baker, who has worked with me now for eight years and who has helped me develop my career and been a good friend.

Thanks also to John Power, who has been such a help to me. At one of the lowest points in my life, when a lot of people doubted me, John dug deep and helped me fight to try and clear my name. I will always be indebted to him for his help.

Thanks to Paul O'Connell for writing the Foreword to this book. Paul has been an inspirational Captain to play alongside and a great friend: Enough said.

Thanks to everyone at Irish Sports Publishing for the hard work that they've put into this project and to Kevin MacDermot for working so closely and so professionally with me. We didn't know each other before this project began but we've spent many late nights in each other's company and I'd like to think that, in the last year, we've become friends as well as book collaborators.

My gratitude also to Dan Sheridan and everyone at Inpho Sports Photography. Dan has been a constant presence at our games and the Inpho pictures featured in my book capture perfectly the passion and joy of playing rugby.

Finally, I'd like to pay tribute to all those unsung heroes in clubs all over Ireland who volunteer their time, their money and their energy to help look after the next generation of young rugby players in this country.

They do an invaluable job, not just for the great sport of rugby, but also for this nation's youth. If it hadn't been for this special breed of sportsperson, the people who work quietly and without reward behind the scenes, I might never have made the transformation from wild, young Tipperary teenager into professional rugby player.

CONTENTS

Acknowledgements   vii

Foreword   xi

Chapter One   In the Beginning   1

Chapter Two   1997/1998 Season: Debut   12

Chapter Three   Up the Junction: Growing Up In Tipperary   19

Chapter Four   1998/1999 Season: The Hand of Claw   29

Chapter Five   The Axeman Cometh   37

Chapter Six   Marching On with Clan   44

Chapter Seven   1999/2000 Season: Never Say Die   51

Chapter Eight   Enter the Schoolteacher   60

Chapter Nine   2000/2001 Season: Axel's Pizza the Action   71

Chapter Ten   Shannon, Contracts and Money   79

Chapter Eleven   2001/2002 Season: End of an Era   88

Chapter Twelve   Rough and Fumble and Rucking Regrets   92

Chapter Thirteen   2002/2003 Season: Miracle Match   101

Chapter Fourteen   World Cup Glory and Pain   113

Chapter Fifteen   2004/2005 Season: Coming Back   126

Chapter Sixteen   Breakdown and Breakthrough   131

Chapter Seventeen   2006/2007 Season: Reality Bites   145

Chapter Eighteen   My Country's Call   150

Chapter Nineteen   2007/2008 Season: Back on Top   163

Chapter Twenty   The Lion King   178

Chapter Twenty-one   2008/2009 Season: In the Lion's Den   186

Chapter Twenty-two   In My Defence   197

Chapter Twenty-three   Battling My Demons   211

Chapter Twenty-four   2009/2010 Season: Regrouping   222

Chapter Twenty-five   2009/2010 Season: C'est la Vie!   228

Chapter Twenty-six   This Rugby Life   236

When I first arrived at Munster I, for some reason, drifted towards Quinny and, in those early days, he looked after me and advised me.

He was an easy guy to be drawn to. He had a raw, infectious personality which, for a young gun like me, was a joy to be around. You could full-on fight with him in training and have the most vicious verbal exchanges, before heading back into the dressing rooms where he would lay on a good half-hour of entertainment by slagging all before him and, in turn, being slagged back.

Every other week, after training, I'd have to apologise to him or he'd have to apologise to me. After we played away games, and particularly if we played well and won, Quinny would seize the plane, train or bus journey as an opportunity to step up to the microphone and entertain the rest of the lads.

He always looked after the guy who'd just had a bad game, who was struggling with injury or who was having a bad run of form.

He would take on anyone at fitness, to this day he still has an incredible engine, letting everyone know when he had won – and leaving you in fear of reprisal if he'd lost.

He trained hard, looked after his body and, on Saturdays, he would do everything necessary to win. He was dedicated to the point where some days he would be upset after games by the result or by how he had played. But his passion and fury for playing this great sport of ours were a mark of the man and they were qualities that I tried to emulate.

I have never played, known or seen anyone play rugby like Alan Quinlan. He is the life and soul of the dressing room but, when a match starts, the game takes over his life and soul.

For eighty minutes he will rage against everything in pursuit of a big performance and a victory. To play with him is to be in the presence of someone who treats every second of the game as a personal battle with all others around him.

The message is simple and direct: Opposing players had better not get in his way, refs had better not get in his way and, occasionally, his team-mates had better not get in his way.

He plays on the edge and for eighty minutes his mind is also on the edge. But this 'edge' is what makes Quinny special – when Alan Quinlan is on the edge, he's one of the best players I've ever had the pleasure of going into battle with.

Running onto a rugby pitch knowing Quinny is in your corner is a good feeling but, off the pitch, knowing he is your friend is a great feeling. He and I live near each other: We travel to training together, cook dinners for each other and, when I can get him out of the house, we sometimes have a drink together.

In rugby, Alan Quinlan is a force of nature but, outside of rugby, he is also my friend, a great guy who loves life.

Enjoy getting to know him.

Paul O'Connell
Autumn, 2010

CHAPTER 1

IN THE BEGINNING

Breathe. Remember to breathe.

Relax. Focus. Don't Stress.

It's ten in the morning. The day of the game. I know it, feel it, as soon as I wake. Everything's changed. The mood's different. The city is different. I'm different.

Everyone around me, ROG, The Bull, Marcus, Wally – everyone has their game face on. They know what today is all about. I know it too. There's a quietness about the place and everyone is serious. They're focused. But it's not fake – it all comes naturally to us at this stage of playing together. There's no need to talk it up. Everyone knows what it's all about. Everyone.

The match against Northampton starts this evening, so I'll get up for a while, have breakfast, go back to bed later on and rest up for a while. Relax. I need to relax.

That's my biggest challenge. It's what Gerry Hussey, my sports psychologist, has told me to achieve above all else – to relax. I need to breathe, let my mind float a bit. Not think about the game yet. I need to stop my mind winding the rest of me up.

That's the hard part. Overcoming your own mind. Being disciplined enough to tell your own mind – your emotions – not to drive the rest of you mad with thoughts of the game.

I can get nervous. I can get down. I can get angry. But they're weaknesses. They're my weaknesses and they've always been there. Now, though, I can get the better of them before they get the better of me. I've trained myself to be disciplined. I've been trained by others to be disciplined.

I'm thirty-five years old now. One of the veteran members of this Munster team and people – team-mates, management, fans – expect more from me. They want what they've always wanted: Ball-winning, ball-carrying, aggression, explosion. But they want more now. They want leadership, they want experience. They want me still on the pitch at the end of the game doing what I'm good at.

But greater expectation equals more pressure and more pressure equals more stress which requires more discipline to stay loose.

Breathe. Remember to breathe. Relax. Focus. Don't Stress.

It's all in the mind. Chill out and head back to the bedroom. ROG isn't there, he's off somewhere. The papers are there and I read about everything except today's match. No relaxing in that. Not interested in reading the book my wife Ruth bought me either. André Agassi's autobiography isn't grabbing my imagination today.

Better off with some music, so I stick on the iPod and listen to The Killers blasting their way through a few tracks. After that, I know I'd better take it down a notch or two – it's too early to get wound up. I always mix up my music depending on what kind of mood I'm in or, more importantly, what kind of mood I want to be in. What kind of build-up I want to the game.

But today it's Northampton and I don't need to build up to play against them. This is going to be monumental. I know it, the lads know it, the fans know it. If you need to build yourself up for a Heineken Cup quarter-final against Northampton, you're either comatose or dead. Either way, you're in trouble.

Maybe a bit of Van the Man or U2, and finally Take That and Westlife to take me through the afternoon.

Breathe. Relax. Focus. Don't Stress.

Remember what Gerry says. Stressing out is going to sap energy, it's going to take away my strength and I need to be strong against Northampton. I need to be stronger than ever.

My back is still sore, still tense, even with the Valium. I've been on Valium since last Tuesday when my back spasmed up. I didn't even know if I would make it for tonight's game.

Last Friday Leinster beat us. That bothered me, still does – you never like to lose to bloody Leinster. But they were up for it. They're physically tough now. Maybe as tough as us, maybe not. But they're mentally tough now as well, which they never were before. They're learning from us – have learned from us. Which is a compliment to us but it makes life harder, too. But, this evening, we have to move on.

I played well against them last week and after the game in the dressing room I spoke to the lads. The lads were down and I wanted to say something, so I reminded them it was only a League match and that we needed to keep our heads up. We could still salvage our season, starting with the next game – tonight's game – against Northampton.

This is the Heineken Cup. Our competition. It's always been like that and everyone knows it. The Magners League is important but if last Friday night Leinster had knocked us out of the Heineken Cup, instead of beating us in the League, then I'd still be sick to the stomach a week later.

But I'm not.

The back's still tense but nothing's going to stop me making the game tonight. When I went into the physio last Tuesday I felt great. He gave me a massage and started getting me set up for the week ahead. Within an hour, my back had spasmed – locked-up completely.

I was flat on my back on the floor for twenty-four hours, taking Valium. Believe me, spending hours lying on the floor is not a good way to relax. I spent the time fretting about the fact that next year's contract is still in negotiation and should have been signed off three months ago. Twelve hours worrying about my family – my wife and my son, AJ – my future, their future. Worrying about where we'll all be in a few months, worrying about the recession, the Heineken Cup, the game against Northampton, how I'll play... Stop! Shut up, Quinny! You're stressing out.

Breathe. Relax. Focus. Don't Stress.

Remember, Quinny, you're lying on a cold, hard floor getting your back sorted for the game against Northampton. Your back's going to be fine. Your contract's going to be fine. Your family's going to be fine. We're still in the Heineken Cup. We're going to beat Northampton. We'll all be where we're supposed to be. You'll play a blinder...

Nice stressing, Quinny. Beat that for preparation for tonight's game! If only Northampton knew – they'd be pressing every button they could to put me off my game. But they don't know, no one knows. No one can use that to put me off my game. Except one person. Me. I'm the only one that can do that. And I've done it before – lost the game before I even left the dressing room.

I beat myself, it's always been that way – me being my own worst enemy – until recently, that is. Now, at the end of my playing days, I'm beginning to relax more, beginning to enjoy playing rugby in a way that I haven't done since the beginning.

Breathe. Relax. Focus. Don't Stress.

Keep taking the Valium. Get on the bus to go to Thomond. I love the bus. That time in the team coach, it's precious. You can feel the build-up to the game beginning. I love driving to the games, driving through the crowds to the match.

I always sit in the same spot. Five seats back from the front on the left side. Marcus usually sits beside me, Hayes and Stringer always in front. I always sit at the window because I want to look out. I want to see. I want to see what's going on outside, to get a feel for what's happening outside our team bus: People walking to the game. Fathers walking to the game with their young kids – I want to see what it means to them. Seeing faces in the crowd that you know, faces that you don't know. I want to see what the whole thing – tonight's match, Thomond Park, Munster – means to people. To see the excitement in their faces and the support they have for us.

I want to hear them cheering the bus. To hear them cheering us. That's something special; to have people not just cheering for you as a team, but to have them cheering you personally.

That works its way into you. It works into me, into the lads.

I can feel the tension rising. It's time to tune in. Tune into the game.

I drift away, find happy feelings. I use these people's positivity to feed my own mental health. Make me stronger. Make me want to fight for them as well as for myself. That calms me down. When I'm like this then I find something relaxing on the iPod, maybe a bit more Westlife. When I'm calm like this, have a good feeling, then I want to stay in that good place. That's where I want to be tonight. On other nights I want to rev it up a bit, hear some up-tempo stuff. Throw on a bit of ACDC. But not tonight, not right now.

This is a Heineken Cup quarter-final and emotions and tensions are running at fever pitch. Later, there will be a moment when I decide to take it up a notch. But, right now, right here on the bus, I don't want to ratchet things up.

Breathe. Remember to breathe. Relax. Focus. Don't Stress.

An hour and fifteen minutes before kick-off we arrive at Thomond Park. I think ahead to my traditions. When we hit the ground, I always have the same ritual. I leave my bag down, have a glimpse at the programme. Then I go out and have a walk on the pitch with the other players.

Once out of the tunnel I pick up a blade of grass and I bless myself. Then it's down the left-hand side to the end of the ground to my usual spot. I go to the left because that's what I've always done. It started before, when I was superstitious. I'd like to sit in the same seat, have things the same way. Jesus. Before, if I didn't have my boots or the right boots, or the right gumshield, or the right bicycle shorts, it'd be a problem. It would have affected me. Why this? Why that? Losing energy. Wasting energy.

But now it doesn't matter what boots I have. I'm not so superstitious any more, not since I started working with Gerry Hussey. Now it's not the end of the world if somebody's sitting in the fifth row of the bus. I mean, is that really going to change the result or my performance if someone is sitting in my seat?

The answer is no. If I sit in the sixth row, I can still play well. So, I've changed my mindset. If I don't go down to the left-hand side of the pitch I can still play well, I can still do my job. Which is a good thing because it takes a lot of pressure off me.

I know now it's about my ability, and my ability doesn't change. I talk to myself now. Tell myself I'm a good player, that I can do this. Now I take things in my stride a little bit more. I take responsibility for myself, the responsibility for how I play isn't elsewhere. It has nothing to do with inanimate objects. It's down to me, and I understand that better now, in a way I never did before. But that comes with experience. It comes with relaxing a little bit more. I understand that and remind myself to breathe, relax, don't stress.

There, standing at the goalpost on the left at the bottom of Thomond Park, I begin my pre-match visualisation. I start thinking about the game, start visualising the things I have to do in the game. I think of happy things, of things going well. I think of myself with the ball in hand, making breaks, just running. Doing well. Tackling well. Doing the little things. Doing them well.

I lean against the post and look back up the ground. Look at the stage. I say a few prayers. A few Hail Mary's, an Our Father. Ask for things to go well, ask to win. But also be thankful for what I've got. Be thankful to God that I'm able to play in such a great stadium, for such a great people, for such a great jersey. Be thankful. This is a little thing, but it makes me happy.

Then I'm set. My piece done. Ready.

I pop back in to the dressing room, don't stay out too long on the pitch. I like to get ready early. Get on my bicycle shorts, get on my shin guards, get on my shorts.

Everything is left out for us. The jerseys are hanging there. The shorts and socks are left folded on the bench for us by our bag man, Jack Kiely. Everything is provided. We wear a different kit for the warm-up so, when we come back in, we take off the T-shirts. We pull on the jerseys before the final huddle.

The only thing that concerns me is that I like to be ready early, so I can get around and stretch and make sure I'm warmed up before we go out for the team warm-up.

I do my strapping. I strap my thumbs and my wrists for a bit of support. Put on my lineout tape. Stretch. Do my own warm-up. Sit down and listen to another song. Chill out. Relax.

There're still thirty minutes to the start of the game. Thirty minutes before we step out there as a team in front of 26,000 supporters, roaring for us, baying for them.

Jesus. I wouldn't like to play against us in Thomond Park. I don't know what our fans do to the opposition but they scare the hell out of me at times. There's no them and us out there. Just us. One big red family. Twenty-six thousand people scrummaging, rucking, sprinting, shouting, spitting, cursing. In victory. In defeat.

Here, underneath the stand, I like to be ready early, but so do a lot of the guys. People have their own routines – some people are sitting down, some people are stretching. As I move around, I do my own exercises and I talk to myself, give myself reminders of the job.

But it's gradual and people might talk in groups. I talk to the forwards, speak about how we need to defend well together and work hard. We need to front up to their pack. Their pack is physically strong and, the last time we met in a pool game, they caused us a lot of trouble.

Here in the dressing room, it's not about one person, it's about a team. People are preparing. The backs are chatting as they're getting ready. We warm up with cables and bands. Do shoulder exercises. I start warming myself up, go onto the floor and start stretching. There's a bike, but I don't want to cycle tonight.

So far, there hasn't been a lot of talk. That will come later, after we warm up together outside on the pitch. Then there'll be a lot of motivational talk. Who'll speak tonight?

ROG will speak, Donners, too, and Marcus. He's just back after a health scare, and played in last week's defeat to Leinster. It's been great to have him back in the team, where he belongs. I'll speak tonight – it gets me fired up. But, right now, we talk quietly to each other in small groups, backs and forwards. Just say things about the game: "Make sure we clean out our rucks properly".

"Remember that the team that we're playing today will come at us hard in the scrums. Make sure we get our scrum right."

"Remember that this is our job. Remember about the things we have to do."

"Remember, remember, remember."

We all come together before we go out for the warm-up. We huddle and tell each other to make sure we warm up well. We go out, we warm up and we come back in.

At that stage it begins. Shouting and roaring. Focus points. We start getting hyped up.

I have three or four minutes left. Then it's action time.

More shouting and roaring.

We pull on the jersey before the final huddle. It feels great to pull on this jersey. So much tradition, history and passion from before I ever arrived on the scene.

Pull on a Munster jersey and you know what it is to walk in the footsteps of giants. Every time I drag that jersey over my head, pride swells my chest and a little trepidation sneaks into my heart – don't let the side down. Tonight is no different. Honour the tradition. Do your best and, if that's not good enough, then do better than your best.

Huddle. In the huddle anyone can speak. The coach, Tony McGahan, spoke before we left the hotel, but that was it. After that it was team time. Tony spoke all week. As coach he provided us with the information we needed. He said one or two things when we arrived in the dressing room at the very start, but dressing room time is player time. He knows that.

That's always been Tony's way of doing things. He steps back. He might go around and talk to individuals and tell them to work on this or that. But he respects the leadership within the group. People outside don't know that – don't understand that. They expect a coach to be roaring and shouting. But it's not like that. There are lots of other guys who do that but not Tony.

Now, ROG speaks up and speaks well. Some lads don't speak at all because it's not part of their routine. But I speak because that's what gets me going, gets me fired up.

That's my thing. Some guys are quiet, don't say anything, they're relaxed. Everybody's different. Every player is different. I've learned that over the years. Just because I'm shouting and screeching and trying to get myself fired up doesn't mean the guy beside me isn't as fired up, just because he's sitting there, quiet as a mouse. You know he's fired up inside, firing on all cylinders.

And he'd better be because, in three minutes flat, he's going to be standing on a pitch in front of thousands of fans – theirs and ours – management, TV cameras, the opposition, his team-mates. If he's not firing on all cylinders, if he doesn't produce, then he'll be found out: He'll be screwed. So, inside that quiet, cool exterior, he'd better be firing on all pistons. We all need him just like he needs us.

I like to get fired up but I don't get as hyped as I used to. I never used to listen. I used to block things out. Before, there were so many things going on in my brain that if someone was making a valid point I'd have missed it. Now, I try to listen and that's a big thing for me.

Tonight Marcus is saying something about the scrums, that he wants his back row on early. His words go in now. I register it. This is what we gotta do. Do the basics well. We gotta defend well. We gotta implement the job we worked on during the week in training. The gameplan. We gotta put pressure on this guy, we gotta find the weak point of that guy.

We're firing the thing up. I like it. We have a bit of a squeeze and get ready to go out.

I love the build-up. I love the excitement. Even though I'm shitless as well half the time. I love that adrenaline rush. You think, "I'm going into the unknown here".

In eighty minutes' time, I could be sitting in the dressing room happy or unbelievably pissed off. The next eighty minutes will either mean the best few days lie ahead, or the worst few days ever.

You can't win week in, week out. I know that. I accept that. But there are pivotal games, Cup games that can affect your whole life. I know tonight will affect my whole life from this point onwards. Tonight will cast me as hero, villain, leader or fool. If tonight goes well, then I'm a hero for two weeks. If it goes badly, then I'm a villain for another year, or maybe forever.

There's massive pressure to perform and it will affect everything. My family, how I'm perceived, how I will behave, my mood swings, my future – everything. If we win tonight, then I'll feel great for the next few days – at least until the next game. But if we lose tonight, then I will be a nightmare to be around. I know, when we've lost games in the past, I've been a nightmare. I've tried to put everything into perspective over the years and not get too high, not get too low. But part of me loves the adrenaline rush of living by the sword and dying by the sword. Going into the unknown. It's a risk. Even though I might be in a great position every time I step out on to that grass, I know I'm playing another high stakes game. I'm risking my reputation, my physical and mental health, my emotions – risking everything.

But it's worth the gamble.

Everything is riding on this performance. People might think I'm crazy putting so much pressure on myself but it means so much to me that I'm willing to risk all of that frustration and disappointment.

But I can deal with it all better now.

To me rugby is a getaway. It's a different world. Once a game begins all the stresses and worries I have in life, just disappear. Evaporate. Being out on the field is natural to me. Muscle, sinew, brain – everything is bent to one purpose.

I know that tonight, if we're leading, I'll be hoping that the time will go quicker and there'll be a voice in my head screaming, "What's left? What's left?"

But, deep down, there'll be another, quietly guilty but unrepentant, voice praying this game doesn't end. Because it doesn't want the curtain to fall. I don't want it to end. I don't want the game to be over, the experience to end. This is what I love to do. I love being out there, being in that competitive arena. Warriors. Gladiators. Measuring yourself against another gladiator.

Even though it's been tough on me mentally and physically, I still love it. It's been a double-edged sword – wonderful but awful at the same time. For fourteen years I've been playing in high-pressure situations and the ups and the downs, the pressure, the good and the bad – all have an affect on you.

"Munster! Munster! Munster!"

"Munster! Munster! Munster!"

"Munster! Munster! Munster!"

The crowd brings me back. The red jersey is on. I breathe in through my nose, hold it, release. Chest in, chest out, chest in, chest out.

Breathe. Relax. Focus. Don't Stress.

Breathe. Remember to breathe.

Now, it's time. It's time to do it.

I always go out last. Most people know that. But if somebody wants to go out last it won't bother me. I say "fine". It's not as though it's going to change the result of the game. Before it would have worried me, panicked me. But not now.

Running up the tunnel, I don't see people, I don't see faces, I don't see anything. It's all a blur, really. I just hear. I feel.

On the pitch, I hear the noise, the crowd.

"Munster! Munster! Munster!"

"Munster! Munster! Munster!"

"Munster! Munster! Munster!"

Northampton are here. More cheering, but I don't see any faces. I don't see anything. Even Northampton are a blur.

I'm in my own zone. I'm... I'm exactly where I'm supposed to be.

CHAPTER 2

**September 7, 1997
Heineken Cup Pool Game
v Harlequins (The Stoop)
Lost: 40-48**

Let me ask you this: Is there a better way to start your Heineken Cup career than lining out in an away game, against one of England's top sides, with players like Gallimh and Claw at your side?

There is not.

At least, not in Munster. There's only one way to begin playing professional rugby for Munster – thrown in at the deep end and left to sink or swim. Men like Mick Galwey and Peter Clohessy will help you, put their arm around you, but, in the end, it comes down to you.

Munster is not somewhere for the faint-hearted or the uncertain of purpose. When you pull on that red jersey and step out on to the green blades, you'd better know what you're at, because in a few minutes' time you'll be under the scrutiny of proud, veteran Munster supporters who will throw a knowing eye over your form.

But at least your fans are on your side. Before they get a chance to size you up, the opposition will have already passed judgement on you. Today, before Harelquins ever left the dressing room marked 'Home', they had identified me and the other debutantes as fledglings who must be crushed before they have a chance to fly the nest. You have only minutes to stake your claim because, in Munster, there are few second chances.

As I walked out to face 'Quins at The Stoop for my Heineken Cup debut, wearing the No. 6 shirt, my chest swollen with pride and my hands trembling with nerves, it struck me for the first time that this was what it was like to be part of a starting Munster Heineken Cup fifteen. This was where I had always wanted to be, where I was meant to be.

I was twenty-three years old and had sacrificed a lot to reach this point in my career, but the sacrifices were not all my own. Lacing up my boots and stretching in those tense moments which exist between stripping off your top and waiting, bare-chested and shivering with cold and nerves, to be handed your match day jersey, I considered the years which had led me to this point.

I thought of the games of rough and tumble rugby that I had played in the fields and lanes of my father's farm and my uncles' farms; of the Sunday afternoon games in which my brothers – John and Andrew – and I, made countless tackles on my cousin, Ian, and other friends and neighbours. My sister, Carol, who wasn't averse to playing a bit of football herself, would get stuck in as my Mum, Mary, watched.

I thought of the countless times Mum had driven me to Clanwilliam matches and training, of the volunteers and coaches who had turned out in the rain and the muck of rural Tipperary to try and mould wild young lads like me into something worthwhile.

They had all watched me develop from a headstrong, mindless youth into a player with something called potential.

The talent was mine, but the vision was theirs: The triumph, this red-shirted debut of mine in the Heineken Cup, belonged to us all – this was their day, their moment, as much as it was mine.

Thank you.

● ● ● ● ● ● ●

My first season with Munster was a tough one. We'd gone on a pre-season tour to Scotland and it was clear I'd a lot to learn about being a professional rugby player.

I'd only signed my first Munster contract about six weeks earlier, a part-time contract that was worth about IR£7,500, with match fees on top. Having worked as a mechanic, it was a dream come true to be paid to play rugby, particularly for a team like Munster which had such a huge tradition.

So, there I was, living the dream, playing professional rugby and not having to work for a living, or so I thought. Things were happening pretty quickly for me, and I was hugely excited, but I had no real understanding of what was expected of me or what I should be doing.

My first provincial cap came in November 1996 against Western Samoa in Musgrave Park, and that same season I'd lined out for the 'A' team and done reasonably well, but still I hadn't made the inter-provincial team. Munster had started well in the inter-provincials that year, beating both Connacht and Leinster, but then lost 12-22 to Ulster at Ravenhill in a game in which I came off the bench to play.

But, suddenly, I was thrown a starting place against Harlequins for the opening Heineken Cup game of the season at their famed ground, The Stoop.

We were still searching for our first European win on the road, and the new coaching team of Deccie Kidney and Niall O'Donovan decided to make a few changes.

Axel was dropped in favour of Greg Tuohy so the starting back row was Eddie Halvey at No. 7, Greg Tuohy at No. 8 and myself at No. 6. Greg was playing well but it was still a shock to see somebody like Anthony Foley being dropped. He'd been playing for Munster for a while by that stage and had a big reputation.

Being selected to play was a huge honour for me and for the other Heineken Cup debutantes that day – Rhys Ellison (a Kiwi and Munster's first, ever overseas signing) and a young out-half, by the name of Ronan O'Gara, were picking up their first starts as well.

There was also a local connection for me because another Clanwilliam lad was lining out for Munster for the first time. Johnny Lacey was one of my best friends – we'd grown up together in Tipperary and soldiered together through years of underage rugby with the Clan. After a brief detour, via Sunday's Well, Johnny had joined me at Shannon and now, here we were, shoulder to shoulder with the three crowns on our chest. The fact that another Tipperary lad, Conor Burke from Clonmel, was lining up beside us made it that bit more special – three tools from Tipperary lining out for Munster in a Heineken Cup match. It was an immense moment for us and for the clubs we came from. Our parents and quite a few people from Tipp had crossed the Irish Sea to support us.

We were bursting with pride to be lining out alongside the Claw and Gallimh – who was captain on the day and one of Munster's most inspirational leaders ever. The presence of players like Claw and Gallimh gave us all confidence that we'd be looked after in our first Heineken Cup game.

The fact we were underdogs was something that Munster thrived on but, at the same time, we were up against a side that contained a lot of household names. Munster and Ireland's very own Keith Wood was Harlequins' captain, alongside French players like Laurent Cabannes, Thierry Lacroix and the English Internationals, Will Carling and Jason Leonard.

Harlequins had an incredibly strong line-up and suddenly, here I was, in the mix for a European game and expected to compete against International legends.

I was part of a rash of red-shirted, raw recruits which signalled a new beginning for the team but only a handful of fans accompanied us to The Stoop to face Harlequins in a game in which no one really fancied us.

We were only starting out as a professional team and we were up against a giant club in Harlequins. Even Deccie Kidney and Naill O'Donovan were learning the professional ropes.

We certainly went into the game with a lot of passion, but there was a fear factor amongst us and, deep down, we didn't really believe we could win it. Of course we wanted to but, in our heart of hearts, we didn't really expect to upset the odds.

We flew out to London two days before the game and I was rooming with Eddie Halvey. The night before the game, the Claw came into our room for a bit of a chat. He decided he wanted to order a Bacardi and Coke to our room and I suddenly found myself under pressure to join in. I thought this was the done thing, so I started ordering some Bacardi and Cokes as well. A few became a lot and we ended up not going to bed until about three in the morning.

It wasn't the best preparation for my first game with Munster, we had a desperate opening twenty minutes, after which we found ourselves seventeen points down. The biggest shock for me was the physicality of the Heineken Cup. In the opening few minutes, I was in awe of some of the hits that were going in.

Our Kiwi, Rhys Ellison, was renowned for his aggressive tackling. But Harlequins had a big Tongan guy in the centre by the name of Johnny Namu. A couple of minutes into the game, Johnny got the ball and started to carry but he only got a few yards when Rhys pole-axed him in a tackle, turned the ball over and won us a scrum. I stood there watching all this unfolding and thinking, "Jesus! I don't know if I can do that, don't know if I'm aggressive enough or tough enough for this".

But, tough as he was, Rhys didn't create the talking point of the game – that came after about thirty-five minutes when, just before half time, Gallimh thumped Woody.

Everyone knew Galwey and Woody were great friends, but Woody's an abrasive character on the pitch – a wonderful player but also a very tough opponent.

We had a lineout, which was followed by a maul. Gallimh was trying to clean Woody out of the maul but managed, somehow, to hit him across the face. I don't think Gallimh intended to hurt Woody, but he certainly swung his forearm with a lot of aggression. It was a sore thump, which dazed Woody and left him with a black eye. Woody left the field and wasn't too happy with what had happened. There was a bit of shock in everyone's faces that two guys who were such good friends, were going for each other. This was all new to me, this was a step up from what I knew from playing in the AIL (All Ireland League). Here were two guys, who were best of mates and who had lined out together many times in the cause of Ireland, going at it hammer and tongs, with Gallimh being super-aggressive. It was an eye-opener for me. I didn't think I'd hit one of my friends that hard – didn't think I could. But it epitomised what Gallimh was about, what playing for Munster meant to him. He hadn't come to London to lose, he'd come to win.

I've known Gallimh a long time and he was never a dirty, malicious player. He was tough and aggressive and honest and that's something to admire.

In the end, we lost by only eight points with the final scoreboard recounting a score-line of 40-48, and indicating a trio of tries scored by three tools from Tipperary, Messrs Lacey, Burke and Quinlan. Mine came after a ruck in the middle of the field. Brian O'Meara made a little break off the side of the ruck and popped the ball to me. I made a clean line break, got through on the Harlequins full-back and threw him a dummy, which he duly bought, and I cantered home.

It was a moment to savour on my first outing for Munster, running half the length of the field to score a try under the posts. To score a try in such a massive match gave me huge confidence, made me believe that I could compete at that level.

I was under no illusion about how much I needed to improve my own game, but scoring against Harlequins was solid evidence that I was good enough, it was proof that I belonged. It was going to be a steep learning curve but this was a great introduction to top-flight rugby.

Most importantly, it was a good result for Munster. Sure, we'd lost, but we'd put down a marker for ourselves and for the rest of the competition. The signs were there that, with a lot of hard work, improvement and some maturing, we could transform ourselves into a unit that could perform at this level.

We were happy that we'd been able to compete and relieved we hadn't been annihilated. Deccie and Niall weren't as happy but, for young players like us, coming close against Harlequins and challenging them gave us confidence and a belief in our own ability.

We'd been twenty points down early in the match and under huge pressure. We could've cracked and been walloped, but instead we'd come within a score or two of beating them. We learned from that performance, and as the season went on we got better and mentally tougher.

Post-game, we stayed over and went out on the lash and got home bleary eyed. That was the norm back then, it was part and parcel of the game. In the years ahead, things would change as we strove for professional perfection but, back then, no one was overly worried about how long it would take a player to recover from a night on the booze. Back then, it didn't take a fizz out of us anyway because we were young and excited. We'd just played one of the big English teams in London in the Heineken Cup and we'd avoided getting trounced.

I'd made my debut for Munster and scored a try. The craic was mighty and the 'Tools from Tipperary' were doing well.

The next few games were a mixed bag. We lost 23-43 in Cardiff and beat Bourgoin 17-15 at Thomond Park, but lost the return fixtures against both Cardiff (32-37 in Musgrave Park) and Bourgoin (6-21 in Stade Pierre Rajon).

We finished the season with a stirring win over Harlequins in the return game at Thomond Park. The Englishmen had come to Limerick with a lot of bought-in talent and a determination to bury us. Their owners had spent a lot of money and expected major success. But, on the night, we beat them 23-16 and deprived them of a home tie in the Heineken Cup quarter-finals. After the game, they disappeared into their dressing room and didn't reappear. They subsequently took severe criticism for not delivering a money-spinning home draw. It was a reminder of the harsh nature of professional rugby – success was demanded from players who were being paid high wages.

For Munster, there was the disappointment that we hadn't qualified for the quarter-finals, but there was huge satisfaction that a team of home-grown players, plus one Kiwi blow-in, had put a team of highly paid International superstars to the sword.

On top of that, Axel, Eddie Halvey and I were beginning to mould into a decent back row unit, and Ronan O'Gara, Johnny Lacey, Rhys Ellison and John Kelly had all made a case for their inclusion.

We had a long way to go, but we were beginning to blend together into a single unit. We still had a lot to learn about being professional rugby players, and about how to build a successful set-up, but by the end of the 1997-1998 season we'd already begun to take our first tentative steps towards that goal.

Personally, things were great. I was a professional rugby player. Was there anything better?

In 1983 there was a group of us that played Russian roulette.

I was only nine at the time so there were no guns or bullets involved, just a bunch of kids on bikes, a railway platform and a frustrated and angry station master. The rules were always the same: About five of us would cycle at speed along the platform, past the stationmaster's office and in full view of the man in uniform.

It was a very long platform and perfect for racing bikes, so we'd tear along at breakneck speed, laughing and roaring, having the time of our lives. And, just in case he didn't see us or hear us laughing, we made sure we gave a good roar as we went past his office. When we hit the end of the platform, there was only one way to go, and it wasn't along the railway track. We had to turn around and exit the way we had come, which meant we had to run the gauntlet of the station master who, by now, was out of his office eyeing up the cycling hooligans and slowly weighing up the weakest link, whom he fully intended to collar.

He wasn't overly fond of the Quinlan boys or our friends, and you couldn't really blame him. It's the task of every young boy to climb every tree, wade every stream and throw every stone but, when you live right beside a railway station, the rules change.

It became our honour-bound duty to explore every parked train, climb onto every roof, walk along every train track and break into every warehouse we came across. We'd climb onto the roof of this man's station, push carts up and down the track and try to get into the trains and engines so we could drive them. We used to torture him; we'd ride down there, torment him, leave and then be back an hour later to play the same trick over again. It was fun for us as young boys but he must have been driven mad.

Every so often, things boiled down to this very personal game of

Russian roulette – five or six of us, aged between seven and twelve years old, lined up across the platform riding early versions of the mountain bikes that were all the rage back then. At the other end of the platform stood the stationmaster, clutching his sweeping brush, just waiting.

A Mexican standoff at Limerick Junction.

He couldn't possibly get all of us – we knew it and so did he – but, if he was quick, he would catch one and that would be enough. So he studied us, weighing up who among us was easy meat, who would be most easily knocked off their bike. He could deliver quite a punch with that brush – I knew from first-hand experience.

So, we'd charge and he'd brace himself for the impact. If he managed to bring one of us down, then the others would have to circle back to rescue their fallen comrade. We'd all jump off our bikes and start pulling his coat to distract him allowing us all to escape.

We had a great time growing up in Limerick Junction. I don't think we ever did anything too bad, but we were constantly dreaming up new ways to doss off chores and inject a bit of excitement into our lives.

• • • • • • •

I was born on July 13, 1974, the third of four children born to John and Mary Quinlan. I've two older brothers – Andrew is the eldest at thirty-nine and John's thirty-eight – next came me, followed by my younger sister, Carol, who's thirty-five. I was always small and skinny: John and Andrew were a bit bigger and tougher, so I leaned on my brothers a lot for protection. We always looked out for each other as we grew up, which was fine for us lads, but I think we made our sister Carol's life miserable. Having three older brothers was tough for her, as we probably scared off every boy that was interested in her. Sorry, Carol.

Our family home had been my Dad's family home as well – my grandfather had bought the farmhouse and the attached land near Limerick Junction back in the 1950s. It wasn't a very big farm, about fifty-five acres, but it was an old creamery so, along with the farmhouse, there were massive sheds for us young boys to explore.

My grandfather was named John but everyone called him Jack: He was a cattle dealer and a fairly successful entrepreneur back in the '40s and '50s. He died when he was quite young, around fifty-four, and left a lot of land – including our farm and those belonging to my uncles, Patsy, Andy and Philly – behind him. That was a pretty impressive achievement back then so I suppose he must have been ambitious. My Dad, who worked long hours as a diary farmer, always reckoned that if the old man hadn't died so young, he'd have amassed a huge quantity of land in the area because he was very driven. But, Jack died of cancer long before I came along and left a huge void in everyone's lives. I've always regretted not meeting him.

With Jack's death, my grandmother, Josephine, was left with twelve children to rear – six sons and six daughters. Some of the older children had already moved out, but it was a harsh life to lead without a husband – it was a hard life for the kids, too, including my Dad.

My grandmother was a tough lady but, I suppose, any woman able to bring up twelve kids on her own in those days had to be resilient. She had to run a farm, milk the cows and pretty much do everything herself, with only her children to help out.

When my Mum and Dad married and moved into the home farm, my uncle, who lived just up the road, built a little house beside their place for my grandmother. So, she spent a lot of time with us and I can remember, throughout my youth, walking her up and down the road, dropping her back to her house.

As kids, we lived in terror of her. We'd hear her coming down the passageway, her walking stick beating out a steady tattoo as she approached and we'd scatter to the four winds. We'd always be up to our necks in some kind of mischief – playing football, breaking windows, wrecking stuff – so there was always some reason for her to be mad at us, and for us to be scared of her. It was probably the natural order of things for a lot of kids the country over.

• • • • • • •

As children, we split our time between the fields around Limerick Junction and the streets of Tipperary town. A lot of our friends lived in the town and that was where we played rugby, hurling, football and soccer. It was always a big deal for us to spend time there: We were country kids intrigued by town life and it was great to have friends to show us around. We had the best of both worlds, really – the freedom of the countryside to roam at will and then the fun and excitement of the town.

Tipp town was also a great bolt-hole to escape the many chores my Dad liked to give us. When you're young, weeding and picking spuds can only hold your attention for so long before you start thinking there must be more to life! The close proximity of my uncles' farms meant that my Dad and his brothers were regularly helping each other out and that usually meant the younger Quinlans had to help as well. Silage wasn't so bad but we all dreaded the hay season and having to pike the hay bales. It was too much like hard work.

But, on Sunday afternoons, we would invite the neighbours round for a big game of rugby out on the front field. The resulting game would ensure that my Mum would spend her Sunday evenings scrubbing the muck of the front field from us, before making us knuckle down and tackle our homework. Nearly every weekend was like that when I was small.

In some ways, we were probably different from other siblings in that we weren't best friends. There was no real competition between us and Andrew and I would have played a lot of hurling together, hitting the ball up and down the field for hours on end, but we just didn't hang around with each other or sit down and chat to each other. We were all fairly independent – we all had our own friends, had our own interests and we did our own thing. But that didn't mean we weren't close, there was always an unwritten rule that we'd be there for each other if one of us needed help.

That rule hasn't changed much down through the years. My family – my brothers, my sister – they've always been there for me when I needed them, and I've tried to be there for them as well. I don't know if I've always lived up to their expectations, or my own, but I've certainly tried to be a good brother.

In those early years, that commitment to each other was always in demand because we got into lots of scrapes and scraps, trying to measure ourselves against the other young clans and gangs around Tipperary.

Not that Tipperary was a tough spot to grow up in – our battles were just part of a normal childhood, really. In some ways, it was a little bit like the Westerns we loved to watch – the cowboys were in the town which, I suppose, meant that us culchies were the Indians.

Our parents always warned us not to mess with the cowboys but there wasn't much chance of us heeding them. Banning us from Tipperary town was like telling Adam to behave himself in the Garden of Eden. Forbidden fruit tastes all the sweeter…

And, when our parents would go out on a Friday night, the easiest way for the Quinlans to access forbidden fruit was to fire up the family tractor and head on into the saloon – or, in our case, the chipper. By the time my parents were ready to leave the house, we'd all be curled up in front of a good fire with a video and my oldest brother, Andrew, would be designated as babysitter. Convinced their kids were settled for the night, my parents would leave by the front door, just about the same time as their saintly children were piling out the back door.

We'd get the key to Dad's tractor and hit the road. Between us kids and our friends there could have been up to six of us hanging off the tractor en route to Tipperary town, we'd reach there by around 10pm. I was probably twelve or thirteen years old at the time and my brother John would drive. At the weekends, we'd often have friends and neighbours, like Niall Crowe and Andrew Corcoran, out to our place for sleepovers. Sometimes, we'd have a friend, like Pakie Roche from Tipp town, who'd stay with us for two or three months at a time. They'd bring their school uniforms with them and just stay because they loved being out in the countryside with us. And why wouldn't they, with the freedom we had to do things like head into Tipperary town on a tractor on a Friday night?

We'd all trundle in, park up the tractor at the rugby club, head down to the chipper for something to eat and go for a walk around town. It was the wrong thing to do and we all knew it at the time, but that's what made it exciting. Luckily enough, we never had any accidents or incidents that came back to haunt my parents, or haunt us. After a while, my Mum figured out that all was not as it seemed, that her little angels tucked up in front of a cosy fire, weren't little angels after all. With my brother in charge, my Mum's biggest worry should have been us fighting over what was on the TV – little did she know. Not that Andrew wasn't mature enough to be left in charge of us: He was quiet and solid and dependable, but he also liked to have a bit of fun.

My other brother, John, was also very responsible when it came to looking after younger members of the family, but his forte was animals, not siblings. Growing up, he was always into looking after animals and he'd always have had a horse or some sort of beast on the go, which was a laugh for the rest of us.

He went from pigs to guinea pigs, from to dogs to cats, from a donkey to a horse, from goats to sheep – or maybe rabbits, for a change. My father's typical refrain was, "Oh Lord, what's he going to bring home this time?"

He'd save his money, go to the pet shop and get something new. Or he'd buy a few calves or sheep, just to have something of his own. He got a horse once and bought a cart and all the tack: He got the horse shod and within a day we were all sitting in the back of his cart, heading for Tipperary town two miles away where we tied up at the rugby club and headed off down the town.

I remember, once, he had a donkey that we all loved. We kept him in a field between our house and the railway track and we were always out with him, feeding him, riding him, playing with him. But, one morning when we went out, the donkey was missing. We looked everywhere but he was nowhere to be seen. I was around seven years old at the time and was heartbroken – we all were. Eventually, after walking up and down the track for miles in both directions, we found him: He'd been hit by a train. It was a tragedy for all of us because we doted on him, but that was part and parcel of a country childhood. You had to take the good with the bad.

As well as the railway line, we lived near the Limerick Junction racetrack – as it was known back then – and we made the most of the place when it was abandoned on non-race days. Slipping out of our beds, we could be there within minutes, galloping, without horses, round the track. Or, at twelve o'clock in the dead of night, we might be up in the announcer's office with his microphone, commentating on imaginary races or directing race marshals to their places.

Maybe we had too much freedom, but my Mother and Father both worked very hard and as long as we were happy, they were happy. For me, my childhood was one of great freedom, great fun. It was a fantastic way to grow up.

• • • • • • •

I suppose if I have a regret from that time of my life, it's that I didn't apply myself at school. We went to school in Tipperary because my Mum worked there – she was a head chef for the South Eastern Health Board. She drove us everywhere and, as she had to arrive at her job by 9am, it made sense for us to go to school there, rather than closer to home.

So, I attended Monastery CBS before moving on to Abbey CBS which was a hurling and football school. I know that a lot of lads who went to Christian Brothers Schools didn't enjoy their time but my school years were happy ones: There were no beatings, there was no physical abuse or any real aggression.

In John and Andrew's time at Abbey CBS, there was one Brother whose office the lads tried to avoid because going there meant you could expect a couple of clatters from his strap. But, by the time I got there, we were lucky enough to have a decent group of teachers. Even the principal, Michael Ryan, turned out to be a great guy, despite his numerous, and sometimes hilarious, attempts at disciplining me.

On one occasion, a gang of us were called into Michael's office for messing around. He lined us up and read the riot act – we were this and we were that, no good, wasters, the usual kind of thing. Unfortunately, he was delivering his judgement on us from behind his desk, improving his vantage point by tilting back and forwards on his chair. As his pronouncement on our general worthlessness reached a crescendo he attempted one tilt too far and, instead of censuring his five errant pupils, he condemned himself to a thunderous fall from power.

Even as the chair and its occupant crashed to the floor, Michael was bouncing upwards again, screaming harder than ever at us. But in his embarrassed anger he ordered us "Out! Out! Out!" and forgot to administer a sentence, so we escaped scot-free.

A true gent, Michael turned out to be a great mentor of mine and, to this day, I get great pleasure out of the letters about life and rugby he writes to me. He never fails to encourage and inspire me in the low points of my career, and he never fails to try to take credit for the successes which he claims are a direct result of the discipline he instilled in me in my time at Abbey CBS.

For my part, I try not to tilt my chair while reading his letters...

Nicky English, the Tipperary hurler, also taught at the school. He was an idol of mine and went on to become a great friend. At one point, I did a coal round with him a couple of evenings a week. His Dad had a hardware store and Nicky would do the coal run for him after school, and I would help.

As a teacher, though, English was fairly strict and he caught me out badly on one occasion. At school, a few of us would sneak off on the sly to puff a few fags. It'd be during lunch or tea break and we'd always have lads watching out. But, one day, as we were puffing in the toilets, word reached us that Nicky was on his rounds. We were looking out for him, but he came by a different route than we were expecting and he caught us on the hop. At the very last second, I took the last pull of a fag in one of the toilet cubicles and then threw it away. When Nicky arrived in the toilets, he asked me if I had been smoking: I shook my head, No, whereupon he hit me straight in the chest and a great puff of smoke appeared before him. He still gets a great kick out of letting everybody know about the day he rumbled Alan Quinlan smoking in the boys' toilets of the CBS.

So, school and the teachers were fine, and I knocked about with a great bunch of friends, guys like Eoin Bresnan, Thomas Martin and Paul Slater. But I have regrets about my time there, though those regrets are all down to myself. I failed to apply myself properly. If I'd shown the same discipline or hunger at school that I showed in rugby, then things might have turned out very differently for me and, if I had my time over again, it's the one major change that I'd make. When my own son, AJ, goes to school, I'll sit him down and try to make him understand how important it is. I'll make him understand that, when you have to work you work – play comes later. Instead of knuckling down and getting stuck into the books, I spent my time waiting for the bell to ring, so I could roar outside and play football, or hurling, or soccer in the school yard. I did okay in the end and just about got through my Leaving Cert, but I was in a hurry to leave and turned a deaf ear to the advice of my teachers that I'd regret not making enough of an academic effort. It would only be in later life that I'd come to appreciate how right they were.

My brothers were off doing their own thing, too. Andrew went to college and travelled a bit, while John started a trade, making fitted kitchens. Carol, was the only one of the Quinlans who applied herself at school.

My lack of academic prowess is not something that I wake up in the middle of the night sweating and screaming over, but I do think about it. Looking back it seems a strange time. After all the good times at school, suddenly the party was over – my mates were going to college but I wasn't. I was hugely determined to get some sort of qualifications: Although I was only sixteen years old, it was time to take a bit of responsibility and start thinking about what I was going to do.

I left school on a Friday and started working for Gerry and Arthur Pierce, in Pierce Motors in Tipperary Town, the following Monday. A few months before, I had gone to Gerry, who was a family friend, and asked him for a Saturday job in his garage. He turned me down, said he already had a youngster who cleaned the cars for him on a Saturday. So, I offered to do anything, even clean up the place for free – anything to get my foot in the door. I think he was taken aback: Here was a kid looking for a break and who was willing to work for nothing. I think it struck a chord with him and, as I walked away dejectedly, he called me back and asked me to come in the following Saturday saying he'd find something for me. After a few months of working Saturdays and showing good initiative, I asked him for an apprenticeship and he told me I could start after I finished school.

I had a good work ethic and never had problems applying myself outside of the classroom, which is something I got from my parents. My Mum began working in hotels after leaving school at the age of eleven or twelve, and my Dad had always worked full-time on the farm.

So, while we all had a normal child's desire to avoid chores, and my folks had to shout to get us out of bed, we also had this huge example of what life was really about, right on our doorstep. The result was that, from a young age, I was motivated and I always had summer jobs.

But, looking back on it now, from around the age of twelve or thirteen I think I made the wrong choices, put myself under too much pressure in some ways and not enough in others. I seemed to do everything the wrong way round. When I should have been working in school I was either messing around or working in part-time jobs. And when I was working outside of school, I should have been playing.

I loved the freedom of playing where I grew up but suddenly, in my early teens, I went from that to, "I have to start earning my money".

No one made me do it. Something in myself, in my own mind, drove me on and now I wish I hadn't rushed into growing up so quickly. I spent a lot of summers earning money that I never even spent. I don't know how I got everything so jumbled up – I think there may have been a bit of me that was already feeling guilty that I wasn't doing well enough at school. So, instead of studying, instead of going to school, instead of doing my homework, I went looking for work.

That decision has had a massive impact on my life. Ever since then, and particularly in my career as a professional rugby player, I've kept my head down, followed orders and concentrated on working, working, working. This need to work, to earn money, has been like a pressure cooker all my life: It's made me stress and worry.

I had great times growing up and I had great times in my rugby career, but I've faced a life-long battle to limit the negative effects of those pressures and anxieties. It's only now, towards the end of my playing days, that I've found a way to do that.

CHAPTER 4

October 10, 1998
Heineken Cup Pool Game
v Perpignan (Stade Aimé Giral)
Lost: 24-41

Pictures and posters of rugby players, flags everywhere. I remember thinking, "This is new. This is different," as we settled into the town of Perpignan back in 1998. "Here we are in a city that takes it rugby seriously. This is cool."

Back then, I still figured rugby was one of the world's more civilised sports, and that its fans were reasonable people. Passionate, yes, but also reasonable.

Just twenty minutes of a survival lesson in the cauldron of Stade Aimé Giral left me under no illusion that rugby in the South of France is unlike rugby anywhere else. It's not civilised, it's bordering on barbaric.

Within twenty minutes of my first appearance against Perpignan, I'd been sworn at, threatened by players and fans, driven back ten yards by two juggernauts in rugby jerseys and dumped on my backside on a bone-hard pitch within touching distance of the Pyrenees.

Welcome to picturesque, painful Perpignan.

It had all started so well! We were coming off the back of a couple of good pool wins against Padova (20-13) and then Neath (34-10) in Thomond Park. We'd been slow out of the blocks, with the Padova coach Vittorio Munari even predicting we'd find it tough to get out of our pool but, heading to Perpignan, we were confident that we were building a nice momentum. We expected a tough game but we also hoped to come away with a win and the points.

This part of the South of France was an unknown quantity for me. The previous season we'd been beaten by Bourgoin away in the pool stages and, while that was a gruelling experience, it hadn't prepared me for a visit to Perpignan.

We travelled down two days before by plane and bus and the whole journey felt like a bit of a road trip. The lads were in great form and the craic was good. Our hotel was right on the beach, a really small, typical three-star French affair. The rooms and the beds were tiny, but we were delighted to be there.

In the lead up to the game, we chilled out, went for a run-out in the stadium the day before the match, and then went back to the hotel for some food.

The first sense that something was not quite right came when we got to the stadium and saw the big wire fence around the pitch. Then, on match day, the full glory of the Perpignan fans was unveiled. The supporters behind the big wire fence were shouting and cheering, bands were playing and hooters going.

It was a carnival atmosphere and sounded fantastic and I was impressed. I was impressed by how much the sport meant to the fans. But only when we appeared out of the tunnel did it dawn on me that this was going to be unlike anything I'd ever experienced before.

They kept chanting, singing and playing their instruments alright but, as soon as they set eyes on us, they went into hyper-drive. They booed us on to the pitch, jeered us as we warmed up and generally did a good job of intimidating us. They weren't throwing stuff but they didn't seem too far off it – I don't think they stopped hurling abuse at us long enough to think about hurling anything else.

The Bourgoin fans of the previous year had been fierce and passionate in support of their team, but this was something else. Whereas the match against Bourgoin had been calm beforehand and got noisy as play progressed, the Perpignan fans looked as though they'd been there all night, waiting for us, and sharpening their knives. To them, the identity of the opposition was irrelevant. Everyone got the same abuse. It was high-octane stuff. Crazy. Visceral. We felt a bit like gladiators hired by the Romans to get slaughtered in the Coliseum for the amusement of the mob.

I thought rugby was a game in which away teams were appreciated for travelling and in which they'd be applauded onto the field of play. In Perpignan that day, I felt as though we'd been lucky to make it onto the pitch in one piece.

We didn't know much about their team, though Raphael Ibanez, the French hooker, was their captain. We also knew they'd have a strong scrum because we'd done our analysis on the team in their previous Heineken Cup games that season, and they looked strong and formidable. But French teams are different at home. They defend as though you're an invading horde who will pillage and plunder the city if they let you defeat them in rugby.

In fairness we didn't start too badly but, within a short while, we were getting blitzed off the field.

At one point, after about twenty minutes, we got a lineout on their 22. We were going to use a well-practised move from the same position, which had come good for us before: Basically, we'd throw the ball to the No. 4 and the No. 4 jumper would pop it down to No. 2. Then I'd run around the front, take the ball off the No. 2, hopefully find myself in a bit of space along the poorly-defended and surprised French touch line, and make a break. It was a good move, and I was confident that it'd work and we could rock them back on their heels.

Anyway, Mark McDermott was the hooker and he was supposed to throw the ball at Mick O'Driscoll who would pop it down to Gallimh, who would wait for me to come round the front before releasing it to me on the charge. Then, up the touchline and over for a try. Sweet.

Trouble was, the noise in the stadium was so loud we couldn't hear the lineout calls. We had a code for different calls but no one could hear which code Gallimh was shouting. A couple of us asked him again for the code and, next thing, Gallimh abandons the code and just shouts, "Four down to two with Quinny around the front".

"This is lights out for me," I'm thinking because, even as I'm thundering around the lads and heading for the hand-off at the front of the lineout, Perpignan's big English-speaking Canadian, who is second from the front of their lineout, is translating Gallimh's every word into perfect

French for his team-mates.

I knew that by the time I got round to the front and began my charge they'd be waiting for me. I could hear the Canadian giving his lads the heads-up. They had so much warning they could have sat down for cheese and sausage, a little wine and some good conversation, and still been ready for me.

I knew I was going to get it, but what could I do? I was committed.

So, the ball is thrown in. It pops down to the front and then pops to me. And, bang! I run straight into two grinning Frenchmen who drive me back ten yards and fire me into touch. They dumped me so hard that I bounced off the ground. Thanks, Gallimh. That set the tone of the game, it was trench warfare – tough, angry, dirty.

They were destroying us in the scrum, pushing us off every time. John Hayes was in the very early days of his career as a tight-head prop and Claw had moved over to loose-head. Deccie had wanted to get The Bull into the team and Niall was trying to make a tight-head out of him but France is a hard place to learn about scrums. They love their scrums and take pride in strong scrummaging.

Every time we were down for a scrum in that first twenty minutes, we were pushed clean off our own ball. We were destroyed in those scrums. So, John got the shepherd's crook from the sideline after about twenty-five minutes. He duly went on to have an incredible career as Ireland's most capped International, but that doesn't save him from being slagged over his Perpignan torment. The Bull was replaced by Ian Murray while Claw went back over to tight-head, and the scrum steadied up a little.

We were still being destroyed everywhere on the pitch. Our defence was all over the place and our set pieces were being annihilated but, for all that, we were still making breaks, still scoring tries, still keeping in range of them.

As a team they were incredibly physical, aggressive and dirty. They were gouging and stamping, and spitting. It was cynical, dirty stuff, which I hadn't experienced before. They were taking great pleasure in welcoming us to the South of France. Our little three-star French hotel on the beach seemed a long way away.

At one point Deccie brought a very young Donncha O'Callaghan on after Mick O'Driscoll hurt his neck. Micko was also very young, but Donncha was about a year younger, maybe nineteen years old.

So, Deccie brought on Donncha for Micko in the second row, but he wound up taking him back off again after just twenty minutes and apologising to Donncha for putting him on in the first place. I think Deccie figured he'd made a mistake putting such a young player into that kind of a cauldron. Donncha was a great prospect, and has become a great player but, back then, I think Deccie just reckoned he wasn't ready for that level of abuse. He sent on David Corkery and moved Eddie Halvey to the second row.

At one point we scored a try and, as I jogged back to the half-way line with Gallimh and Claw, the crowd was banging at the fence and screaming abuse at us. Some Frenchman started to climb the fence and, though he was shouting at us in French, it was pretty clear that he wasn't wishing us well. But Claw isn't a man to be shouted at – he is one tough bastard and he didn't give a damn about any of them. He was an inspirational guy to be around and doubly so when he was with Gallimh – the pair of them were as thick as thieves.

Claw had had enough of the abuse so, he stopped, turned to the guy and flipped him the bird, in full view of a now-enraged crowd. Suddenly, there were ten guys climbing the fence, screaming at us. Claw just stood there, watching them, waiting for them, with Gallimh on one side and me on the other. He was roaring back at them, waving to them, telling them that they were brave men shouting at him from behind a fence and, if they wanted him, they could come and get him.

Gallimh was shouting at him, saying, "Calm down, Claw. You'll get us all killed".

But it didn't bother Claw. Nothing phases him or intimidates him, he isn't afraid of anybody.

I was thinking, "If anyone jumps the fence here, there are only three of us together on the touch-line. I'll have to get stuck in with the two of them but we'll all get killed: I'll get killed. Dead".

In the end, the ten Frenchmen thought better of it and stayed on their side of the fence. We cantered back and the game restarted. In those days, there would never have been an official investigation. It would have been viewed as a bit of hand waving between men.

But it was just one of those games. It was just crazy; really physical, borderline violent. We lost 24-41, but it could have been worse. We got the crap kicked out of us but we also had our eyes opened. Although we scored three tries we were soft in the tackle – missing loads – and we were bullied around the park. Back then, we weren't up to the aggressive levels that were required to go to South of France.

Within a week we had reviewed the video, identified the problem and pledged to ensure that it didn't happen again. No one was bitter about what had happened because France is a top place to play rugby, and Perpignan proved that to us.

• • • • • • •

The trip to Perpignan was important on another level: In the aftermath of the game, we forged a deeper bond as team-mates.

Following the game, we were deflated and dejected, bruised and battered. We'd been picked on, beaten up, spat on and bullied. We left the stadium and, as the coach took us to our meal, Deccie informed us that there would be no night out on the town, we would be leaving very early the next morning and would have our recovery in the sea: A quick dip first thing and then off to the airport.

My head was down and I assumed everyone was feeling as low as me: "That's fine with me, Deccie. Just get me away from here," I said. At times like that, it takes a special kind of man to turn the situation around. In Munster we've always been lucky to have leaders all over the field but, even in Munster, there are the special ones.

Claw is a special one.

Deccie had barely finished speaking, when Claw stood up, strode up the bus and grabbed the microphone. "We're all going on the piss, as soon as we get back to the hotel."

Jaws dropped in amazement, Deccie's too, but what the Claw said, went.

So, we all joined him and got stuck into bottles of red wine at the meal – a lot of wine. Claw was driving everyone on to have a good night out. He wanted to build us into a team.

Deccie and Niallo were doing a fantastic job with us, but Claw brought his own genius to the Munster set-up. He was tough, uncompromising and trully inspirational. Most of us were only young guys in the very early stages of this Munster journey and we all had massive respect for Claw and Gallimh.

And he was right to go against Deccie that night. He realised that, after the kind of defeat and physical beating we took from Perpignan, we had to stick together, get drunk together. We didn't split up and go out to different clubs or pubs, Tom Tierney and Frankie Sheehan led the charge and we all stuck together in one venue, partied together and got drunk together in one place. Just booze, songs and the men of Munster. And the Claw.

At one stage in the evening, I had to go outside to ring my Mum and let her know that we were okay. Unfortunately, I wasn't much of a wine drinker in my youth, and wasn't really prepared for the wine-fuelled drinking games that Claw had been urging us into. So, when I went outside to phone my mum, the fresh air hit me like a train.

"Hi, Mum. Yes, we're all fine. Tough game but the Claw's looking after me. 'Scuse me a sec, Mum…"

In vino, veritas. In vino, vomitus.

I felt better: "All good, Mum. Everything's cool. Gallimh and the Claw are looking after me. See you when I get back".

The next morning, we rose from our sick beds and some big heads were spotted going down to the sea for a dip, before heading for the airport. By the time we returned home after Perpignan in 1998, we were a different team. We'd experienced another low, but this time we'd come through it as a team. That shock to the system had made us tougher.

The season ended with a draw against Neath (18-18), and pool wins over Perpignan in the return match (Claw scored a try) at Musgrave Park

(31-5), and Padova in Stadio Plebiscito (35-21), before losing a quarter-final to another French team, Colomiers in Stade du Selery (9-23).

But, all the while, we were growing, learning, toughening up. We won the domestic trophy that season, the first of three in a row. Deccie, Niallo and Jerry Holland continued to work their magic with us, leading us forward, pushing us on. We were building towards the future, and we wanted the future to be now.

CHAPTER 5

This looks bad. Even by my standards.

Six foot three, twenty years old, standing in a stranger's garden at two in the morning where I have no business being. Soaking wet in the rain, shoulders heaving as I gulp down a few breaths, trying to get some oxygen into my brain and struggling to focus.

But the Gardai facing me aren't looking at my face. They're not even looking at the blood pumping profusely from the sizeable wound in the side of my head.

They're looking down to where my hand hangs limply at my side. To where my grazed and skinned knuckles are still clutching the hatchet.

There's a wide-eyed look of disbelief in their eyes and I have a sudden urge to explain the hatchet isn't mine, that I just took it from another guy inside the house who had been attempting to hit me with it.

But then I'd have to explain why I was chasing the same lad through the garden when the Gardai arrived – with the axe in my hand. That might be hard to do so, in the end, I say nothing. Shut up, Alan.

I bear the marks on my face of a pummelling by somebody else's fists and, when I look at my brother standing beside me, he's grasping a baseball bat. That's not his bat either.

Definitely, this looks bad. Even by my standards.

Okay. Remember; engage brain, then open mouth. Here we go…

• • • • • • •

It really didn't need to be like this. Honestly, it didn't. It could all have turned out so differently, if I'd just minded my own business. But then it wouldn't be me if I didn't get involved.

Even when I have the best of intentions, things turn to crap for me. Whatever the opposite of the Midas Touch is, that's what I have. I'm the anti-King Midas.

The year was 1995, and I was about twenty years old, still working as a mechanic and not yet playing on the Munster stage. I was playing with Clanwilliam and also lining out for Shannon Under-20s and a few senior games with Shannon.

I was going out with a Tipperary girl who was at UCC in Cork. I'd been down there on the Friday night but had come back the next day because I had a Clanwilliam match on the Sunday. It was just a challenge game, so I went out for a couple of pints in The Underground pub in Tipperary on the Saturday evening.

It was a good night's craic, three or four pints with a few old school mates. I wasn't planning on staying out too late so, just after midnight, I made my farewells and headed on my own towards the chipper on the main street.

As I left the pub there were a couple of lads having a row. They were pushing and shoving each other. I knew one guy's girlfriend and I also knew the other fella involved. He came from a family of hard nuts, it's fair to say we knew them and there wouldn't have been any love lost between us. There'd been a few scrapes over the years and they were a tough crowd.

So, I started to walk past them, but the girl asked me if I would intervene and stop the fight. It wasn't any of my business; I figured there was two of them in it and it was only a bit of pushing and arguing, so I had no intention of getting involved. But, as I tried to walk round the corner, the girl pleaded with me to come back and stop the row between her boyfriend and the other guy.

So, I went back reluctantly – a move I've regretted to this day – and stood beside her and said, "Look folks, just leave it off. You've both been drinking, so leave it off 'til tomorrow".

And that was when I got hit. Punched from behind. One of this guy's brothers had been standing somewhere out of sight, watching everything develop. He clearly didn't like the thought of me getting involved, even if it was just to tell the warring couple to calm down and go home.

Anyway, I barely registered being punched from behind before I was being hit in the face as well, with a few fairly serious slaps. After that, the fog of war descended and everything got very confused very quickly. The couple started fighting again and I turned around to see the guy who had just hit me standing in front of me.

He looked a bit surprised that he hadn't knocked me down, or out. So, I grabbed him and we fell to the ground and wrestled each other for a bit. We banged off the door of the pub and rolled around in the street.

Things carried on that way until the guy's brother finished up his own battle and came to his sibling's aid. That meant me getting kicked in the face a few times as the tide of battle slipped away from me. I was left with a bloodied face, a busted lip, a sense of outraged grievance and a raging anger.

People came out of the pub and broke it up and the Gardai arrived a few minutes later. A friend of the two lads pulled up in a car and, as the two culprits jumped in the car to make off, I managed to connect a haymaker with one of them.

There I was, standing on the side of the street with my face busted up, trying to explain to the Gardai what had happened.

I was really angry. I'd gone out for a quiet night and a few pints but these two guys had started a row, they'd fought dirty, beaten me up and now they were getting away. I told the Gardai nothing. I was fuming. All I could think about was retribution. Anger and revenge.

I knew my older brother, John, and a couple of his friends were at a nightclub in Dundrum in County Tipperary – John and his mates were well able to handle themselves. All I could think about was just rounding up a few troops and getting even. There'd already been a bit of a spark between ourselves and this other family, a bit of previous history between us down through the years.

A couple of my own friends, Johnny O'Dwyer and Andy Fogarty, brought me home. They were trying to calm me down, because they knew what was on my mind: To go get my brother and spread a little retribution. So, Johnny and Andy brought me home through the front door, and I promptly took my Mum's car keys and snuck out the back door, took her car and drove to Dundrum to collect my brother and his mates.

One of the other lot was living in a house in Tipperary town and we knew that they hung out there a lot. They were from the country so they would use this guy's house as a crash pad. When we pulled up outside the house in the car, we figured the other crowd was expecting us because the curtains were open.

One of the guys' girlfriends opened the door a little, to tell us she was the owner of the house and that they didn't want any trouble. Hah! Her boyfriend and his family should have thought about avoiding trouble when they were standing on my face.

We were fired up, so we didn't pay much attention. As we barrelled towards her and the door, she stepped aside and suddenly we were inside. There were four of us and about four or five of them in the house. My brother John was first through the door with one of his friends at his shoulder. The space was small and we were all trying to get through the door at the one time, completely aware the entrance was the bottleneck and if we weren't through it quickly enough, they'd pick us off one by one as we got inside.

Through the scrum of bodies, and past John and his friend, I could see someone wielding a hatchet. I could see one of them swing the hatchet at my brother, and I was thinking, "Christ, that's a hatchet heading for John". We hadn't gone into the house with any kind of weapons, so the anger and fear of seeing the other side using a hatchet and baseball bat just increased the adrenaline, which was already pumping.

I blocked the hatchet – just jumped across towards the guy and reached over and blocked it with my hand.

There was pandemonium. Everything was happening very quickly inside a very tight little space. My brother ended up in the kitchen with somebody and I was wrestling with the guy with the hatchet. Two or three of their side broke and ran which only left the two brothers from the other family.

I remember struggling in the hallway with the guy with the hatchet. I was squeezing the hatchet to the ground when the guy broke off and started running out of the house. I took off after him with the hatchet still in my hand. But I slipped on gravel in the back yard and the guy was gone.

With a hatchet in my hand, it could have been the worst slip of my life but, as things turned out, it was probably the best slip of my life. The guy I was chasing escaped and perhaps, in hindsight, I was the lucky one.

At that point The Law arrived.

• • • • • • •

I've often wondered what the Gardai made of us as they piled out of the squad car. In the end, they saw the entire evening's unfortunate events for what they were; the actions of a bunch of highly charged fools involved in a family feud. They questioned us, took the weapons off us, and sent us home.

Barrelling through the front door of the house a while before, we hadn't really given much thought to what we were doing. That was obviously wrong, so when we realised what we'd done, we calmed down. But as we calmed down, the reality of the situation slowly dawned on us. We might have won the battle this evening, but the other crowd were a hardy bunch of lads who were unlikely to take this lying down.

Within a day, we were back in a car with more baseball bats, our own this time, driving around looking for the other crew. By that stage, we didn't really want to find them, we just wanted to know where they were. The only certainty was that somewhere nearby – maybe round the next corner of the road – the other lot was jammed into a car armed with baseball bats and who knows what, looking for the Quinlans. It was like something out of a movie, like something you'd hear about happening in The Bronx.

But this wasn't New York, this was Tipperary. In the back of my mind, I'm thinking, "Here we go again, how do I always end up in the middle of this stuff?" The whole row had escalated into something it shouldn't have, but I was still feeling like the victim in the whole thing.

• • • • • • •

It was a crazy time, a bad situation.

Nobody wants to be walking around their own town like that, worried and looking over their shoulder for fear of an attack. It was a terrible time, and a worry for our parents. That's how feuds start and it would've been a feud with no winners, only losers. We were in a small town in Tipperary and the Gardai were fully aware of what we had all done, and what we were all up to.

We could all have been prosecuted for what we were at – were lucky not to be. I think the Gardai took the sensible option of letting things settle down of their own accord. They'd taken everyone involved aside and warned what the consequences would be if they didn't step back from the brink. Fortunately, the other family was in the same situation as us. Eventually, after a few weeks of standoff, things came to a head.

We all lived in a small area. Everyone knew what was going on, and the rival crew was busy telling people what they were going to do to us. So, we had taken the Gardai's advice and had lain low for a while. We didn't go into Tipperary to socialise. We stayed in our own local pub and out of the limelight.

But one particular night, we went to Tipperary. We had made up our minds that we were sick of lying low; that we just wanted to get the whole thing sorted out one way or another and into Tipperary we went.

They spotted us, and followed us out to a friend's house. There were four or five of us and the same number of them. A standoff developed, until the two older brothers on each side of the feud spoke to each other and agreed that both parties were in the wrong. They agreed the whole thing was best put to bed. And so it was.

Just like that, weeks of anxiety, anger and downright fear just disappeared.

• • • • • • •

For me, it was the best possible result. I was just starting out in rugby and getting involved in that kind of dangerous nonsense could have ruined my career.

In fact, the whole encounter was proof, if ever I needed it, of how much an impact your personal life can have on your professional career, if you're careless.

The first night the whole thing had kicked off, I had taken a few slaps and a few kicks to the jaw. I was due to play with Shannon the following day but my jaw was sore so I went for an X-ray the following Friday night in Cashel hospital to make sure it wasn't broken.

They gave me the all-clear and so, the next day, I played with Shannon and then with Clanwilliam on the Sunday.

As I came off the bench for Clanwilliam in the last twenty minutes, one of our lads was tackled. Next thing I know, he was flung right at me and his two feet smacked me in the jaw. We lost the match and with the amount of pain I was in, Johnny O'Dwyer took me straight back to Cashel hospital.

By this stage, after the beating and that afternoon's two-footed tackle, it would have been fair to say that my jaw and my teeth were going in two different directions.

The X-ray came back clear and the doctor told me there was no break in the jaw, just lots of bruising. "Thanks be to God," I told him, recounting how this was my second jaw X-ray in a couple of days. At hearing this, the doctor volunteered to have a look at my original X-ray and, as he held it up to the bright while light, we could both clearly see it had been broken in the fight. He immediately packed me off to Cork hospital and, within a couple of days, surgeons had inserted two titanium plates in my jaw. By the following Thursday, I was out of hospital, metal in my mouth, upset and sore, and still involved in a running feud. I was feeling a little vulnerable.

So, it was good that the whole thing was finally settled for everyone's sake. Looking back on it now, it's possible to laugh but, at the time, it was no laughing matter for either side. The whole episode did however, show me how important family is in life. We weren't going to take any shit from the other crowd and, when it came down to it, my family stuck together. That was important. That's always been important.

In 1988 I invaded Croke Park.

In fairness, I wasn't alone, there were thousands of us streaming onto the pitch, all decked out in the blue and gold of Tiobraid Arann. We'd just beaten Offaly in the National Hurling League final and, like any other red-blooded teenager from Tipperary, I wanted to celebrate with the team. The first man I ran into was the Clonoulty midfielder, Joe Hayes, who had just put in a towering performance.

"Joe," I shouted at him through the crush of fans, "can I have your socks?"

It was, admittedly, a little more unusual than asking for an autograph but, like the gentleman that he was, Joe Hayes brought me straight into the dressing room, gave me his socks and introduced me to the rest of the Premier County's team, including Nicky English, my Abbey CBS teacher, who immediately demanded to know why one of his students was in the dressing rooms.

Joe made a thirteen-year-old boy very happy that day in Croker and further fuelled my dreams of being the next great thing in Tipperary hurling.

The funny thing is that, growing up, I broke more windows with a sliotar than I did with a rugby ball. I broke them in the house, in the shed, I broke them everywhere. My biggest ambition, then, was to play for Tipp U-14s in the annual Tony Forristal tournament in Waterford. I'd been going to U-14 county trials for months and I was dedicated to making the final cut. It was a big deal for me, a very big deal.

I went everywhere with a hurley and a sliotar and tried to catch every Tipperary match going. I was there in '87 when Tipp beat Cork in the replay to win the Munster final after twenty years and end the great trophy famine: It was a phenomenal day, my Mum brought us, the three brothers, on the train to Killarney with a load of sandwiches and I still remember the atmosphere, mingling with the other hurling fans. It was just a magic day. And when my Mum brought us to Kerry for our summer holidays, I'd catch the train back home on my own to make sure I got to matches and to training. I was the only one from our club, Arravale Rovers – the only one from West Tipperary really – who was in with a shout of making the county team.

In the end, it all came down to that year's County U-14 final. Selection for the county team would depend a lot on the result of that game but, as it turned out, we got hammered and so I missed out on my county team dream.

I was gutted. After pouring all that work, time and effort into trying to make the team, I was pretty much spent. I was no different from the thousands of youngsters up and down the country whose life, at that age, revolves around whether or not they are picked for their chosen team. Love of the game and ambition are big emotions for a thirteen-year-old, but so is disappointment.

In the wake of that setback, I grew disillusioned with hurling: I continued to play, but much of the fun had gone out of it for me and, over the next few years, I played some senior football with Arravale Rovers. To this day, I still love watching hurling and never tire of appreciating the skill of the game, but not even the efforts of a Tipp hurler like Joe Hayes could make up for failing to make that team.

I was increasingly drawn to rugby, for which I found I had a natural talent.

• • • • • • •

My family are part of the fabric of Clanwilliam rugby club and it's part of them. My uncle Andy was a hooker and his two sons, Ian and David, who went on to captain Shannon, both played as did another cousin, Phillip. Many times when I lined out in the black and amber of Clanwilliam, I wore a jersey sponsored by my uncle Andy's Tipperary bar, Quinlans.

The club was down to earth and full of good, ordinary people. In the old days, rugby used to be associated with the class system but there was never any sense of the class system at work in Clan, the thought never entered our minds. It was founded in 1879 and is the fifth oldest rugby club in the country. Everyone was welcome there, you didn't have to be dropped off in a big fancy car – you just had to want to play rugby.

It was a natural progression for me to play rugby and about 90 per cent of the kids playing alongside me were the same gang I played hurling and football with. We were always trying to put pressure on the non-rugby kids to come and play because, if they were good at hurling and football, then chances were they'd be great at rugby.

In fact, the only ones who didn't play all three codes tended to be the kids who stuck to rugby and that was because rugby doesn't require as much skill, it offers people a bit more free license. You can get away with all shapes and sizes in rugby – if you don't have skill, if you don't have speed but you do have strength, then there's a place for you on a rugby field.

I grew up playing all codes and making friends with a great bunch of kids – but a core group of us went all the way through the Clanwilliam system, playing with the U-8s, U-10s, U-12s, U-14s, U-16s and U-18s. We had a decent amount of success, winning the U-16 Limerick Cup, which was almost unheard of for a Tipperary team.

Unfortunately, I missed out on the honour of being in the starting line-up for that particular triumph. I was still U-14 at the time and, though I'd played for the U-16s most of the year, my older cousin, Ian, was returning from injury and took my place. Ian and I were more like brothers than cousins – we acted as best man at each other's weddings – but I've never forgotten that he took my place on that Cup final team.

Worse, his Dad (and my uncle) Andy was the team manager: Ian was the better player back then, but I always ribbed him that he only got the start because his Dad was picking the team.

"I'll get you back," I told him, though I had to wait for my revenge for almost a decade until Clanwilliam won the Munster Challenge Cup with me in the starting line-up and Ian on the bench.

Growing up in Clanwilliam was a great way to be introduced to rugby.

We did everything there, played rugby, went to teenage discos and had some great social nights and sing-songs – we felt we had a bit of ownership in the club, that we were part of it. The parents of a friend, Johnny Lacey, owed The Royal Hotel in Tipp town and, between it and the Clanwilliam clubhouse, we were never at a loss for a place to go, a club to gate-crash, or a bit of craic.

On the playing side we had great coaches – guys like Michael Hogan, Liam O'Dwyer, Willie Cotter, Billy Brett, Vinnie McCormack, Tommy Crowe and my uncle Andy.

It was to those men that I owed my selection to the Munster U-18s, and my Irish Youths captaincy for a game against Scotland. That was a great moment for me and I was delighted my parents travelled over to Ayr to watch. It was a big day, too, for Clan. Club representatives, Tod O'Rahelly and Billy Brett, came over to support me. It was great to see how much pride the club took in my achievement, but it was a mark of what a close-knit set-up Clanwilliam really is that they put such great store in their young players.

In 1993, Clanwilliam won the Munster Junior Plate with Martin O'Sullivan as the coach. Martin brought us up from the Third Division to the First and then we won the Munster Junior Challenge Cup with Declan Madden in 1995/96. That period from, 1993 to 1996, was great for Clanwilliam and I was thrilled to be a part of it.

• • • • • • •

It wasn't all about rugby, though. I was training to be a mechanic at Pierse Motors for Gerry and Arthur Pierse and, while the money was low and the identical twin brothers were hard taskmasters, the garage was a great place to work.

On more than one occasion, Gerry pulled me out from under the chassis of a car to wake me up as I tried to sleep off a hangover. Or he'd check up on me as I disappeared under the bonnet of a car, to see that I wasn't reading a newspaper instead of working.

My mate, Johnny O'Dwyer, nicknamed me 'Mudflap' for – allegedly – putting mudflaps in front of a car's wheels instead of behind, and, in return, he was labelled 'Lamb Chop' because he was a trainee butcher.

One of the main aims, in those early days, was to secure as much money as possible so you could go out at the weekend. There weren't too many opportunities to increase your pay packet but there was local racing tycoon, John Magnier – or, more accurately, there was John's driver, Trevor, who used to bring the Magnier cars down to Pierse's for a regular service.

As soon as the lads in the garage saw Trevor pulling into the forecourt, there'd be a scramble to reach him first and get the keys, as it was well know that a decent effort sprucing the car up would be rewarded with a IR£20 tip from Trevor, which was a lot of money in those days.

So, I made sure that I was at the front of the queue every time Trevor arrived, and I made sure that the cars were washed and cleaned and left sparkling for his return.

But, apart from the money, I had another incentive to be the first to meet Trevor at the door – I had a weakness for driving around in top-of-the-range Mercs. Back then, the only one of my friends to have use of a car was Justin Flynn, who regularly brought Bressie, Skin, Mikey, Thos Martin and me cruising in his Dad's motor. We had great times but, when presented with a golden opportunity to drive around myself, it was impossible to say no. So, John Magnier's car provided me with the perfect opportunity to indulge myself.

Sometimes, after finishing at the garage, I'd pick up my old schoolmates and take them for a spin, at other times, I'd be happy driving around on my own. On one memorable occasion, as I was cruising down the main street in Tipp in John Magnier's Merc, who should drive past me in the opposite direction but Arthur, my boss.

Arthur's jaw dropped as he drove past, his head slowly rotating as his gaze followed me and the car – his mind trying to take in the sight of his young employee travelling in the other direction in a Mercedes belonging to his friend and one of his most important clients. He narrowly avoided crashing.

Like a deer caught in the headlights I stared back at him and high-tailed it back to the garage.

When Arthur finally caught up with me, he gave me a rollicking. He screamed and shouted at me and threatened to fire me. But I was only seventeen or eighteen years old at the time so all I could do was laugh and, eventually, Arthur started to laugh as well, roaring at me to get back to work. Deep down, I think he knew it was the kind of stunt he'd have pulled when he was my age.

• • • • • • •

The years at Clanwilliam were as much about having fun as they were about playing rugby. There was a gang who knocked around together: Lamb Chop O'Dwyer, my cousin Ian, Fergal Gallagher, Paddy O'Callaghan, Justin Quinlan, Steve Nugent and Johnny Lacey. Not all of us played rugby – Johnny O'Dwyer was our kitman for years and served on various club committees – but we were all involved with Clanwilliam somehow.

The club was the reason we all met in the first place and it provided the glue that held us together. If we weren't playing rugby there, then we were dancing or messing or, in later years, having a few pints and plenty of craic. Like any good club should be, it was the constant thread that ran through our lives and lives of the community.

After gaining promotion to the first division in 1995, Clan went on to have quite a lot of success and stayed in Division One of the Munster Junior League for the next fourteen or fifteen years.

But things were changing for me. I was beginning to play with Shannon U-20s and was wondering how I could progress my own rugby career. I tried to stay with Clanwilliam as long as I could, as a dual status player, because I wanted to try and help the constantly improving team.

But, nothing stays the same forever and, when we won the Munster Junior Challenge Cup in 1995/96, I'd pretty much played my last game for my old club.

• • • • • • •

In the two decades that have passed since I invaded Croker and secured Joe Hayes' sweaty old socks, the pair of us have become good friends and keen golfing rivals. We can often be found out in Dundrum House in Tipperary along with the owner, Willie Crowe, who's the third wheel in our golfing trio.

These days, as Joe hacks his way around the golf course, and I smoothly make the greens, he often asks me for a pair of Munster socks, which I'm only too happy to pass on, so he can keep warm as he gets closer to drawing the pension.

Joe thinks I'm mad, I think Joe's mad and Willie thinks we're both mad – I think Willie's right.

As for Joe's socks – it's quite possible they're still at home in a GAA sports bag somewhere, hiding in a dark corner or lying at the bottom of a cupboard, waiting for a thirteen-year-old, would-be Tipperary hurling champion to come and fetch them.

November 28, 1999
Heineken Cup Pool Game
v Saracens (Vicarage Road)
Won: 35-34

I couldn't help reflecting on how far my own career had come as I stood there, on a Wednesday night, down at my home club, Clanwilliam.

I was giving them a dig out, doing a bit of coaching, helping the lads to face battle against our greatest rivals, Kilfeacle.

Games against Kilfeacle were always intense, nerve-wracking affairs that everyone looked forward to and dreaded at the same time. Sunday's game would be no different so I was talking to some of the lads about it, trying to help them prepare for the massive derby.

But, try as I might, I couldn't stop my mind wandering to the Sunday after and to one of the biggest challenges of my career. Munster were about to face a Saracens team packed with International stars and great English players.

I was experiencing the two extremes of the changing face of Irish rugby. On the one hand, my home club was facing a tough and familiar adversary while, within a couple of days, Axel, Wally and I would be facing a Saracens back row of François Pienaar, Richard Hill and Tony Diprose.

Pienaar was South Africa's 1995 World Cup winning captain, a huge man and a fantastic player. On top of that, he was an icon of the game and a personal hero of mine. Life was becoming complicated.

For our part, Munster had signed up John Langford from Australia and we'd brought Keith Wood back home from Harlequins. Langford was an eye-opener for us in terms of fitness and conditioning. One look at John and his training regime was enough to convince us we were way below par in weights and fitness training. And, of course, the entire province was excited by Woody's return home. He wanted to base himself in Ireland in preparation for the upcoming World Cup. Like Langford, Woody's arrival really raised the bar for us.

Alongside those two, we'd signed a New Zealander who'd been playing in England called Mike Mullins. Mikey was a great signing for us, he gave us a new dimension in the back line at a time when we were primarily known as having a strong forward unit, and as a team that mauled and kicked a lot. That season we wanted to be more expansive and move the ball around more so that Munster wasn't just all about the forwards. He added a bit of flair and an extra dimension to our midfield and gave us more of an opportunity to move the ball a bit wider.

The previous year we'd made the quarter-finals of the Heineken Cup but been beaten away to Colomiers. We were just starting to build some self-belief; Declan and Niall were instilling that into us and we were starting to improve as a squad. But we would be up against a newly-strengthened Saracens team boasting Argentinean, French and South African Internationals and English players like Danny Grewcock and Richard Hill. A new financial backer had come into their club a year or two before and was investing heavily in big-name players.

It was a Sunday match and we travelled to London on the Friday, two days ahead of the game, to check into a hotel in Watford because Saracens shared their ground with Watford soccer club.

On the Friday night were having a meal in the hotel and, in those days, I loved a pint of Coke with my dinner. Although we didn't have the huge financial support that other clubs had we were allowed to order a drink. So, at the start of the meal, I ordered a pint of Coke from the waitress. But it never arrived.

I was sitting there watching everyone else eating and drinking but I had no Coke. Halfway through the meal I asked again but, again, the waitress forgot to bring my Coke. Finally, towards the end of the meal I started getting annoyed and asked another waitress to get me my pint of bloody Coke, please.

I don't know what she thought she heard but two minutes later the doors of the dining room swung open and waiters and waitresses appeared from everywhere carrying trays of pints of Coke – thirty pints of Coke, to be exact.

All the Munster players just sat there with their mouths open, amazed. I didn't know what was happening but Deccie was livid that there were an additional thirty pints of Coke on our hotel bill. He called me in afterwards and gave a rollicking over it. After that, my pint of Coke and I kept a low profile at the dinner table.

The Coke fiasco notwithstanding, it was a brilliant trip. Watford were playing Sunderland in soccer on the Saturday so we all traipsed along to watch the match. It was a great distraction for us all but I had managed to embarrass myself, as normal.

• • • • • • •

Niall Quinn was lining out for Sunderland in those days and, while he wouldn't have known much about me, or perhaps even Munster rugby, we all knew him and I'd even met him on a couple of previous occasions.

Anyway, he was busy warming up when I spotted him and started cheekily roaring at him to come over and say hello. I wanted to shake hands with him and wish him well, and I didn't really have the cop-on to leave the lad alone to warm up.

If he'd ignored me, I'd have been mortified but, as it was, he came over for a quick chat and we wished him all the best. It's a mark of the guy that he was relaxed and confident enough to break his warm-up to come over and talk to a bunch of Irish fellas that were shouting at him from the stands.

I admired him hugely as a player and was excited to meet him – and I was trying to impress the boys. Niall had an incredible career, both at club and national level, and on top of that, he's a genuinely nice guy. To this day, Gallimh, ROG, The Bull and Axel still slag me about embarrassing them but it was wonderful to meet him, and they secretly got a real kick out of it as well.

Sunderland went on to win the game with Niall scoring. It was a great occasion for us because it gave us an early look at the ground and also took our minds off the impending clash with Saracens.

• • • • • • •

We didn't have huge expectations going into the battle with Saracens, but things were starting to build within the Munster squad. Our skill set and our fitness levels were improving under Fergal O'Callaghan who had come on board full-time. 'Foggy', as we called him, came to be an integral part of our plan to build for the future. He was a competitive rower and a fitness freak who loved nothing more than to get out on the running track and train with us, push us harder and harder.

Overall, there was an air of excitement about the squad. We were beginning to believe that we could compete and maybe start winning games away from home. That was one of the main targets we'd set ourselves for the coming season – winning consistently away from home and putting an end to the constant accusations that we couldn't travel.

We were also beginning to develop a healthy paranoia that the whole world was against us when we stepped outside Munster. That's not a difficult frame of mind to achieve when you're playing a massive English team on their home patch with not a lot of support of your own.

On top of that, Deccie had the perfect opportunity to wind us all up when the hotel's fire alarm went off in the middle of Saturday night, just hours before the game. We were all hauled out of our beds at around 3 or 4am, and ordered to get out of the hotel, until they decided whether it was a fire or just a hoax. Needless to say, it turned out to be a false alarm, but it gave Deccie the chance to tell us all that someone connected to the Saracens camp had set the thing off deliberately to disrupt us.

Looking back it was probably nonsense but we swallowed his allegations hook, line and sinker, and went into the game pissed off and paranoid.

The fire hoax may have robbed me of a few minutes' sleep but that was nothing compared to how much shut-eye I missed thanks to my room-mate, Anthony Horgan.

Hoggy was a good friend and a great player and was chosen to room with me that weekend. He is a light sleeper and any noise in the room, such as a room-mate's snoring, is enough to wake him, so, he would wear earplugs. Which would be grand except that Hoggy is a bit of a snorer too, so, instead of wearing earplugs, he should have been handing them out to everyone else.

I had nothing to stick in my ears to dull the noise of Hoggy – not that the noise of the snoring was the only problem, the room also felt like we had the London Underground running directly below us because the vibrations were so strong. I was worried that I'd go to sleep only to wake up to find my bed slowly vibrating its way towards the toilet! Every hour I'd wake up, time and again. At least when the fire alarm went off, it was a bit of variety. All I wanted to do was tackle Hoggy, and dump him in the corridor. It's fair to say that he took a lot of pillow slaps to the head that night.

It all added to the tension and the nerves in the lead up to the game – I was worried for myself, worried for Munster. I tried to dwell on the positives: How we had improved, how we had a lot of big characters of our own like Woody, Gallimh, Langford and Foley, who were all inspirational leaders in their own right. Back then, even in those early years of playing beside Anthony Foley, you could see he was a special player. He was always so calm in the middle of adversity, nothing phased him. Wally was on the other side of the back row and was an incredibly powerful guy but also one of the quickest guys in the squad making him one of Munster's biggest assets. He was also a great guy to play with and to know.

So, there were plenty of positives to cling onto. Munster were confident deep down. Nervous, yes, but quietly confident. We had a big forward pack, then Strings was there beside ROG, we had Mikey Mullins and Killian Keane – as a unit we were coming together and as young players we were starting to show off our ability and express ourselves on the pitch.

Deccie was turning us into a good team. He and Niall were drilling the mental side of the game into us. That was something we had never really worked on in the past. Before Declan and Niall came in, we hadn't really understood the need for mental preparation prior to games; hadn't really analysed how having self-belief and self-confidence could be translated into success on the pitch.

Still, despite all the mental preparation I found myself thinking: "How the hell are we going to compete against these guys, never mind beat them?"

Early on, we were hit by a few sucker punches which led to us standing back a bit. We'd put a lot of these Saracens boys up on a pedestal and suffered the consequences. I got caught up in the circus of it all. I remember thinking how strange it was to see Paul Wallace playing for Saracens against his brother – I couldn't imagine playing competitively against my brothers, especially at that level.

It didn't seem to be a problem that many Saracens were dwelling on. By the end of the first half, they had given us a lesson in rugby. Although we managed a couple of penalties they torpedoed us with a couple of tries and a few penalties of their own. Worse, they had us under all kinds of pressure. Trooping in at half time, we knew we'd have to up our performance but, as the game restarted, we found ourselves in dire straits, behind 9-21. We were dead in the water, or rather we should have been.

We were playing in a great stadium against a team of wonderful Internationals, and no-one expected us to win or come close to winning. Essentially, all we had to do was follow the Saracens script and, if we didn't disgrace ourselves, in a few hours time we'd be on our way home, our bellies full, drinks in our hands, with some happy memories of a great away loss against Saracens. Morally victorious. Not a bad outcome, all things considered.

We were gone. We were beaten. They could smell blood and all we could smell was defeat. But then, something strange happened. We reached a crossroads. We had a choice. We could roll over and get hockeyed. Or … we could roll up our sleeves and fight for our lives.

We rolled up our sleeves and went for broke. The team came alive and we inspired each other to fight, and keep fighting. We began to get the true measure of these International legends.

From the stands, or from the sofa in the living room, these guys had looked unbeatable. But up close, they began to lose their cloak of invincibility. We started to believe that the gap in the scores was more a reflection of our mental timidity rather than a deficit of playing ability. Saracens weren't beating us so much as we were beating ourselves.

So, gradually, it stopped being about Saracens and started being about Munster. For me, we were turning a corner. For me it was the beginning of something – it was the start of never say die.

We came right back into the game, scored a couple of tries and stole the momentum from Saracens and, afterwards, it seemed to me that it was the nature of our comeback that shocked them more than anything else. We became much more physical and aggressive; a team with fight and grit and possessed of some individual brilliance. Mikey Mullins was a giant. He began to make line breaks, create plays and tries for other people, and he began to inspire people.

And I caught up with my idol François Pienaar. Near the start of the second half he made a break; I anticipated him, got across to make the tackle and managed to get back on my feet and steal the ball. I turned possession over and we passed the ball out along the back line to Killian Keane who scored a great try.

For me, that tackle was a revelation: "This guy is only human. He's not a freak. I can take him. I can get stuck in and I can take the ball off the World Cup winning captain."

Towards the end of the game, we were six points behind and we had to score a try and convert. So, we did: Jeremy Staunton went over for a great try and ROG converted to give us a one-point lead. Saracens were a great team and weren't prepared to go quietly so they battled back to set themselves up again with a scrum near our line, and Thierry Lacroix prepared to strike a dropped goal.

But we weren't to be denied. The pack surged forward and turned over possession. The ref's whistle shrilled across the stadium and up through the thin November air: 35-34 Munster.

Munster had won, unbelievable. We'd beaten Saracens on their home patch in an amazing game. They seemed to be in shock, I know we were.

•••••••

A lot of us matured that day and really came out of our shells. Time and time again we'd lost games we could have won. Time and time again we'd tasted bitter defeat and embraced heartbreak, but we'd learned our lessons well. We refused to be second best any more.

In the aftermath our critics poked around for excuses for the win. People said we rode our luck, people said Saracens helped our cause by pulling off some of their players and changing their game because they thought the match was already won. They were right. I couldn't argue with their observations. But, so what? These things happen in rugby matches. We've lost games because of bad decisions.

But the fact was it wasn't all about Saracens and their decisions, good or bad. The victory was down to us. Our backs had been to the wall, and in the end Saracens were beaten by a team that was fighting for its life, for its future.

It was an incredible game to be involved in, just fantastic. I felt honoured and proud to be in the thick of it with those guys. In the dressing room afterwards, we just jumped around with delight and relief.

There was very little media on hand to record what was an historic win for us. The match wasn't being shown live on TV, there was only Len Dinneen from radio and a few newspaper reporters. But even that insult, that we weren't important enough to warrant live television coverage, was turned into motivation. Knowing that we were away from home, that we were ranked as underdogs galvanised us further. At least the handful of travelling Munster fans were delirious after the game, fifteen or twenty of them clapped us off the field and roared with joy.

Liam McCarthy, the groundsman at Thomond Park, couldn't stop hugging me and congratulating all the players. To this day, his face stands out for me, he made me realise that we'd won that, against all the odds, we'd just done something special.

The Saracens game was a key game in the whole 'Munsterolicy' of the Heineken Cup, and immediately put us in a pretty strong position. Walking off the pitch at Vicarage Road, we were the team that had beaten Pontypridd in Thomond Park in the opening game, and had just taken the Saracens' scalp away from home in our second match.

We followed it up with two wins against Colomiers in Stade des Sept Deniers [31-15], and Musgrave Park [23-5], a massive return win against Saracens in Thomond Park [31-30] before being pipped by Pontypridd [36-38] in Wales.

Munster beat Stade Français 27-10 in Thomond Park to set up a semi-final against Toulouse in Bordeaux which was won 31-25 but, by that stage,

I was on the outside of the team looking in.

The final ended in heartbreak with Munster beaten 8-9 by Northampton at Twickenham, and earned us that most unwanted of titles: The Nearly Men.

On top of that, Woody was leaving us so, by the end of the season, we weren't sure whether we would ever achieve our ultimate dream.

But I had a bigger personal challenge. I'd injured my shoulder in our last pool game against Pontypridd, which put me out of the game for a few weeks. We went back to our clubs for three months while we waited for the April quarter-final against Stade Français.

I lined out, along with The Bull, Gallimh, Axel and Eddie Halvey for Shannon but my concentration slipped and my form dipped as I took my eye off the ball. I trained badly, I played badly and I started arguing with my team-mates. Deccie dropped me for the quarter-final, the semi- and for the final, preferring Eddie Halvey as a lineout option. I didn't regain my position for the rest of the Heineken Cup. By the time the season ended, I was having a crisis of confidence, on the point of failing to have my contract renewed and being kicked out by Deccie.

I was asking tough questions of myself: "Did I want to be a professional rugby player? Did I want to dedicate myself to the job and did I want to make a career out of it?"

Just two years after I'd become a professional rugby player, my dream was in danger of being over.

CHAPTER 8

I waited at the top of the stairs for Deccie Kidney.

When the bastard appeared out of the dressing rooms I was going to cleave him from head to toe. Then I was going to tell him to feck off with his Munster team, and his professionalism.

Or, maybe I'd do it the other way round: Tell him to feck off and then take his head off. I didn't know what I'd start with. I was just too angry to think straight. But I knew one thing, I was done with Declan Kidney and with Munster, for good.

As soon as he appeared out of the dressing room, I would let him know what I thought of him. I'd had enough of his schoolteacher ways. I was sick of him.

However, the first face to appear wasn't Deccie's. It was Brian O'Brien, my Shannon manager, who'd come along for a look at the Munster training session and who, by the time he'd asked me what was wrong, must have been wishing he'd stayed at home.

I told him I was going to kill Deccie when he came out. "I'm sick of this crap, I'm going to bust his head and I'm going to kill him," were my exact words.

It was, I think, a bit of a shock for Brian. He'd been very good to me when I first went to Shannon and had been a great mentor to me, so I think he wasn't overly happy at the prospect of one of his lads going postal on his provincial coach.

So, he pulled me away, sat me in his car and had a long talk with me. He listened patiently to me explaining what had brought me to the point of violent confrontation with my Munster coach. I explained that, even though a lot of us were only part-time players, Deccie was acting like a teacher, being overbearing and controlling.

I told him that being a part-time Munster professional was like going to school every day: If you messed up or stepped out of line you'd have the teacher giving out to you. And I was a prime example of that.

I explained to Brian how that particular day had started off very badly. It was a summer's day and quite sunny, so I had stripped off my top and was sunning myself on the pitch. It wasn't what Deccie Kidney wanted us to do. He wanted people to warm up on their own, to be stretched and ready to train.

So, when he arrived, the other lads were jogging around and stretching but there was Quinlan, lying on the grass, sunning himself. The only stretching I was doing was lying splayed on the blades catching a few rays. That really annoyed him.

After that, the morning session went from bad to worse. Deccie had done a lot of shouting and roaring – "Do this!" and "Do that!" – and had been giving out to me about the way I was training. He shouted at me if I dropped the ball or if I didn't concentrate.

Then, towards the end of that morning session, he gave us an option. Either we could finish training straightaway and come out for a second session in the afternoon, or we could carry on training for a while as a team, and he'd call off the afternoon session. So, I opened my big mouth and said, "Sure we'll train on and get it out of the way".

I didn't mean it badly, but he took it the wrong way and ate me out of it in front of everyone. He shouted at me for my bad attitude, he said I needed to cop on and get a better attitude. Attitude, attitude, attitude.

By the time we finished training I was bloody fuming.

"And that, Brian," went my closing argument to my Shannon manager, "is why I want to kill Declan Kidney".

As juries go, Brian didn't deliberate long. He told me to, "Calm the hell down," and not say a word to Deccie. He told me I was only going to harm my career, my future and myself by opening my trap again. According to Brian, I needed to become a bit more disciplined, keep my head down more, and apply myself. I needed to cop myself on.

Within a few minutes he had calmed me down and turned me around. I didn't wait to confront Deccie. I don't think I was ever going to hit him but I was probably going to abuse him and tell him to feck off and, ultimately, I would have paid the price.

I'd only been trying to play the role of professional rugby player for a short while by the time I planned to 'ambush' Deccie after training. Turning myself from a raw, country boy into a focused rugby professional was a magic act that I just couldn't seem to master.

• • • • • • •

In 1996 the first coach to be appointed to Munster as part of the new era of professional rugby was a Welsh guy. I remember going to the first meeting with him. He addressed us at length and spoke to us about the team and getting to know everyone. That was the last we ever saw of him. I think he was under the impression that the Munster players were all going to be on full-time contracts and got a bit of a shocker when he arrived and found that wasn't the case. We all figured he hadn't the will or energy to be involved in something still in its early stages, he just didn't want to do it.

There weren't too many other candidates for the job. Declan Kidney was the Irish Schools coach and he was having a lot of success at that level, so Declan and Niall O'Donovan, who had been very successful as both a player and coach with Shannon, were appointed to Munster: Niall as forwards coach and Declan as backs coach and head coach.

Jerry Holland arrived as team manager and Dave Maheady of UL was our fitness adviser. Dave was a great character who managed the difficult task of making our fitness training an enjoyable and rewarding, experience.

I knew very little about Declan at that point. I remember meeting him the first night at training in Musgrave Park and having a bit of a laugh with him. But, underneath everything at that first meeting, you could tell that this was something new – Deccie's time in charge of Munster was going to leave its mark one way or another. He was clear about what he was going to do – he was going to have a go at the job. He wasn't first choice but he didn't care, he was determined to give it his all.

I had problems with Declan right from the start. He was an ex-teacher who wanted to be in control of his team and I had never been one for discipline. I was still a bit wild and totally unprepared for becoming a full-time rugby player. I messed around a lot because it was all new to me: I'd never been in an environment where things like time-keeping were important.

Of course, Deccie was obviously a very bright guy: Educated and very organised so, when he first saw me, I've no doubt that he saw someone in dire need of being put back in their box.

Deccie was a disciplinarian. He was a guy coming in to do a job with a team. He demanded the respect of the players and intended to organise us all but, of course, when you're young you don't really see the benefit of discipline, you just think of the person behind it as a control freak.

For the first while we settled into our respective stereotypes and got on okay: I did my thing and he pegged me as a messer and treated me like a pupil. He wanted me to concentrate on my rugby and get focused on and off the field, but I didn't really know how. All I knew was that playing rugby for a living beat having to do 'real work'.

That year the team went on a pre-season tour to Scotland. I was only twenty-three years old and I'd never been away with a group of lads before, going abroad and staying together in a hotel for an entire week.

So we ran wild, drinking, going out and turning up late for training. When we did show up, we didn't train well and acted up. It wasn't especially bad but I was being a bit too cheeky and cocky for Deccie and Niall's liking and I knew I was irritating them.

When the starting team for the first game in Scotland was picked, I wasn't on it, which was frustrating. So, at the next training session when the starters played the reserves, I did my usual thing of being a bit of a nuisance and practically messed up the session.

At one stage, I went in to ruck the ball for my side and Brian O'Meara hit me with his hand so I pushed him back. Next thing I know, I get this almighty haymaker from Gallimh in the back of the head.

Gallimh is a big, strong man so it was a fair slap. He just reckoned he needed to put a few manners on me and, in fairness, he was probably right. Gallimh was a Shannon team-mate and one of my best friends in the team, so I figured if he was whacking me, I probably deserved it. True to form, though, I didn't learn anything from the episode. I spent the rest of the week being as giddy and wild as I had been at the start of it.

But things got worse when I screwed up during one of the warm-up games against the Scots by getting involved with someone during a match. I gave away a bad penalty, a couple of them in fact, and I knew Deccie was annoyed with me. He was right to be. This was pre-season stuff, his first pre-season in charge, and he had a right to expect all of us to be focused and to try hard.

The final straw came after a mid-week match when we had a few post-game beers. I'd already had a few and I walked over to the bus and sat down with a beer in my hand. It wasn't the done thing, but I didn't know any better, so I drank the beer and afterwards threw the bottle in a hedge. Deccie spotted me and I think he made his mind up that this Quinlan was a bit of a wild one who needed to learn at thing or two.

So, the next morning I was called into a meeting with Niall O'Donovan, Jerry Holland and Deccie. They informed me, in no uncertain terms, that I needed to change my attitude. I had to be more disciplined and I needed to start listening, learning and behaving myself. They warned that if I didn't I wouldn't be involved any more, I'd be out on my arse.

At the time, it came as a shock to me. But I pretty soon figured out the lay of the land and got up to speed on what was required of me.

After that first meeting I was a little wary of Deccie. I had to bide my time for a while, but played well in a few 'A' games and got my chance with the senior team.

But I didn't really shake off the tag of being a messer and I still had a long way to go before I really understood what it was to be a full-time rugby professional. I still relied hugely on people like Brian O'Brien to help me understand what was expected of me.

• • • • • • •

In the 1999-2000 season I played the six Heineken Cup pool games and performed well in them but then we faced a lay-off of a few months before the quarter-final.

I went back to play for Shannon but my discipline and my attitude began to slip. I wasn't training very hard and I didn't really know what was required to better myself, or how to act like a professional.

I didn't play particularly well with Shannon and started to get frustrated when we were losing matches. My match discipline began to go and, before I knew where I was, I was giving away penalties and arguing with team-mates on the pitch.

I'd been at a point in my career where we were winning games easily, but suddenly here at Shannon we were losing games that we weren't supposed to. Things weren't going according to the script. I was irritating people and my body language was poor. My training standards were low because I wasn't pushing myself, which only served to make me more angry and frustrated as time went on.

Of course, Munster were watching me deteriorate through all of it. They were watching everyone's performances and they didn't like what they saw. At that point I just wasn't much good and, worse, I was talking a lot on the pitch: Bitching, giving out, annoying people.

A week and a half before the Stade Français quarter-final at a team get together, Declan called me aside and told me I was dropped for the game. I still remember being told in the hallway of the University of Limerick. Deccie informed me I wasn't giving 100 per cent and that was frustrating him. He could certainly see that I was a good rugby player but I wasn't applying myself properly. Other guys he'd looked at had their heads down and were working really hard, giving themselves, giving everything.

It was a real hammer blow. At the time, I didn't really understand it, how could I? I still had no idea what it meant to be a professional and was still years of experience away from understanding how to really apply myself 100 per cent.

I was genuinely surprised. I wasn't playing well with Shannon but no one was. I wasn't the only Munster player there. What about John Hayes, Axel, Gallimh, Eddie Halvey? I knew I wasn't playing well but I didn't think my Munster place was in danger.

But Deccie told me that Eddie Halvey was a great lineout option for him. Eddie had only just come back from Saracens and was still part-time with us while he worked part-time. Deccie said he wanted to put pressure on Stade at the lineout and that Eddie gave him a better chance of achieving that, which, if you look back at the game, he was right about. Eddie was a great player with bags of talent – a really athletic guy who was brilliant at defensive lineouts and at being lifted at the front of the lineout. Still, it was a hammer blow to be told I was being left out. It was a defining moment for me, though I didn't know it at the time.

Deccie told me I'd definitely be coming on at half time, or just after, and would play a good part in the game. But that never happened.

I sat on the sideline during that quarter-final, thinking to myself, "I'm going to come on in the second half... I'm going to come on in a few minutes... I'm going to come on in a few minutes... I'm going to come on in a few minutes..."

I came on in the seventy-eighth minute. Taking off your tracksuit and warming up at that late stage in a big game isn't a pleasant feeling. I was gutted: After playing all six pool games and contributing massively to getting the team to this point, here I was coming on at the last minute to play a bit-part in an historic day, a two-minute cameo.

On a big day like that, no one remembers the last six games you've played, they only know what they see in front of them. It's not a case of being as good as your last game, it's more a case of only being as good as your current game.

A few weeks later, the lads faced Toulouse in Bordeaux and had a fantastic win. But I didn't get any game time. It was the same story in the final. Eddie had played well in those games, had taken his chances well.

There, on the sideline, I was suddenly faced with a massive challenge. I've always been a worrier and watching my team make history without me I began to sweat that I was irrevocably slipping down the pecking order. The consequences would affect everything – my contract, my life.

If you're a rugby player, then you play rugby. If you're not playing rugby then you're not a rugby player. Simple as that.

I was mad at Deccie. After all, he had been the one to drop me, the one to cause me all this pain and stress, the one to leave me out of the team. I'd been an automatic team choice but now, because of him, I was on the outside.

Of course, that wasn't true. I was the only one to blame, I just couldn't see it back then. In fairness to Deccie, he was protecting me from myself at the time. He didn't tell me the real story of why he was dropping me – that my attitude stank, that my game wasn't any good, and that I was within a hair's breadth of losing everything. He understood me and knew that I was always hard on myself, never giving myself much credit for the good stuff that I did.

His approach was probably the best thing for me. He was treading carefully with me. He didn't want to destroy me. But it was difficult to appreciate that at the time. All I could see was a guy who had robbed me of my rightful moment of glory.

My fall from grace had massive consequences for me. At the end of that season I failed to be picked to go on the tour to Argentina, America and Canada with Ireland – another incredibly disappointing set-back – and I made up my mind that I was going to work hard in pre-season training and try to get back. But the clock was against me. It had taken me too long to get my act together and I knew it. I had new contract negotiations coming up in a couple of weeks and I was deeply uncertain about my future.

Back then, there were no agents so contract negotiations meant talking directly to the coaches. Mind you, contract negotiations was a misnomer. You went in, the coach told you what he was offering and that was that. No negotiation.

All of which meant that, at some stage in the summer, after a tough period in my rugby career, I had to go and talk to Deccie about my future, or lack of one. All summer long I fretted about the meeting and then, finally, Deccie phoned me and asked me to meet him in Cork.

He didn't pull his punches. He came at me with accusations about the way I was training and the way I was playing, about my attitude, my lack of discipline and that I wasn't applying myself fully. He hammered away at me for twenty minutes or so, and it was so bad that at one point I remember, thinking, "God, why's he doing this to me? Are things really this bad?"

Eventually, I just couldn't take it any more. I was only in my early twenties and this was new territory to me: My eyes welled up and I got embarrassed. I felt vulnerable in front of him and I broke down, got very emotional. I apologised to him and spilled my guts, I told him my entire story, explained to him why I was such an emotional and mental screw-up. I said I wasn't happy and that I'd spent the last few months pressing a self-destruct button on something that I loved. I wasn't training hard enough, was going out on weekends and having a few pints. I said I'd gone from being a mechanic on low-ish wages to being paid a good salary, and even given a sponsored car, to do something I loved. I had got carried away and lazy.

"Help me," I asked him. "Help me."

In that moment, the mood of the meeting changed.

He told me he would help me, said not to worry, that things would be okay. I made a commitment to him – to learn from the knocks of the last few months. Deccie spoke of the need for me to maintain a level playing field by not allowing myself to get too high when we won, or too low when we lost. He wanted me to strike a better balance. I left the meeting with ten grand cut from my salary and a short-term contract, but I was happy – I was still a rugby player and I felt stronger and better than I'd done for a long time. I was determined to prove myself all over again.

• • • • • • •

Looking back at that point in the summer of 2000, I have only one regret – that the meeting with Deccie hadn't come sooner. With his help and his influence, I could have achieved a lot more in the early part of my career. But, from that point on, he saw a change in my attitude and, in return, he gave me great support. He was still tough on me, still made me do my job. But I improved the quality of my work and my attitude so that there was a huge improvement in my whole application to, and appreciation of, being a professional player.

I still infuriated him sometimes over the years and he didn't always pick me, but a new relationship blossomed. He was never a guy for favourites but we were able to get along a lot better, have a bit of fun together and we got to know each other really well.

Deccie was one of the people who helped me get there in the end, Deccie, Niall and players like Gallimh all played a part.

By the time I had walked out of Deccie's office that day we had got everything out into the open and it was a painful, sobering experience to go through that kind of process. It was, in truth, a cathartic moment for me and for my career. At that time, I was someone who was actually quite fragile. I obviously had this macho reputation and a tough exterior but I was quite soft on the inside. He began to understand me better, he realised he didn't always need to roar at me to get results and was more patient with me. He'd take time out to ask me how I was, how things were going. He'd tell me to be more positive with myself and to come and talk to him if I had problems or needed help. That was a massive thing for me, just massive.

Here was a guy who had twenty-five or thirty other players to look after, but was taking time out to deal with me, personally.

That was one of his true strengths, and all the players knew it. Deccie has a great heart and a caring side. It wasn't just rugby players he was training, he grew to understand that we all had lives, we were all people. He was building a team, but much more than the school teams he was used to. He was learning to deal with adults who had hopes, needs and desires and he was doing a superb job of learning how to deal with us all.

In fact, though none of us really understood it at the time, we were all on a learning curve together.

And again, though none of us really understood it back in the summer of 2000 when we had just embarked on what would be known as the Munster Journey, Deccie was building more than just a rugby team. He was building a family.

All that was ahead of us, ahead of us all. In the summer of 2000, all I knew was how I felt when I walked through the doors of Deccie's office at the end of our meeting. I felt a great weight had been lifted from my shoulders, from my mind. I was being given a second chance but, more

January 28, 2001
Heineken Cup Quarter-Final
v Biarritz (Thomond Park)
Won: 38-29

Were we a one-hit wonder?

Were we a team that had more to give, or was last year's march to the final, which we lost 8-9 to Northampton, the pinnacle of our journey?

People had already labelled us 'The Nearly Men' a tag that we were anxious to shake off. Woody had departed back to Harlequins, but Frankie Sheehan was battling his way into the side as hooker.

We'd beaten Castres 32-29 in France, a game in which I'd been sin-binned in the first half. At one stage we were fourteen points down, 6-20, but Gallimh and Axel led from the front and we managed to turn things around. After that, we swapped results with Bath, beating them in Thomond Park and losing to them away. But wins against Newport in Rodney Parade (39-24), and a great victory over Castres in Musgrave Park (21-11) left us with a quarter-final against Biarritz in Thomond Park.

All winter long we'd been putting together good results. The wins over Castres at home and away were huge triumphs, but beating Newport was a massive, massive result. The game was a tough, hard slog with ROG pulling the strings, and important tries from Anthony Horgan and Mike Mullins sealing a great win. Beating the Welsh meant our quarter-final clash with Biarritz would be at home.

The French fought like fanatics on their home turf but they still weren't great travellers so making them travel to the west of Ireland was brilliant for us – we would need every advantage we could get if we were to make it past these guys.

• • • • • • •

In the midst of some terrible weather, we'd just lost against Bath, 5-18, in a Saturday night match at the Recreation Ground and, as I was trudging off the pitch, three friends from Clanwilliam, Frankie Nolan, Liam Downey and Stan Waugh, approached me.

They broke the news to me that my uncle Andy had died. In fact he had died the night before, Friday, October 28, in hospital but my extended family, including Andy's wife Olive and my cousins, Ian, David and Andrea, had decided to keep the news from me until after the game. Andy loved rugby and had played a big role in my making it through to the Munster team, and his family knew that it's how he would have wanted it.

We were very close and I was very fond of him. Andy was my Dad's brother and he and his family lived and farmed very close to our home, so, I would have spent a lot of my childhood up at his house, playing rugby with my cousins.

He was a great character – always good craic – and he was a Clanwilliam stalwart, taking a great interest in the players there and in how his own youngsters, and nephews, progressed. His son, Ian, and I were roughly the same age and we were very close friends, playing rugby together and hanging around.

All through our childhoods, my uncle had been there for us, coaching us, training us, shouting at us, encouraging us, playing with us as we moved through the Clanwilliam underage set-up.

It was hard to believe that he had died. Like his own father, my grandfather Jack, Andy was only fifty four years old when he died of cancer. He'd been ill for three or four months and, while we had known his illness was serious, the family had been trying to stay positive.

Losing to Bath in a disappointing game, the emotions and the adrenaline were already running high, but the shock of hearing, so far away from home, of Andy's death was a blow. My parents were at the Recreation Ground and came into the dressing room to talk to me: Deccie arranged for them to fly back that night with me and the team.

I still miss Andy. His death marked the end of an era in many ways.

Over the coming decade another two of my uncles and one of my aunts also passed away – all from cancer.

Their deaths were hard on my Dad. He had grown up in a big family – there were five brothers and six sisters – but they'd all stayed in contact, despite some of them moving abroad.

My uncle Billy, a building contractor who lived in England, died on October 10, 2005, and my aunt Joanie, whom I stayed with many times in London, passed away on April 12, 2008. Both Billy and Joanie came home regularly and my Dad's family remained very close knit.

Then, soon after Joanie's death, my uncle Philly died on July 22, 2008. Uncle Philly was another Clanwilliam stalwart who was active in the club until he became ill. He had started life as a hurling man but, over the years, he became very passionate about rugby in Clanwilliam, Munster and Ireland. His son, Phillip, and his three daughters, Josephine, Catherine and Toni still live close to Limerick Junction and growing up we spent our summers going backwards and forwards between all the farms.

Looking back now, I recognise how hard it has been for my Dad and my surviving aunts, Peggy, Eileen, Nuala, Brigid and Mary, uncle Patsy and uncle Nick, who lives in Australia. To lose three brothers and a sister is a hard thing.

●●●●●●●

The quarter-final against Biarritz came early in the year, right at the end of January and at the outset of the Foot and Mouth crisis.

By that point, we'd won five out of six pool games and bringing a French team out of France for the quarter-final was seen by us as a massive boost, particularly when you considered what kind of a side they were. They were one of probably three or four teams in France, alongside the likes of Toulouse, Stade and Perpignan, who had massive budgets. With money came the capability of signing players from all over the world to play alongside their home Internationals. One word describes their pack: Huge. I hadn't seen a team that big before – they were bloody massive and, watching them trundle out onto the pitch, just looking at their size and physicality, was an eye-opener.

I was feeling good, confident and optimistic in the lead-up to the game. There had been a couple of injuries on the Ireland team, Simon Easterby was out and Eric Miller, so I figured there could be an opening there, an opportunity to break into the Six Nations squad, which was going to be announced the following week.

Just a few months previously, Munster had reached a Heineken Cup final but instead of lining out with my team-mates in the most important game of my life, my career was hanging in the balance – only a heart-to-heart with Deccie Kidney had saved it. Now, I was only one good performance away from cementing my provincial return to form with a potential call-up to the International squad again so, there was a lot at stake for me and I desperately wanted to play well. But, having missed out on so much the previous year, I wasn't taking anything for granted.

There were some significant talking points leading into the game. People made a lot of the fact that Claw's old friend, Olivier Roumat, was lining out for Biarritz.

A couple of years previously, Claw had been suspended for six months for stamping on Roumat's head in an International game in Paris. So, people were trying to talk-up that rivalry. We expected a few sparks to fly as well but, in the end, that didn't happen.

In fact, the game started well for us. Early on, Axel and I were out on the blind side when the ball was passed along the back line. I caught a pass really low at my feet and made a little bit of a break, before passing it out to Anthony who forced his way over in the corner for a try.

According to Axel, he used his speed and power to get over but, to the rest of us, it looked like it was more his weight and bulk that got him through it. He was only a couple of yards out so, after my precision pass to him, all he had to do was put it under the arm and drive his way in. He'd have been hard pushed not to make the line!

It was a great start to a match in which Axel went on to score three tries – and I had a hand in two of them. His second try came when we broke up the field from a lineout. Gallimh and Axel stayed out on the blind side and

I went to the bottom of the ruck. Strings was giving out to me for going for the ball and playing his role. But I cut back to the blind side and threw a big long floaty pass out to Gallimh who drew in the cover of Serge Betsen and then passed to Axel who marched up the sideline and just about reached over for his second try.

He scored a similar one for his third try and, suddenly, the rest of us were faced with the prospect of a lifetime of having to listen to Axel's triple try tale. In fairness, it was a unique achievement for a No. 8. Especially as his tries were all scored out wide.

Woody once described Axel as, "… the smartest player I have ever played with or against". Woody was right, Axel was a great player and, by scoring a unique haul of three tries, Axel was rewarded with an equally unique prize. Unknown to us, any player who scored three tries in one game for Munster would win the prize of free Domino's Pizzas for life.

We were convinced that Axel had known about the offer before the game, and that's what inspired him to hang around on the wings for his three tries. He could even have passed for one of them but, clearly, the pizzas were on his mind. Not that he has the physique of a man who eats pizzas, but still, it was no mean prize. But he's very decent about his lifelong freebies. The pizza chain has a place quite close to the Clarion Hotel where the team stays in Limerick before each game so we often get a pizza on Axel's account.

Match-wise, I didn't do too badly myself. I picked up the Man of the Match award and got plenty of congratulations, but Axel was the man who finished the night with free pizzas for life!

Unfortunately, we took our eye off the ball in the last fifteen or twenty minutes of the game and let Biarritz back into it. In that last period we felt really good. We were two or three tries ahead and Biarritz were throwing the ball all over the place. The game looked well and truly over, but they scored two tries in the last few minutes and came right back at us.

The last few minutes were absolutely nerve-wracking. We managed to hang on and win the game, but it was no stroll in the park.

It was a big, big night for us all. Axel had secured pizzas for life, while I'd picked up the Man of the Match award and put myself into a very strong position to get into the national squad the following week. I was happy with my performance, I'd played well, I'd been involved a lot and made a few line breaks.

But I didn't get too carried away with myself. It's always nice to pick up an award like that – anyone who tells you differently is lying – but it's not something I ever dwelt on. I just wanted to play well and do my job, especially after the previous year.

Twelve months on, from a tough period in my career I was now starting the quarter-final for Munster in Thomond Park, playing well and making a significant contribution to the success of the team. In that twelve-month period, I'd moved on and my career had moved on with me. I was back at the heart of the Munster team and on the point of launching my Ireland career.

That was the most important thing for me, not a Man of the Match award. As it turned out I was selected the week after in the Ireland squad and two weeks later I was selected for my first start against Italy in the Six Nations, and my second-ever Irish cap.

The Biarritz game was massive for the entire Munster team. We were back in a semi-final and within striking distance of putting right the previous year's disappointment against Northampton.

Losing to Northampton could have caused us to slip away. It's happened to a lot of teams – to get within inches of the winning post only to lose, and then allow the disappointment to overcome the desire to win.

But we were growing as a team. We hadn't had huge changes in team personnel and we had developed and improved. That idea of growing together as a team, rather than as a disparate group of individuals is the reason why a lot of us have stayed with Munster for so long. We stuck together through thick and thin; we progressed and developed and learned from each other and with each other, getting better together.

We developed our ambition together and shared a drive to succeed. That win against Biarritz was proof to me that we were going to get back up there – that we weren't going to be one-season wonders.

We were starting to win away from home, and starting to consistently beat significant teams at home. Our performances were much better and we were eradicating the mistakes from our game. We weren't the finished article, by any means, but we were aware of that. We knew we had a long way to go, but we also realised we were in a good place.

There was a real buzz about the place. Brian O'Brien had come in as manager when Jerry Holland stepped down for work reasons. I knew Briano from Shannon. He was a great guy who was very important to us in both Shannon and Munster. He would be important to us that year as Munster manager. It was the first year of the 'Stand Up and Fight' song, and Briano started coming down into the dressing room to sing that song with us after games.

It's well documented how far the song has gone; it's become synonymous with the team, and we all took inspiration from it. So, when we beat Biarritz, there was a buzz about the place. It felt good to be back in the semi-final of the Heineken Cup.

Post-Biarritz, Deccie congratulated us, but he also took us to task over our mistakes and for letting the opposition back in. One of his main strengths has always been that he doesn't get carried away with big wins, or too angry or low over losses. If he thought we didn't try or give 100 per cent, he would get really annoyed at us.

As it turned out, there was a long delay before the semi-final against Stade Français. By the time the two teams met on April 21, in Lille, I was out of the Munster team with an injury. I'd broken my thumb playing for Shannon in the AIL against Young Munster two weeks before the semi-final, so I was condemned to watch the encounter from the stand.

The game ended in a 15-16 defeat which included the disallowing of a perfectly good John O'Neill try. The ref also ruled out a perfectly good penalty by ROG, and the French winger, Christophe Dominici, was allowed back onto the pitch after serving only eight minutes of a, supposed, ten minute sin-binning.

In the end, Munster ran out of time. Looking back on it, we'd faced a strong Stade squad who badly wanted revenge for their quarter-final defeat in Thomond Park the previous year. But bad decisions also cost us.

It had been a huge achievement to get that far, but there was no getting away from the fact that the season was a disappointment. On top of that

John Langford, our honorary Munster man from Oz, was returning back home and losing such a great player was disheartening. At the end of April 2001, it was hard to lift ourselves up after another disappointing defeat.

But we did. Within a year, we'd be back in the final of another Heineken Cup, pushing hard to land that elusive trophy.

When I first went to Shannon my nickname was 'Cheeky' because I was a mouthy kid from Tipperary. The truth was, I was in awe of guys like Mick Galwey and Eddie Halvey, and I was excited to be around them, stepping up to a higher level.

I'd been going with my Dad to watch these guys playing with Shannon for the previous couple of years and now, here I was, in the midst of them, playing alongside them.

I was still a young kid working at Pierse Motors and, suddenly I found myself rubbing shoulders with great players like Brian Rigney, Ciaran Maher and Mick Fitzgibbon.

It dawned on me this was what I wanted to do. So, agreeing to play U-20s with Shannon was the right decision to make at that stage – after all, I was still going home to play with Clanwilliam as well, so I had the best of both worlds.

The move itself was straightforward: Melvin McNamara, who used to deliver fuel to the garage, got me involved. He knew that I'd played with Munster U-18s and with the Irish Youths and asked the club to contact me. Garryowen had been on to me as well, but I just liked the idea of playing with Shannon. Mick Galwey was playing there and, when I joined the U-20s, Brendan Foley – Anthony's Dad – was our coach.

I was lucky enough to play in an unbelievably good U-20s team, which swept the board in all competitions. We won the Limerick Cup, the Limerick League and the Munster Cup.

James Hickey from the Irish U-21s was there, so was Alan McGrath, Andrew Thompson and a certain John Hayes. There was a core group of players who'd been successful in Schools rugby with St Munchin's: Axel Foley was the captain and, even at that young age, he had a fearsome reputation. He was a former Irish Schools Captain and, right from the start, I was in awe of him. The thing that stuck out about Axel was that nothing ever phased him, he had a calmness about him. I loved playing with him: I fed off him, listened to him, watched him.

We still slag the hell out of him for being an ignorant sod because he can appear quite rude to people – he often just grunts at them and turns his back. But, in reality, he's quite shy and is a lovely bloke.

Then, after those early years with the U-20s, the senior coach, Niall O'Donovan, asked me to tour Canada in 1995 with the senior team which was a huge step. Eddie Halvey and Axel were just back from the World Cup and I was touring with the likes of Mick Galwey, Pat Murray, Conor McDermott, Billy O'Shea, Niall O'Shea, Noel Healey and Colm McMahon.

In 1996, Shannon won the AIL title following an incredible run, which saw them win ten games out of ten. I wasn't on the team that first year – I was still playing U-20s and lining out at home for Clanwilliam. But Niallo thought I was ready to take the step to the senior Shannon team so, finally, I had a decision to make.

The following season – 1996/97 – I opted to go full-time with Shannon and left Clanwilliam for good. It was a difficult call to make but it had to happen – I'd exhausted the dual status situation and I felt I'd given Clan as much as I could.

If I experienced some tugs on the heart-strings about leaving my old club, I knew that it was the right decision for my rugby career. I joined Shannon at an incredibly fortunate time – they'd just won the first of four-in-a-row AIL titles, and I became part of the team that won in 1997, '98, and '99.

That early success in the AIL helped my career. I was playing with the likes of Pat Murray, perhaps the most underrated back in Munster and Ireland back then, and probably the unluckiest guy never to play for his country.

Playing with Pat and the others and winning trophies was ideal for me because I was still so young. I wasn't fully developed but there were a lot of big strong, experienced guys to look after me during games. Their successes on the pitch meant that I was being propelled into the national spotlight.

But, at the start of that first season with Shannon, I wasn't overly concerned with ambition – I was just excited to be playing senior rugby. I'd gone from playing against the likes of Kilfeacle to playing against the big Dublin teams like St Mary's and in local derbies against Young Munster and Garryowen in front of 10,000 or 12,000.

• • • • • • •

Who doesn't know Mick Galwey? He's a great character with a huge heart and over the years I've grown very close to him. Everybody knows him as a great rugby player and as a great leader of Shannon, Munster and Ireland teams but Mick has been much more than that: He's been a great leader of men, someone who didn't just look out for his team-mates, but for everyone.

Gallimh would drive down from Kilkenny and pick me up for training if I couldn't borrow my Mum's car. Although he was always a good friend to me he could get very thick as well, and he gave me a few verbal – and the odd physical – warnings over the years. But he loves the craic as much as I do and there was a bit of a bond there between us so we started to spend a lot of time together. On one occasion, he phoned me up in the garage and pretended to be the rugby journalist, Ned Van Esbeck. I gave him almost a full interview – telling him how great I was and waxing lyrical about my future and playing for Shannon – before I copped on that it was Gallimh at the end of the line, doing his best not to burst out laughing.

But, if you can't beat 'em you gotta join 'em, and, pretty soon, I was a fully paid-up member of Gallimh's unofficial press corps. Noel 'Buddha' Healy became a regular panellist on local media shows which, inexplicably, never seemed to air, while John O'Neill must be wondering to this day why most of his interviews were never published. Sorry, lads.

It wasn't just players that we targeted – my plumber mate, Fergal Gallagher, received the odd emergency call from shops asking him to urgently deal with a burst pipe. Fergal's work van would screech to a halt outside the shop and he'd disappear inside, only to emerge a few minutes later, enraged and looking around the place to see if he could identify the spot from where Gallimh and I were watching the fun unfolding.

In those days, we would play AIL games in Dublin and myself and John Hayes would go and stay with Gallimh in his home in Kilkenny. We all became solid friends and, later, some of the Clanwilliam lads like Johnny O'Dwyer, Johnny Lacey, Fergal and Ian started to come down with us.

It was all part of the fun: We'd play a Saturday game, head down to Kilkenny for the evening and then travel back to Tipperary the next day to take in another game. It was nothing for Gallimh to have maybe seven or eight of us staying in his house and his wife Joan – God be good to her – always welcomed us and fed us, looked after us and put up with us.

Mind you, it was her husband who was the biggest messer of all. Often, Hayes and I would open our kit bags at Tuesday night training to discover a nappy belonging to Mick's little daughter, Neasa, buried deep inside. The nappy would have been in there since the weekend and the smell would have knocked you out. Or, sometimes, I'd find one of Neasa's nappies under the seat of the car.

Nappies aside, it was a special time. The Shannon connection wasn't just introducing me to a new part of my rugby career, it was introducing me to a new chapter in my life and a group of friends who blended in perfectly with my old mates.

John Hayes was a perfect example of that. Today, John is the most capped player ever to don the Irish jersey and he sets the standard for quiet dependability. But The Bull has a wicked sense of humour and is one of the greatest slaggers in the Munster team.

When I first moved to Shannon, I had an apartment in Limerick and John would come and stay on Saturday nights and we'd go for a few drinks together. Neither one of us were big drinkers and that was part of our connection – some of the other lads could murder a load of pints but The Bull and myself were slower drinkers who liked to pace things. We got hammered alright, but compared to some of them, we were just amateurs. Mind you, if he paced himself in the drinking stakes, there was no such restraint with The Bull when it came to his grub. On one memorable night

Backed up by his Mum and Dad, AJ faces the media in his first Munster jersey.

Aged just one day old, AJ catches a few
zzzs on his Dad's chest.

AJ has brought incredible joy to our lives.

Little Munster Monster

If only I were allowed to carry the ball in one of these!

Ruth introduces AJ to Thomond Park.

Ruth and I take a helicopter trip over the Grand Canyon during our Vegas trip.

Alan junior looks a little unsure about the busted lip his dad got during the 2009 Heineken Cup quarter-final against the Ospreys.

Smile!

The Brothers Quinlan – John, me and Andrew.

(Left to right) My sister, Carol, me, and my brothers,
John and Andrew with my Mum, Mary.

My cousin, Ian, and I pose in our school uniforms.

Some pictures need no explanation!

Mum makes sure I look presentable for my Communion.

On holiday on the Costa del Tipperary.

Animal Farm – growing up in Tipperary.

The gang poses with one of our many donkeys.

Nice hair!
Captaining
Munster U-18s
in 1993.

Mum poses with the Munster Senior Cup and Dad
holds on to the AIL trophy.

My parents, John and Mary.

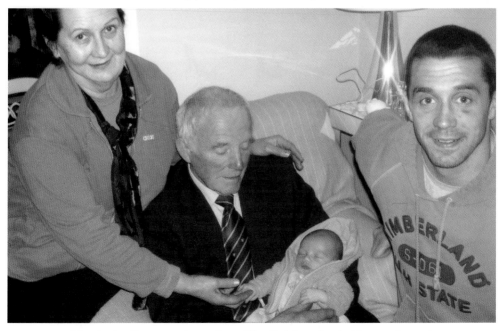

Introducing the newest member of the Quinlan clan to his grandparents.

*Ruth and me on
our wedding day.*

*The lads get ready for the
off. I'm joined by Fergal,
Pat, Ian and Johnny.*

AJ and his cousin, Peter Paul, at their joint Christening with (left to right) proud parents, Peter and Gillian Smith, and Ruth and myself.

AJ and I take a moment out to ourselves.

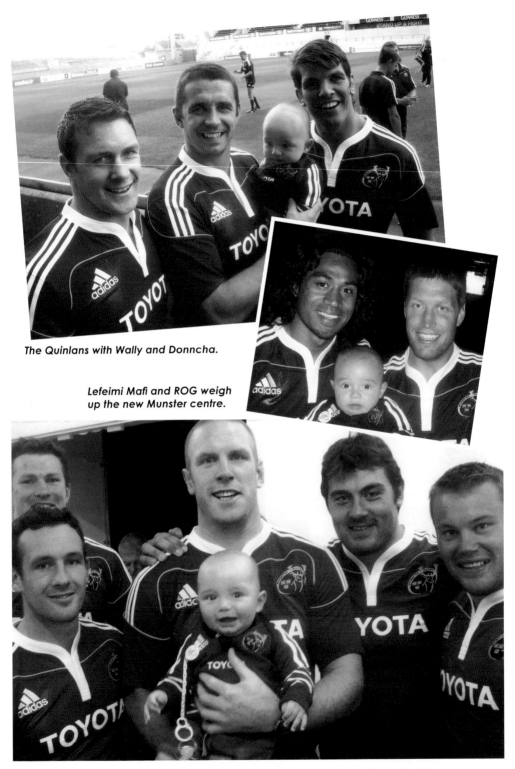

The Quinlans with Wally and Donncha.

Lefeimi Mafi and ROG weigh up the new Munster centre.

Meet the Feckers: AJ with (left to right) Donnacha Ryan, Danny Riordan, Paul O'Connell, Tony Buckley and Denis Fogarty.

The guys get ready in 1997 for the holiday of a lifetime in Crete.

On tour: (Left to right) Ian, me, Stevie and Johnny.

Turkey '98 (front left to right) Johnny O'Dwyer, Fergal Gallagher, Ian Quinlan, Paddy Maher, Paul McMahon, (back left to right) Colm McMahon, Mick Lynch, Alan Quinlan, Anthony Foley, John Hayes, Johnny Lacey.

It's tough work being a toddler.

*AJ joins me at Thomond Park to help me
celebrate reaching 202 caps for Munster.*

out in Kilkenny, Gallimh, Lamb Chop, myself and The Bull all headed to the chipper for some food to soak up that evening's alcohol. Problem was, there was a queue ahead of us and we were all starving, especially The Bull. But where there's a will, there's … no depths to which a rugby player won't sink and, as we progressed along the queue, Hayes started picking at some of the scraps left by departed diners. He made his way along the counter stuffing his face with half-eaten burgers, chewed-up chicken legs, discarded onion rings and abandoned chips. By the time we reached the top of the queue and were ready to order, John put his hand in the air: "No thanks," says the Bull, "I couldn't eat another bite!"

So, John and I became close and we'd look after each other on nights out. We've developed a close bond, which is just as well because when we went to Gallimh's home in Kilkenny in those early years, John would invariably be my room-mate. It was usually Hayes I'd wake up with on a Sunday morning, with him farting across the top of me, his big hairy back looking out at me. It was no surprise that, years later, following my shoulder injury, it was The Bull that I entrusted to scrub my back in the shower.

• • • • • • •

When I joined Shannon full-time in 1996/97, the new dawn of profession-alism in Irish rugby was already a year old. There were a handful of contracts in existence but we were informed that twenty new, part-time contracts were due to come out at the end of that season – I made up my mind that one of those contracts would have my name on it.

I'd qualified as a mechanic but I decided to down tools six months before the contracts were given out and dedicate myself to trying to win one of them. People told me I was crazy, that I was giving up a good job for something unknown. But I reckoned I had to take a chance: I had enthusiasm and talent and I wanted to find out just how far could I go.

We were all delving into the unknown. Professional rugby was in its infancy, there were no rules and no-one knew how it would work out.

Money and rugby were relative strangers at the time, with Shannon you got your travelling expenses and a few bob, but that was all. So, I ended up selling Lottery Tickets for Clanwilliam to make a few quid. Michael Hogan from Tipperary was running the lottery for the club and he had heard about my plan to leave my job and give myself six months to have a crack at winning a professional contract. He offered me IR£50 a week to run the lottery and see if I could get the numbers of participants up. I accepted and hand-picked a few sellers who knocked on doors and asked people to support their club. We ended up doing pretty well – I got IR£50 a week and the club were making IR£400 a week.

There were other part-time jobs too. My long-suffering plumber friend, Fergal Gallagher, got me a part-time job taking down suspended ceilings for his Dad. Fergal and I had a great time and earned a few bob and when we weren't working, he helped me in the gym.

My goal was to train full-time and I was lucky enough to be awarded a scholarship to train in the local sports centre – the Canon Hayes Recreational Centre in Tipperary – because of my involvement with the Ireland and Munster U-18s.

I'd get on my bike and cycle from Limerick Junction to Tipperary every day and train for a couple of hours in the Canon Hayes gym. I was tall but quite slim back then and I realised that I had to get bigger, to strengthen up, so my main focus was bulking up a bit with weights – something my brother, John, helped me a lot with.

It was an exciting time for me. I never questioned the decision to quit work – I knew I had talent but, more than that, I knew this was a once-in-a-lifetime opportunity, a chance for me to do something different with my life. I wanted to play rugby and be paid for it.

At the end of that first season with Shannon, I planned a holiday with the lads at the end of June. Johnny O'Dwyer, Johnny Lacey, Fergal Gallagher, Ian Quinlan and I were heading to Crete along with Davie Donovan, Brian Gallagher, Eddie Nugent and Eamon Buckley.

The holiday turned out to be one of the best of our lives, and we still talk about it to this day – discreetly. But, if the Crete trip was notable for things that can't be included in these pages, then it was also a key time for

Johnny Lacey and myself, as we were both waiting for news from Munster regarding those crucial part-time contracts.

It was a bit like waiting for exam results. I was phoning home to my Mum to see if anything had come in the post. Eventually, I got the news that I'd been offered a contract and so had Johnny. From then on it was party-time, celebrating our elevation to the ranks of part-time rugby professionals. We couldn't wait to get back home and get started.

It was hard to believe how far we'd come. I'd quit my job as a mechanic to get to this point and, to be given a part-time contract was such a boost to me, a reward for the gamble I'd taken.

But the rollercoaster ride wasn't over yet. I played my first Heineken Cup game for Munster that autumn against Harlequins and scored a try, and then followed that up with another try in the next game against Cardiff. After that, I was contacted by London Irish and also Bath, who actually travelled over to Tipperary to meet me.

Life was going at a-mile-a-minute as London Irish offered me in the region of Stg£45,000 to Stg£50,000 to sign. I'd just bought a brand new mobile phone and was trying to keep up with Willie Anderson from the Irish, and with Bath's representatives, as they tried to persuade me that my future lay across the Irish Sea.

Unfortunately, my immediate future was thrown into danger when Lamb Chop O'Dwyer discovered my mobile number and realised I was talking to the English clubs on it. Suddenly, and very strangely, every time I climbed onto my bike to pedal in to the Canon Hayes sports centre, I began to get calls from potential clubs anxious to talk to me. It took me a while to discover that Lamb Chop and the lads were driving around behind me every time I got on the bike, making hoax calls to my mobile and breaking their arses laughing at me, wobbling all over the road, every time I tried to answer my mobile.

A the time, I wasn't sure who to turn to for advice – professional rugby and contracts were a brand new entity so, in the end, I spoke to Jerry Holland and Deccie. Within a week Jerry sat me down and offered me a full-time, two-year Munster contract, worth around IR£25,000.

Within three months of being offered a part-time contract worth

IR£7500 plus match fees, and within nine months of packing in my job as a mechanic to have a crack at this whole professional thing, I was now being offered triple that amount.

But more was to come: I'd trained a few times with the Ireland squad and within a couple of days I received a full-time, eighteen-month Ireland contract for IR£35,000 plus a Mondeo car, plus match fees.

It was phenomenal money for me – less than a year before, I'd been earning IR£140 a week as a mechanic, borrowing my Mum's car to get around, cadging lifts with people or cycling. Jerry Holland still gives me a sore touch about claiming expenses for travelling up and down to training in Cork that summer when I didn't have a car and was being driven everywhere by Johnny Lacey!

Now, I was only one of five or six players in each province to be on a full-time contract though more players would be upgraded as the season went on. It's hard to describe what the mood was like in rugby circles back then. Guys were being faced with decisions about whether or not to leave their jobs, sign rugby contracts and take a chance. A lot of good rugby players passed up contracts because they didn't think the whole professional thing would last. In the event, it was a massive change for us all. Suddenly, guys were training full-time and giving up work. It was unheard of. What was professionalism, being paid to do your job? But how did you do that in rugby? How much to train? How little to train? How much recovery did you do, what kind of training did you undertake?

• • • • • • •

Fortunately, in the midst of the chaos of contracts I could always rely on the mayhem of my friends at home to lighten the mood. On one memorable trip home to Tipperary I found myself touring around the town with Andy Fogarty, a friend of mine who was working as a mobile security patrol at the time.

Andy was called out to meet the Gardai at a suspected break-in at a local filling station, so I tagged along for the ride. It was early in the morning so the petrol station was closed down and empty, except for the Gardai and Andy.

As the men in uniform discussed crime in the Tipp area, I amused myself by playing with the forecourt's Tannoy. Johnny O'Dwyer lived just across the road so I decided to wake him up by calling to him over the PA system.

"Lamb Chop, Lamb Chop... Get out of bed, Lamb Chop... Come out with your hands up, O'Dwyer," I called softly into the microphone, pleased with the effect I was creating outside in the darkened forecourt. Johnny actually woke up and started peering out the window to see what was going on but, by that stage, I had got fed up trying to waken him and had spotted a better target on which to try my disembodied voice.

Mikey Morrissey, a friend of mine from the town, was on his way home after a night out and he was clearly the worse for wear. Staggering through the forecourt, between the petrol pumps, Mikey was stunned to hear a voice calling to him quietly through the dead of the night.

"Mikey... Mikey... Mikey Morrissey. Yes, Mikey, I'm speaking to you," I intoned in a deep voice. Mikey, clearly four sheets to the wind, stopped staggering and peered up into the darkened heavens – actually the roof of the forecourt – wondering who owned the invisible voice speaking to him. "This is God, Mikey, and I need to talk to you about your drinking and about your wicked ways. I want to hear your confession, Mikey."

An awestruck Mikey, thankfully, was too drunk to realise he was talking to a rugby player and not God, so he dutifully dropped to his knees and, clasping his hands together, rapidly cried out to his God, praying and apologising for his wicked ways.

Spreading his arms heavenwards, Mikey cried out: "I'm sorry, I'm sorry, what can I can do?"

"Mikey, you must give up your aul' sins, and you must give up the drink. Then, Mikey, you will be forgiven," said the voice.

Beseeching God to give him a second chance, Mikey crawled on his knees across the forecourt where, according to the watching Lamb Chop O'Dwyer, who was now weeping tears of laughter, he made his confession and, "prayed for forgiveness from pump No. 4".

CHAPTER 11

April 28, 2002
Heineken Cup Final
v Leicester (Millennium Stadium)
Lost: 9-15

The 2001/2002 season brought with it a lot of hope and a lot of controversy. In the pool stages we'd put together wins at home and away to Harlequins and Bridgend and we'd beaten Castres in the season opener at Thomond Park.

But then came the return game against Castres in France. It was our last pool game and we were pushing for a win and a home quarter-final, but we ended up losing in a typical South of France battle. The game in Stade Pierre Antoine was tough and intense – they dominated us but, all through the game, we'd held on and notched up a few scores which secured us a bonus point.

But the talking point of the game wasn't the result, it was a hugely contentious incident in which the Claw was bitten on the hand by one of the Castres players.

I was right behind Claw in the scrum when it happened, but it all took place so quickly that I wasn't at all sure what had gone on.

We were in a scrum in the middle of the field and Peter was trying to push back the Castres No. 8, Ismaella Lassissi who had moved to wing forward. Next thing I knew, Claw was letting out a roar, closely followed by a couple of expletives, and I was thinking, "What the hell happened there?"

After the scrum there was a break up and a bit of pushing and shoving and Claw had a serious mark on the inside of his hand. Claw was pretty angry as the mark on his hand looked like it had been left by teeth, so after the game the doctor treated Peter's hand and Munster took pictures of it and examined the video evidence. It was fairly conclusive that some sort of an incident happened and Munster decided to cite the player.

Castres decided to counter-claim and accuse Claw of making, "racial and discriminatory remarks," about their player.

Lassissi was found guilty of biting Peter and got a lengthy ban. It wasn't something Peter, or any of the other Munster players, wanted to see – he would have settled for an apology but in the absence of that, there needed to be some kind of action taken, because of the seriousness of the incident. Castres withdrew their allegations against Peter but appealed Lassissi's ban. They brought a forensic scientist from France, who argued the point that the bite wasn't human. Much to the annoyance of Munster, the player was cleared and the ban was reversed.

The incident added spice to the knock-out stages because, after beating Stade Français in the quarter-final, we once again faced Castres in the semi-final so the two boys were going to be locking horns again.

We beat them 25-17 in a game in which the Claw played with burns on his arms and face which he'd received trying to light the family barbeque! After the match Lassissi came into our dressing room and, unofficially, apologised to Claw for what had happened in the first game. It was enough for Peter and the two men swapped jerseys, which was a good way to put an end to the whole affair.

I was lucky enough to be in the side for the semi-final: I'd lost my place in the quarter-final when Wally returned from injury and, when the lads beat Stade Français, I reckoned it was going to be another case of déjà vu for me and that I'd miss the quarter-, semi- and final again like I had in 2000.

But, two weeks before the semi-final, our new Australian signing, Jim Williams, tore his calf in a friendly against Leinster down in Cork. I was back in the starting line-up and, despite Jim and Axel both recovering from injuries in time for the final against Leicester, Deccie selected me at No. 6, Wally at No. 7 and Axel at No. 8 – with Jim on the bench.

The four of us in the back row knew that we were up for three places but we also knew that the competition for places was a sign that we were becoming a strong squad. Lots of teams had Internationals on the bench, so not starting wasn't seen as being dropped.

• • • • • • •

I remember watching the other semi-final between Leicester and Llanelli. The Welsh team was very strong that year with players like Scott Quinnell and Guy and Simon Easterby but, deep down, if you were to pick which of the two teams you wanted to face, it would have been Llanelli. Leicester was full of world-class English Internationals and were a powerhouse in both the Heineken Cup and the English Premiership.

Llanelli played above themselves that day and should have won, but Leicester pipped them to the post when Tim Stimpson kicked an injury-time penalty.

We'd had a good year ourselves, and the semi-final win over Castres had been superb, but I remember thinking that Sunday evening that, maybe, we'd have had a better chance of beating Llanelli.

Going into the game, the big threat from Leicester was their rolling maul and their scrum. In the game, we counteracted their maul really well but they still managed to score two tries, while we failed to get over the line at all. We only lost 15-9 and could have scored a couple of times but, still, to concede two tries and not score any ourselves was significant. Our discipline was good and our defence was strong but they beat us in the lineout. Paul O'Connell had just emerged that year and was playing superbly but, two weeks before the final, in a friendly against Ulster, I dropped him in a lineout and he rolled over on his ankle and wasn't 100 per cent going into the Leicester match. It was an accident on my part but Paulie wasn't too happy with me at the time.

His injury, plus the fact that Leicester had clearly done their homework on our lineout, resulted in them stealing quite a few balls from us. They were grizzled and experienced and their defence was up a notch from anything we'd faced before.

Their first try came when they stole the ball from our lineout and passed it out their backline to an Irishman, Geordan Murphy, who managed to score against us in the corner.

That try was a big blow. We knew going into the game we'd have to defend really well, we'd have stop Leicester from scoring and, when Austin Healy scored a second, opportunistic try, we were always chasing the game. Before Healy's try, Leicester had kicked into the corner and had tried to maul us over the line, but we defended well and stopped them at source from getting any momentum. But then they passed it to their out-half and Healy made a break and scored under the posts.

One of the most significant moments came near the end. We were 9-15 down, chasing the game and putting pressure on them when we won a scrum in a good position. We knew we needed a try and a conversion but there were only a couple of minutes left, so we were trying to keep the momentum going when Neil Back knocked the ball out of Stringer's hands and the ref failed to spot the foul. Seconds later the game was over and we'd lost our second final.

There was a lot made of the incident but, at the end of it all, Back did what he had to do – he made a decision and his team won. They're the ones in the history books. Sure, it would have been interesting to see what might have happened if we'd been allowed to carry on with the scrum but, at the end of the day, we didn't deserve to win that game and, deep down, we knew that. We gave it our all, but on the day they were a better side.

After losing to Leicester we came back to Limerick, accompanied by the tens of thousands of fans who had swollen the Millennium Stadium. It was Deccie and Niall's last game with us – they were departing to work with Ireland under Eddie O'Sullivan. It was also Claw's last game as he was retiring, so we'd really wanted to win the Heineken Cup for him and Deccie and Niallo.

We ended up going back to Claw's nightclub, The Sin Bin, where we had a few pints and drowned our sorrows. The next morning was very somber and emotional as we nursed sore heads and said our goodbyes. We would cross paths with Deccie and Niallo in the years ahead, but Claw had played his final game in a Munster shirt.

An era had truly ended.

CHAPTER 12

ROUGH AND FUMBLE AND RUCKING REGRETS

I don't know who grabbed my testicles but somebody did. It was in a maul and they were trying to turn us around. Everything was going at a frantic pace and you're playing as much by instinct as by design. All you know is that you're in the middle of a very physical confrontation and you're pressed up tight against your own team-mates in a maul against the opposition. Everyone's heaving and straining and busting a gut and then, suddenly, in amongst the pushing and shoving you feel someone hauling on your nuts. I don't know who did it or how it happened, but I remember it being a frightening experience: And ... well, feeling a bit shocked.

• • • • • • •

In France there's always an added bite to games and playing French teams on their home patch is a very different prospect to playing them in Ireland. There's a history, in the French Championship, of teams doing badly even when playing away in France, never mind their record of playing in another country. Certainly, in the early days of the Heineken Cup, Munster profited from a combination of being underestimated by a lot of the bigger French teams, and the apparent lack of French spirit in away games. They are overcoming that now, they no longer underestimate us and they prepare far better for their away games than they used to. Bottom line, they are trying harder. Their old mentality appeared to be that they'd win their home games in the League and lose their away games. We suspected that they were happy to pick up the odd away win but that the coaches would be inclined to accept that they would lose away from home.

That suspicion was confirmed for us when former Munster scrum-half, Mike Prendergast, left us in 2006 to play in Bourgoin. Mike played in

France for one year and, when he came home, he spoke of his frustration at the French mentality towards away games.

The flipside of this mentality is that playing at home is a totally different proposition for them. Essentially, it's a sin to lose at home so their determination, their level of effort and their levels of aggression seem to rise dramatically on home turf.

We witnessed this at first hand when we played Colomiers in 1999, in the Stade des Sept Derniers. We went into the game expecting a hard physical battle but I didn't expect to wind up having my testicles yanked by a Frenchman. I remain convinced that there are some encounters that should remain strictly between those of the opposite sex.

We were away from home in the last pool game in 1999 and qualification was on the line. Munster were really developing as a team: We had Woody playing with us and John Langford from Australia and we had a lot of young players coming into the squad. I remember we had a lineout and were driving Colomiers back in a maul when someone grabbed me and tried to pull me out of the maul. I was grabbed from the front, it was quite a frightening experience.

I don't want to castigate the French teams and, certainly, I'm no angel, but there is a bit of a history of their game being very physical. Today things are different, French teams are not known for dirty play, but it's still very tough.

In the end we won the match 31-15 – the first time we had won in France – but it was a baptism of fire in many ways and the first time I had ever been grabbed in that way in a game of rugby. There's nothing quite like playing the French in France. Expect anything and everything when you play down there. It's rough and very tough and a hell of an experience. Pushing, shoving, thumping, grabbing, spitting. Every team wants to win at home and, down through the years, we've made it an absolute point of principle that we would turn Thomond Park into a fortress.

I mean, rugby's a physical game, so there's no point in going out on a pitch expecting to be left untouched. I've been on the receiving end plenty of times, but nothing too bad. No one leaves the field of play surprised to see stud marks on their calves, hamstrings, their back, that kind of thing, though I've been lucky enough to be head-stamped only once – that was in a game for Ireland in Dublin against France. Whether it was deliberate or not, I don't know, but it wasn't a major thing – just a small gash on the head. You just get on with it. If you believed it was a deliberate head-stamp out in the open, you might swing for somebody, but otherwise you let it go. I figure it all goes with the territory when you play as a No. 6 and you're on the ball, trying to turn over possession and you're playing on the edge. It's something I've come to accept.

Punching, now that's a different matter. I haven't received any punches during a match, thanks be to God, which is a bit ironic really given my reputation. I've probably deserved a few punches from time to time, but no one ever took it upon themselves to land one on me.

Even though I've gotten into a few scrapes over the years, I've never intentionally gone out to hurt someone. Sure, I've stamped on people and rucked people off the ball when they've intentionally killed it, but I've never punched or spat at or gouged anyone.

I'd say there are a few lads out there who would have loved to have given me a good thump but, in my own mind, I've always played the game. Mind you, how Rodney So'oialo restrained himself from landing a haymaker on me when Ireland played against New Zealand, I'll never know. It was in 2008, and So'oialo dived over the ball and I rucked him out of it. He jumped straight up off the ground and I was bracing myself for a right chinning but, fortunately, it never came. He was a hardy sort of a fella and I'd say it would have hurt if he'd connected. In the event, the ref gave a penalty against Rodney So'oialo. The only thing the ref said to me was, "Well, mind your feet".

Unfortunately, I was cited after the match for the incident and was suspended for three weeks. That was a nightmare, considering the referee had been standing right beside us and hadn't even deemed it a penalty against me. The stamps had been a very passive, backwards movement. You could say I haven't had much luck against New Zealand, but there you go. So, while I may have rucked people out of it, it was never done to deliberately hurt anyone or be dirty. If I ever did it, it was to get someone off who had rolled over our ball and killed it for us. Rucking used to be in the rules of the game. Now, everything's changed and you're not supposed to put your feet near anyone, only move your feet in a backwards motion. Nowadays, there are a lot more cameras and citings so everyone has to be very careful.

I do have one regret.

It was against Cardiff in 2006, and we were driving forward, going for a bonus point. We had a pretty dominant maul that night and they were pulling our maul down all evening long and, in the midst them doing it again, I stamped on Mark Lewis' calf.

I'd been hacked off with him because we were going for a bonus point and he was illegally pulling on our maul and it was just getting frustrating. In the build-up of frustration, I stamped on him.

A little later, after the maul had collapsed, Mark fell and twisted his knee and was out injured for a couple of weeks. It hadn't been my intention to hurt him and he didn't blame me for his injury, but I just regretted it anyway and it kinda played on my mind. I ended up getting cited for it and suspended for six weeks. It was costly for me, personally, but that wasn't why I felt bad about it. I felt bad because the lad got injured and I knew how I would have felt if it had been me. I later apologised to him and he accepted and was very decent about it, but the incident has always stood out in my mind as something I wished hadn't happened.

• • • • • • •

In 2003, five years after Munster's first baptism of fire in Perpignan, we returned to the Stade Aimé Giral. The match was notable for a number of reasons, not least because it was the first game in which a player spat directly at me.

We had played Perpignan the week before in Ireland in the Heineken Cup, and beaten them at Thomond Park. A few of the Perpignan players threatened us coming off the field. Saying stuff like, "We'll see you next week!" that kind of thing. It had been quite a physical game at home but we had won.

We travelled to France the following week and the crowd were baying for blood. It's a funny thing when a crowd is like that – some games you can tune the crowd out but, in others, the crowd just seems to get in on top of you. The Perpignan game was like that.

They had an excellent home record and it was as though they were a different team to the one we had played a few days before. They were well up for the match and it turned into a very tough encounter. They were much more physical than they had been at Thomond, much more aggressive, and they were doing a pretty good job of kicking the crap out of us.

I was having a bit of a pushing match with my opposite No. 6. We'd been having a heated conversation all match long and exchanging pleasantries, which was funny given that he was speaking in French and I was talking in English.

So, at one stage, he's shouting in French and I'm shouting in English and we're abusing each other and pushing and shoving each other. You might not know what he's saying but you have a fair idea. We continued like this throughout the game and, in the middle of a heated conversation, he spat towards me. It didn't actually hit me, so I didn't make anything of it, but it happened.

I'd heard from some of the other boys over the years that they had been spat at during various games in France. For me, there's a line you don't cross and spitting is on the far side of that line. I've been no saint in the game, but I never contemplated anything like that. It was just something I'd never seen before. It was never going to affect the outcome of the game, Perpignan just seemed more determined, they were physically more aggressive and in our faces.

Fighting it out in the scrums with French teams is tough, slogging work. The first few scrums of any game in France are a good indication of how the match is going to go. They pride themselves on their scrum, so you have to take them on there if you want to compete. It was no secret that Perpignan were going to target our set piece, and that we'd have to front up against them.

When we got to Perpignan that weekend, they mauled us and carried the ball more aggressively than they had in the previous game. They were hitting us off the ball, just cleaning us out of rucks and pushing and shoving us. They were late tackling, streaming into us, trying to take us out, pushing us onto the ground after a tackle. They were trying to hit any red jersey they could.

That's what happens down there – intimidation is an important weapon in their armoury, both the players and the crowd try to intimidate you. When they get moving in a scrum or maul the crowd gets off their seats, they bang their drums and the players get huge encouragement from that, it inspires them.

We were down a notch from the week before and they were up a notch, which manifested itself in a strong performance by them. We were a bit shell-shocked by the atmosphere, by the surroundings, by the dominant body language. We should have expected it after our last experience there and, over the years I've, personally, learned not to allow myself to be intimidated by French teams when they are on the front foot. As a team we've learned from our mistakes in the past and we no longer underestimate French teams at home. On the other hand, in recent years, French teams have changed the way they prepare for, and approach, away games. They bring a positive attitude to the away matches believing that they can now win. A lot of their top teams have developed an expectation of winning.

Anyway, that game away to Perpignan was a massive lesson. We tried our best to stem the tide but they were more clinical in holding onto the ball, kicking the ball better, putting us under pressure.

Mentally, maybe we weren't as tough as we would have liked and, perhaps, they wanted it more than we did. They put the points on the board and beat us 23-8. A pretty comprehensive win by anyone's standards.

• • • • • • •

As Munster, we've worked hard to develop a mix of enthusiasm and energy and turn that into dominance. Other teams have picked up on what we've done and the bar has been raised over the years.

People have looked at the Munster team for many years and said, "Look, it's not as though they're world beaters. Take 'em and break 'em down individually and you can see they're not as good as us". And then they ask themselves, "How the hell did those Munster fellas manage to win so much?"

I've noticed from speaking to people – in France and England especially – that they're perplexed by how much Munster has achieved, how much we've won. At this stage, they've long since figured out that the majority of it comes down to a collective determination, a work ethic and a will to win which has spurred us on down through the years and has allowed us to dominate the opposition, even win big matches that we, perhaps, weren't expected to win.

Sometimes, you have to get a hiding to become mentally and physically tougher. Certainly, that's what has happened with me. I never went onto the pitch intending to intimidate, but definitely to dominate. My ability to dominate improved hugely when I learned that the first battle you have to win comes long before you ever set foot on a pitch.

Early in my career, I didn't understanding how a player ought to compete against his opposite number. I concentrated on running after him and trying to stop him playing. Now, I try and dominate the player without running headless around the field after him. It's a case of just showing him: Show your opposite number your eyes, look at him, nod at him, give him a stare and show with your body language that you're not going to take a backward step. More often than not, they'll be attempting the same thing. It's like going into battle, you find out who wants the game more and whoever wants it more will probably win. Simple really.

When the game means everything to you it just gives you an edge – that extra bit of energy, that extra spurt, that extra bit of enthusiasm to go down on a loose ball, to make that tackle, to get off the ground quicker.

The first few minutes of any game are crucial. That's why you need to be in the right place, mentally, before you ever set foot on the field. In those first few minutes, you've a chance to set the tone for the contest ahead. You need to have that determination. You've got to be ready, focused – ready to make your tackles, ready to do what you do best. If someone runs at you, you'll knock them back. You're going to make a statement. You're going to carry the ball well.

In the 2008 Heineken Cup final against Toulouse, I was lucky enough to play the full game and pick up the Man of the Match award.

My opposite number, Thierry Dusautoir, the French captain was a big, dominant player for them, a class act who always had a massive impact on the game with big carries that got the rest of them going forward. Going into the game, it was about how I was going to compete with him: I would wait for him to pick up the ball and carry it, then track him, reach him and drive him back. Ball, man, and all.

Five minutes into the game, I stood on the backline and there was a ruck over on the left hand side of the field. I was defending in the line in the middle of the field and I was numbered up and nominating who I had to watch: it just so happened to be Dusautoir.

They were all fairly flat across the front so I just came up and I looked at him. There's a mix of emotion and thoughts at a point like that. You know what you have to do, what you want to do, but you also know how much respect you have for the guy, because he's top class. When you play at this level against quality players, you have to respect your opposition because you need to be on your toes.

So, I was standing on the backline watching the ruck over on the left-hand side of the field. I was defending in the line and I saw him three or four yards away when he got the ball. I sprinted out of the line at him and I hit him as hard as I could, pumping my legs backwards to take him out. At the time I was thinking, "This guy's a fabulous player and if I don't hit him as hard I can and keep pumping then it's gonna be me that gets dumped".

I knew that, just five or six months previously, he had inspired France to beat New Zealand and Wales, so I was in no doubt about his quality as a player. I knew that if I didn't try, if I didn't hit this guy hard, he would force me back which would give him the upper hand for the rest of the game, rendering me useless to the rest of the lads. I'd be a beaten bloody docket.

It was all going through my mind. Heart pumping, adrenaline coursing, I was focused and just ready to get going in front of tens of thousands of Munster fans in a Heineken Cup final.

It was imperative that I made an impact. I wanted to play well for the fans, for my family, for myself.

But most of all I wanted to play well for the lads. It is never about the individual, it's about the team. This was obviously a chance to make an individual statement to my opposite number, but also to try and do something for the team.

Dusautoir saw me before I hit him. He knew what was coming, but there was nothing he could do about it. He was a bit passive and a bit hesitant but he still had to get on with it, he still had to play. I hit him in the midriff and picked up his leg and drove him back with my right shoulder. Drove him back five yards and dumped him. Ball, man, and all. I got up from that thinking, "I can do this, like. I can dominate this game. I can play at this level". The confidence boost that kind of thing gives you is indescribable. Your blood pumps and your chest swells … there's no feeling like winning that individual confrontation because you know that, for the rest of the game, you won't let anyone down. Instead, you're going to help drive the team on to victory and you know that everyone around you in a red shirt is thinking the same thing.

Then it's on to the next job.

Focus and re-focus, because when you play in high intensity games against a quality team like Toulouse, it's easy to sit back and rest on your laurels and think, "That's great, now, I'll take it easy for a few minutes".

That's a weak spot for me. When I play in games that are not as intense and not as high quality, sometimes I drift in and out of the game, lose my concentration a bit. I'm at my best in high-tempo, intense battles. I'm on my toes and playing hard – no quarter asked for and none given.

CHAPTER 13

January 18, 2003
Heineken Cup Pool Game
v Gloucester (Thomond Park)
Won: 33-6

All change.

Deccie and Niallo are gone. Dominic Crotty has left for the United States, Claw has retired and Gallimh is on the bench. We need a new captain.

But, before we ever get to that point, we find ourselves embracing an even bigger challenge – the arrival of Alan Gaffney.

Deccie and Niallo had left their mark on the Munster team. The question facing us, facing Alan Gaffney, was whether their mark was indelible.

It was an exciting time for us all. We were a good team and we figured it was an attractive proposition for Alan. He was coming into a team that had enjoyed a fair amount of success, and was poised for even greater things. It was a big leap for him to move from being Matt Williams' assistant coach in Leinster to being Munster coach, but he was renowned for his emphasis on skills and back play. And times were changing.

If there had been a criticism of Munster, it was that we had a strong set of forwards but we didn't play expansive rugby. It's not something that the players would have felt, but our critics were constantly wagging an accusing finger at our backs.

So, Munster's Chief Executive, Garrett Fitzgerald, went out and recruited the best man he could.

We figured that Alan would be good for us, and were excited by the prospect of his joining. To get someone of Alan's quality, someone with his depth of knowledge, and his emphasis on skill and attacking players, could only benefit the team. He brought with him Brian Hickey as forwards coach, another master technician with great knowledge of the sport and a superb work ethic.

Alan also delivered our first defence coach in Graham Steadman. Graham was a former rugby league player and a big coup for us. The nature of the game had changed and there was more emphasis now on defence, and we had to move with the times.

Rounding off the new coaching staff was the scrummaging coach, Paul McCarthy. The four new coaches were proof that Munster, as a club, wanted to move forward. Garrett Fitzgerald and his senior management committee wanted to give the team every opportunity by re-investing in it. What's more, Garrett had obviously witnessed the changes occurring in the game internationally. Rugby was getting quicker. Players were getting stronger and fitter. They were becoming more professional.

Defence was becoming a big issue in the game, as were tactics, the scrum and the lineout. So, it was a significant move on Munster's part to bring in four new coaches. It showed Garrett, and his team behind the scenes, were anticipating the development of professionalism in the sport, and were planning to help add another dimension to our game.

But, with all the changes, we knew we were standing at another crossroads. The team needed to select a new captain.

We had new players coming through, players like Paul O'Connell. Everyone could see his quality, but Paulie wasn't alone. Donncha O'Callaghan was coming through, Mick was there and Jim Williams had joined from Australia, passing John Langford going the other way.

The younger boys had matured into supreme athletes and now Munster had four great players fighting for two positions.

Gallimh realised that Micko, Donncha, Paul and himself were the four second rows, and that he might not make it into the team all the time.

So, Gallimh made a big decision to relinquish the captaincy and just concentrate on fighting for his place in the team.

There was an assumption that Axel would be the next captain. After all, he was the ideal candidate. But, surprisingly, Alan announced there would be a vote for the captaincy. That had never happened before, certainly not during my time in Munster, I'd never seen two players going for the captaincy.

At first I didn't think Jim Williams would express an interest in being captain because, although Jim had great leadership qualities and was a wonderful player, he was new to Munster.

Even when her put himself forward it didn't enter my mind that Jim would get more votes than Axel. Axel had been there for years, toiling at the coalface and leading us by example. But, in the end, Jim won the captaincy by a single vote.

I was disappointed for Axel, and worried that it could set up a divide in the camp. Thankfully, Axel accepted that Jim had won fair and square and a split was avoided. We all got behind Jim, and he was a superb captain that year. Axel's time would come, but not yet, not yet.

It says a lot for Munster that, although its proudest traditions are rooted firmly in its connections with the local community, it can still accept players coming in from the outside and allow them to take the captaincy and lead from the front.

Jim's ascendancy to captain complicated things for me. Axel was going to be on the team but now Jim was captain, and it looked like he would be a permanent fixture as well – he wasn't going to captain the team from the bench.

There was another young pretender coming through who went by the name of Denis Leamy. Denis had been involved with the squad a little bit the previous year but he really put his hand up and came to the fore during that pre-season.

He was only out of Schools and played with Rockwell and the Irish Schools. But he was very strong and you could see he had a big future. He played a number of the early games at No. 7 and was phenomenal when he came into the team. You could see just how tough he was. Hard as nails. I liked that in him, admired him for it. So, now there was another problem – we had five really strong lads going for only three positions: Williams, Foley, Quinlan, Wallace and Leamy.

Obviously, we had a lot of games coming up and there would be player rotation, but things were going to get really difficult when we got down to the important games.

In the end, Denis trained with us but didn't play many games and Wally was out injured a lot of the time.

Another great signing was Rob Henderson from Wasps. Most of our players were home grown and Rob fitted in – an Irish International who scored three tries the previous year in a green shirt. He was a former 2001 Lion and was in the form of his life.

So, Alan Gaffney was changing us on many different levels. He was changing personnel, he was changing our leadership, changing how we approached the game and how we played it.

He put a lot of emphasis on our skill levels, on our handling ability. We trained more often and for longer. We did more scrummaging, more forward work and certainly there was a lot of emphasis on trying to make the team play more expansive rugby.

However, we lost in our opening match to Gloucester 16-35 in Kingsholm. That was a bad start for us. We followed up with a win against Perpignan at home (30-21) and another massive win at Musgrave Park against Viadana (64-0).

We beat Viadana again (55-22) in the return match in Italy, which left us with three wins out of four games. To be guaranteed a home quarter-final in the Heineken Cup, you really need to win at least five out of six, so the pressure was on us going into the pool game against Perpignan.

We were headed back to the cauldron where we had lost in 1998, and we knew it was going to be a very difficult game. Wally was still out injured so the back row was Jim, Axel and me, with Denis on the bench. It was another physical encounter that we lost 8-23. It wasn't as comprehensive a beating as it had been the last time we played in Stade Aimé Giral but, on the day, we were just beaten by a better team.

The dressing room afterwards felt a bit like a morgue. We had played poorly and lost and now we were left facing the prospect of not even making it out of the pool.

It was now down to a three-horse race; Munster, Gloucester and Perpignan. But Gloucester had a much better point difference and could afford to lose to us by less than twenty-seven points and still qualify top of the group, though they'd have an away quarter-final.

Still, going into the game, the main feeling was one of utter confusion. Everybody had their own version of exactly by how much we needed to beat Gloucester to qualify, and how exactly the scores needed to come.

It looked like we would have to score four tries against them, but nobody really knew.

I certainly had no clue that we had to win by four tries and twenty-seven points in order to get through. My own calculations were a little more straightforward: they were five points ahead, so I reckoned if we beat them with a bonus point, that would do.

I left the permutations of the necessary final score to everyone else. Beating Gloucester, even at Thomond Park, was a tall enough order at the best of times. Beating them out of sight was the stuff of dreams, or miracles.

It had been a year of great change. Gallimh was still in the squad but on the bench. Paul O'Connell was out with a bad back injury, and Wally had been out for much of the season, too.

But, despite being bench-bound a lot of the time, Gallimh was still a leader to us. The night before the Gloucester game, he arrived in the hotel and gave us an amazing speech. He spoke with passion and pride about what it meant to wear the Munster jersey. He laid it on the line for us, told us how disappointing a season it had been, to date. He warned that no English team would be allowed to come into our back yard, into Thomond Park, and bully us and beat us out the gate.

There'd been stories reported in the newspapers that Gloucester players said they didn't fear us and that they were confident about leaving Thomond Park with a win. As a team, we were always on the lookout for some kind of ammunition that would fuel our anger, something that we could use to fire our motivation.

Gallimh insisted that we weren't being respected as much as we deserved to be and his brilliant speech that Friday night was just the push we needed. He was close to tears and I think a lot of us players felt the same way. Here was a guy who wasn't starting in the team the next day, a guy coming to the end of his career but, in the space of a few minutes, he laid bare for us all what it meant to be a Munster man, a Munster player. Pulling on the Munster jersey to play in Thomond Park represents so much to so many people and those people aren't strangers – they are our family, our friends, our neighbours.

A massive English team was coming to do battle with us and we needed to front up to them. Gallimh didn't mention the quarter-final or how much we had to win by. No one, not the players nor the coaches, talked about how big the winning margin had to be, which was a good thing. Playing a game like that with one eye on the scoreboard and doing mental arithmetic, would have been disastrous.

Before the game, Jim Williams spoke well, Alan Gaffney, all the leaders. But Gallimh's speech the night before really stood out. I think before Gallimh spoke, we were a bit giddy but he focused our minds. For me, Gallimh, made the difference to the Munster team that weekend. He led us to victory without ever playing a minute of the game.

Gloucester were a fantastic team and they'd beaten us comprehensively at the start of the season. But we had so much energy, so much adrenaline, so much intensity, we felt that nothing could stop us. Our intensity fed into the crowd and back into us. We were absolutely buzzing; nothing was going to stop us that day. Nothing. In the dressing room before the game not much more was said. You could see in people's faces what their intentions were. Players were ready to give it their all.

As a rule, I don't remember much about matches, or the build-ups. But I remember that day, Thomond Park was a special place.

John Kelly got us off to a great start when he scored a try in the corner after a break by Stringer and then, crucially, just before half time, Jason 'Dutchy' Holland put a great little grubber kick through for Mossy Lawlor to go over.

The timing of Mossy's try couldn't have been better and we went into the dressing room knowing that we were halfway there. We still weren't clear on the exact permutations needed to go through, but by that stage we knew we needed four tries. Scoring two in the first half meant we needed to score two more in the second half – and that seemed do-able. There was a lot of excitement at half time, the adrenaline was really pumping and I, and a few of the other lads, spoke. I felt the body language of the Gloucester players said it all: They just didn't seem to want it as much as we did, our desire was taking us to a different level in the game. There, in the dressing room, we were just buzzing off each other, people were encouraging each other to push on to go out at the start of the second-half and crank it up again. To show them that they were playing against a ruthless pack of animals.

And we did.

We went back out onto the field and put them under a lot of pressure but, still, we struggled to score. Then Jason Holland launched a great crossfield kick for Mick O'Driscoll to score from. Dutchy was a Kiwi who had travelled to Ireland to play club rugby for Middleton but went on to have a massive impact on Munster. A case of New Zealand's loss being Munster's gain.

Now, we had three tries on board. We were pummelling them but they still hadn't cracked, punch drunk but refusing to go down for the final count.

Then we took a ball from the lineout and set up a maul in midfield. With just a couple of minutes to go, it looked like we were going over the line for the final score. It felt amazing.

But we were stopped just short, and left facing heartbreak until Stringer passed the ball out to John Kelly who went over for a try.

The place just went absolutely crazy. It was just amazing. We didn't realise where that score left us. But, before ROG kicked the conversion, someone actually ran out and gave ROG the message that we still needed the conversion to put us twenty-seven points ahead on a scoreline of 33-6. Can you imagine the pressure that must have been on him at that moment? To be told that everything – all of his team's blood, sweat and tears and all of Munster's dreams – would be for nothing, unless he scored. But ROG is made of strong stuff. He's an unbelievable character. I didn't doubt for a minute that he'd kick the conversion. He's won so many games for us over the years that nothing phases him any more.

So, he landed the kick.

More messages started flooding onto the pitch. "Don't concede any more scores. You need to win by twenty-seven points. Don't concede any more points."

We retreated into the trenches. Gloucester suddenly realised they needed a score, grasped that they were about to be on the wrong end of one of the most amazing scorelines in the history of the Heineken Cup. They were about to enter the history books for all the wrong reasons and they threw the kitchen sink at us.

In a near catastrophe, I almost wrecked the whole night. I tackled one of their players and stayed on my feet as I tried to poach the ball. I thought I was legal in doing so, but the referee thought otherwise and penalised me. I don't think he realised the significance of the score line.

But, that wasn't the final twist on that amazing night, there was still one twist left.

Gloucester had been handed a soft penalty and all they had to do was split the posts and they were through. But, if we had been perplexed by the necessary scoring requirements before the game, now the Gloucester scrum-half, Andy Gomarsall, fell victim to the same fate. Instead of landing three points on the board from a kickable position, he opted to run the ball quickly.

It was a huge mistake for them, but was a massive relief for me. If they'd kicked the penalty I gave away, we'd have lost and I would have been to blame.

The gods were smiling down on me.

The whistle went and the crowd invaded the pitch. We were carried off like heroes. We came back out of the dressing room after the game and went up into the stand and 'The Fields of Athenry' was pumped out of the speakers along with 'Stand Up and Fight'. It was just amazing, as though we'd won the Heineken Cup.

Against all odds, we were now in the quarter-finals again, after beating a very good Gloucester team by twenty-seven points. It was the stuff of dreams, really. The game was named the Miracle Match and, in many ways, it was a miracle. It was amazing to be involved – the atmosphere, the crowd, the buzz in the dressing room afterwards.

After the game, the Gloucester team came in for food and drinks and they were really decent lads. They looked pretty taken aback by our performance, a bit shell-shocked, but they stayed with us for a few drinks and we had a great night out in Limerick. The city, the whole province, was alive.

We woke up with sore but happy heads, and began to take in the fact we were now facing an away quarter-final against Leicester.

That was enough to sober up the drunkest of us.

• • • • • • •

We weren't believed to have much of a chance of beating Leicester. They were a tough prospect – reigning Heineken Cup champions – and taking them on at home at Welford Road just added to the task ahead.

However, we knew we were an improved team from the one that had lost in the previous year's final at the Millennium Stadium in Cardiff. We'd learned from the defeat and, most importantly, we figured that this was a good opportunity for us to get a bit of payback.

Before that incredible result against Gloucester we'd been dead and buried, so a quarter-final against Leicester, in England or wherever, was a bonus to our season. We had nothing to lose, so we decided to go for it.

There was a hangover of bitterness going into the match because of the Neil Back episode of the previous year's final and his comments afterwards when he said, "If it was a boxing match it'd have been over at half time," were still in people's minds.

More motivation came from the Ireland-England Six Nations game in Lansdowne Road a few months previously when, en route to winning another Grand Slam, Martin Johnson had snubbed our President by refusing to move his team off the red carpet and instead making her walk on the grass.

There was a lot of respect for Martin Johnson because he was a fabulous player but, when we went to Welford Road, we used this episode to give us a lift, give us an edge.

There were other niggles which we used to our advantage, including the way our huge travelling support were dealt with by Leicester. The Munster fans were entitled to 25 per cent of the ticket allocation, which was quickly taken up. Our supporters then plotted and schemed to buy more tickets in England so, by the time the match came around, there were thousands of Munster fans with match tickets. But Leicester split them up and put them in different pockets around the stadium to try and dampen the noise they'd make. On top of that, they delayed the kick-off by ten minutes to let fans take their seats but neglected to tell us, so we were out on the pitch waiting an extra ten minutes for the Tigers to appear.

Welford Road is an inspiring place to go – great stadium with great supporters who know their rugby – but seeing the Munster people, including family and friends, who had fought tooth and nail to be there, gave us a massive lift. By the time the game got going we were on fire and reckoned we had a few scores to settle. We picked up where we'd left off against Gloucester.

We had done a lot of analysis on them and Paulie, Donners and I had spent a couple of weeks examining their lineouts, looking at things like their short lineouts.

In the event, we defended their lineout really well: We took a lot of their ball, stifled them and put their scrums under pressure. We knew that the only way we were going to beat them at home was to up our intensity a level and get into their faces, so we got stuck in to them from the word go.

The match was a tight affair: ROG kicked a couple of penalties and we went through most of the game 6-0 up. Then we made a mistake and they scored taking them to 7-6 up, with only twenty minutes to go. Nobody panicked, we felt in control. ROG scored a try almost straightaway and, suddenly, they were on the back foot again, on the wrong end of a 13-7 scoreline.

Then we went half the length of the field and, as Mikey Mullins was tackled down the touchline, he popped the ball, basketball-style, over two or three Leicester players' heads and I caught it on the run. I knew I wouldn't make the line, that I'd be tackled just short of it, but I managed to free the ball up to Strings who ran around to get in under the posts and put some daylight between the two teams.

A lot of the Munster support was at that end of the ground, and I knew my parents were in there too, it was amazing to see their reaction. It dawned on us we were going to win the match. We'd just scored an amazing try and you could see on the Leicester lads' faces that they were astounded. We'd put them away.

At the end, we kicked a penalty into the corner and won the lineout. We did a Leicester-style job on them where we mauled the ball twenty yards upfield, into the corner, and saw the game out. That maul, out-Leicester-ing Leicester in their backyard, summed up the whole day, summed up how dominant we were and how much we'd learned since the previous year's defeat.

After the game, we came back out of the dressing rooms and we went up into the stands which was incredible. Here we were, in Welford Road, the fortress of one of the great teams of the Heineken Cup and English rugby, and there were thousands and thousands of Munster fans in the middle of the pitch, singing songs and cheering.

The Leicester set-up took the pitch invasion in good spirit. I think they accepted they'd been well beaten on the day, and they knew how much it meant to us. Martin Johnson and Austin Healey came into our dressing room afterwards and they were very decent, very humble in defeat. It was a great gesture by them and I think they maybe reckoned that our time was coming – we'd endured a lot of disappointments and we'd been knocked down many times, but we kept getting back up again.

They acknowledged we were the better team on the day and wished us well. There was no bitterness at all and the Leicester fans – who are real rugby people – gave us a great reception at the end of it all. To get that kind of reaction away from home, and from a people with such a proud tradition of their own, meant a great deal to us as a team.

The Leicester match was one of the greatest wins of my career and was a perfect example of why so few Munster players opted to go abroad and play for another team. Something was building back then, and we all knew it, we could all feel it. Days like that are special, and they come around only rarely. To back up the Gloucester win, away from home against a team like Leicester was a big statement for us to make, not just to the other teams in the competition but to ourselves.

• • • • • • •

Even though we'd won, we felt a bit guilty about going back out onto the pitch, after all, we'd only won a quarter-final. Alan, Gallimh, Jim Williams and some of the players reminded us all that we needed to keep our feet on the ground and keep building. So, when we returned to Limerick, we went out and had a few pints but nothing too extravagant – we were aware of the job at hand, facing Toulouse in a semi-final in the South of France.

That game, and our season, ended in disappointment after an epic battle against a team which featured another Irishman – Trevor Brennan.

Trevor was always a great competitor but, over the years, he has turned out to be a great friend of mine as well. His career down in Toulouse was a great success although, sadly, it ended prematurely. But nothing can take away from his achievements both in Ireland and France. He lined out for a legendary team down there and the French fans loved him and considered him one of their own: Compliments don't come much better than that.

After the match, Trevor told a great story of how, the night before the semi-final against us, he had endured a sleepless night and vivid dreams. "I dreamt that Quinny and myself beat the crap out of one another, that we were both sent off. I dreamt that they beat us, that we beat them, that it was a draw and went to extra time, all sorts of things: My mind was obviously all over the shop. Sitting here now, I'm still not convinced we won, it was that close."

Trevor's dream was prophetic as far as the closeness of the game was concerned. The match ended 13-12, but to Toulouse.

CHAPTER 14

I can see the line just ahead.

The ball is tucked in under my arm and I can see the line.

I'm going to make it.

The Argentinean appears in the corner of my eye. He's coming fast and hard but he's not faster and he's not harder than me. He isn't going to stop me. No one's going to stop me.

Scoring for Ireland in the World Cup. No one's going to take that away from me.

He's coming at me from the right. The ball is in my right hand. I should switch it to the left and protect myself. But if I do that now, I know I'll never make the line. If I do that, I won't score, and scoring this try is what my life is about.

Take the hit Quinny. The pain will pass. Scoring a World Cup try for your country against your bitterest rivals will last forever. Take the hit.

I'm on the line. The Argentinean is on me. Get the ball down, get the ball down.

In a split second, almost without thought, I reach out and place the ball. I make the line. In the same split second the Argentinean hits.

He gets me on the way down. Gets me around my legs, which shouldn't be too bad, but my shoulder hits the ground wrong. A stab of pain strikes at me.

But I've scored. The roar of the crowd is in my ears. The World Cup. I've just scored in the World Cup!

I roll onto my back and try to figure out what the hell has just happened here. I try to take it all in.

Bang! The lads pile in on top of me: Strings, Humphs, Marcus Horan. Marcus lunges to grab me and ... Oh, Sweet Jesus! The pain is phenomenal. It's indescribable.

This is the worst pain I've ever known. It's the worst pain I could ever imagine. The angle my shoulder hit the ground was bad. My arm nearly came back over my head with the force I hit the ground.

I know something has gone, I felt something. I put my hand inside my shirt and, although I didn't really feel it pop, when I put my hand to my shoulder there's such a pain that I know this isn't good.

I can feel my shoulder sticking out. I'm screwed.

But, no, it'll be alright. The shoulder is probably just dislocated, it'll be fine. I'll be fine.

But the pain is unbelievable and growing. All thoughts of scoring the try are gone from my mind because all I can think about is the pain.

Ailbe McCormack, our physio, and Dr Gary O'Driscoll arrive beside me. Thank God, help's here. They feel my shoulder and they know. I can see it in their faces. But it's just a dislocation, right? It'll be fine, yeah?

I see and hear nothing as I limp from the pitch. I concentrate only on putting one foot in front of the other, keeping a lid on the pain and getting to the dressing room. The lads bring me in and lay me out on the treatment table. They know how much trouble I'm in, but I don't.

In my mind, I've come to terms with the fact that the game is over for me. But there will be other games in the coming days. I've just got to recover, stay healthy, get ready for the next game.

God, I need something for this pain.

•••••••

A few days before the Argentina game in the 2003 World Cup in Australia, Eddie O'Sullivan took me aside and told me he was picking me, said he was giving me a chance.

He said it would be very physical and that I brought that physicality to the game. That's what he wanted from of me – to try to be physical and get in their faces.

That was pretty much it. He didn't go into the details much and, because I was in shock, I didn't question him. I thought, "Just sit down and shut up, Quinny. Don't pinch yourself or you might just wake up from this dream".

I knew this was a big call for him, too. He'd been hacked off with me for a long time and we both knew that. My temperament and my discipline had been poor at times, so this was a big deal for both of us. For him it was a gamble but, for me, it was the ultimate shot at redemption. I wanted to get my Ireland career back and make up for my past sins.

To get to the World Cup was just unbelievable, but to play in it … it's impossible to explain what it's like to play for your country in a World Cup. It's phenomenal, just phenomenal.

At that stage, between 2001 and 2003, I was involved full-time with the Ireland 22, either starting or coming off the bench, but getting at least twenty minutes per game.

In the first World Cup game we played, against Romania, I came off the bench and I started the next, against Namibia. I scored two tries and was selected to start in the crucial pool game against Argentina on October 26. We had to beat them to come out of the pool and make the quarter-finals.

But there was a lot more riding on the game than just a result. Ireland were at a crossroads in rugby. Poor results against Argentina in the past had left us on the brink of dropping out of the top rugby nations, about to be overtaken and left for dead by The Pumas. Argentina had dumped us out of the last World Cup by beating us in Lens and sending Irish rugby into a tailspin of introspection.

But, if we lost this time around, then we'd have to qualify for the next World Cup. There was a lot on the line: Pride, honour, money, jobs. The stakes couldn't have been higher and for me to be picked for that game was a personal watershed. Nobody was out injured, everyone was available, but I was still selected.

I felt I had finally reached a point where I was carving out my own spot on the Ireland team. I was getting the biggest opportunity of my life and I couldn't have been more ecstatic at the faith being placed in me.

The players I was up against for the back row berth were Keith Gleeson, Anthony Foley and Victor Costello along with Simon Easterby and Eric Miller. I was chosen ahead of Keith Gleeson, which was a bit of a shock for me and it was probably a shock for him, too, as he'd been playing particularly well for Ireland.

But the Argentinean game was always going to be physical, and Eddie clearly picked me for my physicality. When he finally sat down with me before the game he said as much: "Watch your distance, but get stuck into the Argentineans. Rough them up. Be physical and be in their faces. That's why I picked you." Right. My chest puffed out.

It's a massive compliment to be told you're the cutting edge of the team. It made me feel immensely proud – Eddie and Ireland were putting their trust in me. What a boost. After a pre-game chat like that, there was only ever going to be one outcome for me: Win or bust.

From the first minutes of the game, I got stuck in. I made a good start; carried a lot of ball, made a lot of tackles. Then, twenty minutes into the game, Woody makes a break off the back of a lineout, passes to me and I start running for the line. Twenty minutes into the game, and it's all about making the line. Nothing else matters.

• • • • • • •

I open my eyes and try to focus on who I am and where I am, but the pain crowds in on my mind. I feel my vision going dark and I can feel, or imagine, blackness beginning to seep in at the peripheries of my mind.

For a moment the confusion is complete: It's frightening. Then the blackness ebbs away and I can see again. I'm in the dressing room in the Adelaide Oval, the Aussie cricket stadium. Ailbe and the Doc are here and I'm laid out on the treatment table.

I'm groaning with pain. I can hear myself. All I want to do is curl up into the foetal position and make the pain go away … just go away. They give me oxygen and tell me to breathe in deeply, but the oxygen does nothing for me.

With your standard shoulder dislocation – if it's not traumatic – the injury is definitely sore, but the pain is manageable: Grin-and-bear-it kind of stuff, run-it-off pain.

But this is not standard and definitely not manageable. I'm not going to run this off. I've ripped my bicep off. I've damaged the bones. I've spoilt the socket. I've injured the soft tissue. I've torn the ligaments – it's like a set of instructions about what not to do to your shoulder.

I need real pain relief. I need drugs – just give me the drugs. They turn me over, somebody yanks down my shorts and somebody else produces a huge bloody needle and presses it into my buttock.

Praise the Lord and pass the morphine.

Other medics come into the room. They're with the World Cup. The World Cup? Ah yes, the competition in which I just scored and which has banjaxed my shoulder.

"What are you doing to me?" They keep trying to lay me flat down on my front to put my shoulder back in. They keep trying to press down on my back. But my shoulder just won't go back into place. Forget the morphine: The pain is back – they've brought it back. They can't keep doing this, I can't keep doing this. After the third attempt they give up and sit me in a chair.

Somebody produces a pair of surgical scissors and cuts my jersey from me: My Ireland jersey – the jersey I just scored a World Cup try against Argentina wearing. It now lies in shreds around me – like my World Cup, except I don't know that yet.

Then off come the shoulder pads: God, now they want to try to put my shoulder back in again. Just one more try, Alan, one more try. Come on, son, get your game face on.

They turn me around on the chair and put my arm over the back of it. Then they pull down my arm and my shoulder just pops back into place. Massive relief: I've been given oxygen and drugs and the shoulder has been popped back in.

They can do no more for me in the cricket stadium so an ambulance reverses up to the door and I'm bundled into the back of it. Ailbe and Gary aren't coming with me. There's a game on up top in the stadium and their place is out there, with the men playing against Argentina, not in here with the dead and the dying. Our assistant manager, Ger Carmody, comes with me instead. So there's just me, Ger and the ambulance driver bumping along in the ambulance en route to a hospital where I don't know anyone. I'm woozy and thinking: "Where has everyone gone? I'm on my own. Any more morphine?"

By the time I reach the hospital, I'm coming around again. Ger is with me and now I know where I am, I know what's going on. But there's not even a TV with the game on, so I keep asking Ger, "What's the score? Tell me the bloody score!" He's running in and out every few minutes, getting updates on the phone, and filling me in. The game's unbelievably tight.

I should be there, I shouldn't be lying here in this hospital bed. I grip the side of the bed and then immediately wish I hadn't as the pain stabs again.

But Ireland win and the morphine finally kicks in while the doctors take an X-ray to check for structural damage and bone damage. Back comes the X-ray and the medical prognosis – they've done everything they can for me, so they put my arm in a sling and send me back.

The game is only over about fifteen minutes when I arrive back in the dressing room: We won, 16-15 and everyone's in the showers. The lads are ecstatic and so they should be, they've just turned around the fortunes of Irish rugby. They've just saved Irish rugby, they're verifiable Irish rugby heroes. They really are.

They cheer me, congratulate me, give me sympathy. Marcus Horan begins to ship some stick for being the one who caused me the shoulder injury by jumping on top of me in the try scoring celebrations. It'll be years before he lives it down!

You have to laugh. Kind of.

The pain in my shoulder is easing off but, here in our dressing room, watching my team-mates celebrate, the pain of missing out on the game is finally kicking in. I feel like crying – great, heaving gulps of salty tears.

But I don't. I focus on the pain in my shoulder and concentrating on the physical pain of my torn bicep takes away the hurt of knowing my World Cup – the tournament that was going to turn my Ireland career around forever, is over.

• • • • • • •

My Mum had travelled to the World Cup and I met her after the game. She was upset and worried about me but I tried to reassure her that I was fine, as long as I was standing, and that I wasn't in that much pain.

The lads went for a few beers that night in an Irish bar somewhere in Adelaide and I joined them, along with Anthony Horgan and Mike McGurn – the fitness coach who had spent so much effort getting me into great shape for the World Cup. We had to get up early the next day for a flight to Melbourne. The lads had a tough game against Australia ahead of them while I was booked in to see a local specialist.

It was really only when we reached the airport that it began to dawn on me that something major was happening. There were lots of guys there taking pictures of me with my arm in a sling. When I turned on my phone there were around two hundred text messages waiting for me. My profile had gone through the roof. I was being portrayed as a hero, as the 'man who saved Irish rugby' – a title which had originally started off as a slag by our physio, Ailbe, but which seemed to be sticking.

It was a very strange feeling. On one hand, I was feeling hugely proud of how people were treating me, happy to be an Irish hero, but, on the other hand, I was still gutted over the injury. I wanted more than anything to be back playing and I was still naïvely thinking that everything would work out fine and that I'd be back playing in two or three weeks. If only the lads could make the quarter- and semi-finals, I might have chance of getting back... Sometimes the shoulder can pop out and go back in, and you can strap it up, play away and defer an operation until the end of the season.

So, it was with that in mind that Gary O'Driscoll and I went to the specialist in Melbourne. The Doc said he thought there was a chance I could avoid surgery and that I could strap up. I remember being delighted, but Gary was pessimistic. Very quickly he was proven right: We went to see a surgeon and had a scan which showed a lot of damage.

Decision made. World Cup over.

The Ireland management team of Eddie, Niallo and Briano was

wonderful. They gave me the option of staying on for a week with the team, which was great because I just didn't want to go away. It would have been too heartbreaking to leave just then, the end would have come too quickly and proper closure would have been impossible.

So, it was a case of just relaxing, having a few beers and finally enjoying being part of the team that beat Argentina, being the guy who scored a try against Argentina. My Munster team-mate, Wally, was flown out to join the squad and Frankie Sheehan and I amused ourselves for a few days by winding up Briano and Wally over expenses. Before I got injured, I'd already been given some expenses for the days ahead so, when Wally came out to replace me, he discovered there was nothing left in the kitty for him for those first few days. Frankie and I proceeded to wind Briano up by telling him Wally wasn't happy about losing out and, generally, did our best to trigger a row between the two of them – it was great craic and passed the time nicely for me and Frankie.

With my arm the way it was, it was nearly impossible to even have a shower without being in danger of wrecking the shoulder again. So, for the rest of my time in Australia, John Hayes became my favourite washer boy. I needed a lot of help with the most personal of tasks. Marcus Horan and Frankie Sheehan volunteered to rub moisturiser into my back – Marcus even let me use his.

But it was The Bull who got the job of scrubbing my back in the shower. He thought it was disgusting and crazy to have to do it, but he carried out his task like a man. Even as he washed my back and scrubbed me with a bar of soap, he gave out about it. Considering the number of times I'd had to put up with looking at his hairy back all those years ago, during our trips to Gallimh's home in Kilkenny, it was the least he could do. I still reckon you haven't lived until you've had The Bull Hayes scrub your back. Thanks, John.

Staying on for that extra week also gave me the chance to spend some time with my cousins and my family. We got together to watch the match the following weekend as Australia squeaked past Ireland. The lads just barely lost against the Aussies, in fact, they should really have won that game. And if they had, then they'd have avoided France in the quarter-final and pulled Scotland instead, which could have meant a clearer path to the semi-finals.

But for me, my World Cup adventure was already over. I went on the rip with the lads on Sunday and John Langford, one of Munster's Australian heroes, brought me to the airport. I flew home on the Monday, sad to be leaving the boys with an uphill battle against the French in the following weekend's quarter-final.

And that was that.

• • • • • • •

It was only when I got home that I fully realised the impact my try against Argentina and my injury had had on my profile. I reached Shannon on Tuesday and I was to be on The Late Late Show that Friday night. Radio stations and newspapers were ringing around the clock. Everybody knew me, or wanted to know me.

I went to see the shoulder specialist in Dublin the Friday morning before I went on The Late Late Show. The specialist looked at the scans that I had brought with me from Australia and didn't pull his punches: All the ligaments were damaged, I needed surgery and I'd be out for up to six months. I was stunned, six months is an eternity. In the end, though, my recovery would be a lot slower than that, but I had no idea, at that stage, just how long the fight back to fitness would take me.

All I knew was that I didn't want to waste a moment. How quickly could have I surgery? The quicker I got fixed, the quicker I could start recovering, and the quicker I could get back to playing.

Woody told me about his specialist in London, a guy called Iain Bailey, and Gary O'Driscoll set up an appointment. I flew over from Shannon, the specialist examined me, confirmed I needed surgery and performed the operation the next morning. It was a hectic turnaround but I felt I was finally on the road to recovery. I was wrong – it was a long, slow healing. In his initial examination the surgeon believed I'd only be in a sling for three weeks but, during the operation, he discovered that the top of my bicep had been ripped off my shoulder as well. He had to pin my shoulder down heavily, because of the amount of damage, so I ended up in a sling for six weeks and lost all lateral rotation and movement in my shoulder.

I couldn't do anything, just sleep, see the physio, see my friends, sleep, see the physio, have massage around the clock – every day the same thing. But you can only read so many books and watch so many movies before you start to go mad. I wasn't supposed to drive, because I couldn't change the gears, so I had to get an automatic car from the garage. At least then I could go over to Limerick University and watch the Munster boys training. I got out of the sling just before Christmas but I could hardly move my arm. I couldn't rotate it, could barely put my hand up over my head, and I was all crooked.

I finally got back by the end of April, and played an away game against Cardiff. I knew my shoulder was sturdy but I hadn't much use of my arm, and had lost a lot of power, lost a lot of strength in the left side of my body. But I played against Cardiff, and played a few more games for Munster before Eddie O'Sullivan picked me to go to South Africa for a two-Test tour against the 'Boks.

I knew I could barely tackle or catch a ball on my left side, which maybe isn't ideal when you're playing against the South Africans. But I was desperate to get back. I worked hard in training and came off the bench in both games. But my shoulder just wasn't right, there was no flexibility or movement there. In the end I played in the Tests in South Africa and presumed I'd have a good pre-season with Munster and get back, but I hit a wall for five or six weeks and couldn't do any shoulder presses.

I was literally crooked on the shoulder press because they couldn't really get my hand over my head. It was an unbelievably frustrating injury and one that I had to accept had left me badly damaged.

So, down through the years, I've had to adapt. The shoulder no longer bothers me when I'm playing but it ruled my life for those first couple of years. It was always tight – tight and sore. For two years the muscles keep locking up and the shoulder kept getting tighter. The surgeon had obviously pinned the shoulder down as tight as he could so that it wouldn't dislocate again.

Looking back on the injury now, it's sometimes hard to believe you can recover from that kind of hurt. I had somewhere between five and ten surgeries and I've still got the scars from where Iain Bailey had to cut into my chest.

But the hardest part was accepting I had been injured. It was a huge setback. Before the injury I was exactly where I wanted to be: I'd made the Ireland team again and I was in great form. I was looking forward to the best years of my rugby life, nailing down an Ireland spot and helping Munster conquer Europe. Everything, my entire life, was poised.

Then came the shoulder injury. Instead of conquering Europe in a red jersey I could only watch Munster, barely able to raise my hand above my head. As for nailing down a spot on the Irish team? I was watching from the terraces when the boys went out and won a Triple Crown after Christmas.

Even when I came back and Eddie picked me for the 'Boks Tour, I still wasn't right, wasn't happy in myself. The following season, my shoulder still wasn't right and I didn't make the Munster team, I was on the bench. I was in pain, I had a lot on my mind. I was disappointed and frustrated with my shoulder. Where had my good arm gone?

That's how it was for the guts of two years: I missed out on a lot of opportunities with Ireland and Munster. But I was still just twenty-nine years old, so I clawed my way back and tried to overcome the frustrations, tried to work hard and concentrate on getting better.

• • • • • • •

I can see the line just ahead.

The ball is tucked in under my arm and I can see the line.

I'm going to make it.

The Argentinean appears in the corner of my eye. He isn't going to stop me. No one's going to stop me.

Scoring for Ireland in the World Cup. No one's going to take that away from me.

He's coming at me from the right. The ball is in my right hand. I should switch it to the left and protect myself. But if I do that now, I know I'll never make the line. If I do that, I won't score, and scoring this try is what my life is about.

Do you want to take the hit Quinny? Maybe the pain will pass, maybe you'll be on The Late Late Show, in the papers, in the history books. But you're staring into the jaws of a two-year battle in which you'll be sore, frustrated, angry, depressed carrying an injury that will rob you of your place in the Munster and Ireland teams. You'll watch your Ireland mates lift two Triple Crowns while you go to the physio.

I'm on the line. The Argentinean is on me. Get the ball down, get the ball down.

Do I take the hit? Do I get the ball down?

In that split second, thinking about everything it will mean, I hesitate.

• • • • • • •

People ask me about the injury. They ask me am I bitter about it? If I'm angry about the guy who hit me? But I'm not. Honestly. The man who put in the tackle was Ignacio Corleto, who played with Narbonne. He was a very good player, and I hold no bitterness towards him. The guy had a job to do, defend the Argentinean line against the Irish, and that was what he tried to do. It was a perfect tackle. No hard feelings.

Then people ask the other question, the one they really want to know the answer to: If I had the chance to go back to that moment in the Adelaide Oval, would I do it all over again? Would I make the line against Argentina, score the try and take the hit? Accept the injury? Would I swap two years of pain, frustration and hurt, in exchange for personal pride, the tag of saving Irish rugby and a place in the history books? That's the question they want answered. Was it worth it? I think about that moment a lot. I re-run it in my head. I tell them that I don't know.

Truth is, I'm not sure I would.

For my career the shoulder injury was a turning point. Up until then

I'd had the usual stuff – broken jaw, broken thumbs, that kind of thing – but this was, potentially, a career-changing injury.

The dynamic had changed massively for me on one level. It was undeniably great to go to Lansdowne Road to watch an Ireland game and have everybody stopping me, saying hello, thanking me for scoring against Argentina and asking for my autograph and to have their picture taken with me.

And I was in demand for lots of corporate stuff, businesses keen to sign me up to give talks and promote their companies. I wasn't used to that stuff, so it was fantastic to be treated like that, like a genuine hero in a green jersey.

But I missed out on other things which were more important to me – time with Munster, more caps with Ireland. In my absence from the Ireland set-up, Simon Easterby went on to nail down the No. 6 jersey on the team and, within six months of the World Cup, the guys were Triple Crown champions, a feat they repeated a year later.

I gave my left shoulder to be the hero against Argentina but I'd have given my right hand to have won those Triple Crowns – my Triple Crowns. That should have been my time. No one remembers the World Cup any more.

The man who saved Irish rugby? Fine, but who was going to save me?

CHAPTER 15

April 1, 2005
Heineken Cup Quarter-Final
v Biarritz (San Sebastian)
Lost: 10-19

The 2004/05 season was big for me. I was returning after recovering from the shoulder injury which I'd sustained playing for Ireland against Argentina in the 2003 World Cup. I was nervous about coming back but determined to win my place in the starting fifteen.

Alan Gaffney was in his third, and final, season in charge of Munster. He was a good coach and his knowledge of the game was excellent. He had also resolved to encourage us to play a more expansive kind of rugby.

Under Alan, Munster made a number of overseas signings. Up until then the team had, with the exception of one or two players each season, been homegrown. Unfortunately, not all of the imports worked out. There were some great signings, such as Christian Cullen, who tried hard to repay Munster the money they had laid out for him but who, unfortunately, was plagued by injuries. Shaun Payne, an Australian, came in as well and Shaun fitted in so well as a player and as a Munsterman that he has never left – he remains the Munster manager to this day.

But, there were other overseas players in our squad who weren't singing off the same hymn sheet as the rest of us – perhaps they weren't used to the Munster mentality and the Munster work ethic and didn't fit in as well as we would have liked. Some of them just weren't good enough. When you sign someone from overseas, you're always taking a chance. Some players are great in their own countries but when you bring them away, they may not be able to fit into a whole new culture.

But, back at the start of that season, I was more concerned about my starting place in the team: I was facing a battle for the back row with Jim Williams, Axel, Wally and Denis Leamy.

Denis had missed part of the previous season through injury but, like me, he'd come back again and had played some early games at the start of the 2004/05 season, before the Internationals returned from national duty, and he'd been superb.

Alarmingly, it was beginning to look like Wally and myself would be surplus to requirements. There were five good players for three slots and, with Jim, Axel and Denis looking like they were the starting line-up, Wally and I knew there was only one place on the bench, so one of us was going to lose out.

I was on the bench for the opening game against Harlequins, probably because I gave the management more of a lineout option, and Wally found himself playing club rugby for Garryowen. The starting line was set and, whatever Wally or I thought about it, that was that.

I came off the bench in the win against Harlequins (15-9) and then Wally was back for the win over the Neath-Swansea Ospreys (20-8): The lack of a starting position put paid to any chance I had of being in the Irish squad. Missing the Autumn Internationals was disappointing and frustrating but I tried to remain objective about it – one minute you're flying, the next you're crashing.

Despite having a good run of wins in the Celtic League and the Heineken Cup, we hadn't been too convincing and an away game to Castres ended in a 12-19 defeat, though we managed to pick up a bonus point. But by that stage, Wally and I were knocking at the door, asking the coaches what we had to do to get back on the team. We understood they were in a difficult situation – they had five good players but only three could start. Still, making a decision that someone like Wally couldn't even make the twenty-two was a massive call. Plus, Wally and I reckoned that if we were all so close as players, then maybe the coaches could rotate the back row.

The loss in Castres gave me my chance and I was back in the starting line-up for the next game, which was the return fixture against Castres, in Thomond Park. We won the match 36-8, which was a big turn-around from the result a week before, and I held my starting place for the last two pool games against Ospreys and Harlequins, which we won 20-10 and 18-10, respectively. By the end of the pool stage we had topped our group but faced an away match to Biarritz. We knew they'd be aiming to get some payback for what happened in the 2001 quarter-final, when we beat them in Thomond Park.

Significantly, they moved the game from their home ground to a 32,000 capacity soccer stadium in San Sebastian in the Basque country of Northern Spain. It was a big call for them but they see themselves as Basques and they figured they could fill the place.

The game came at the end of a disappointing season and represented a new type of challenge for us. We hadn't played particularly well that year, there wasn't the same flow to our game. We were a bit predictable and we'd struggled a bit. Teams were no longer underestimating us – they were analysing us and looking for ways to break down our game and put us under pressure and, ultimately, beat us.

Reaching the quarter-final was a great achievement but we weren't firing on all cylinders and that caught up with us in the game against Biarritz.

We struggled badly in the first half, conceded a lot of penalties and a try in the first forty minutes, which ended with us being down 0-19. Unfortunately, on a personal level, I had a very disappointing match. I got pinged for three or four penalties in the game, two of which they kicked. It was stupid stuff – I got caught offside on two occasions and I came in from the side for another, the last one was for pushing in the lineout. Ultimately, it hurt the team and it hurt me a lot. I questioned myself afterwards: I was on edge, tense and jumped the gun a few times – got caught in the wrong place at the wrong time – but most of the decisions against me were 50/50 calls.

In the dressing room at the interval, Alan Gaffney and Brian Hickey let us know they weren't too happy with us. They ripped into us, and rightly so. We came out a different team in the second half and Wally scored a try, which Paul Burke converted and then Burkey added a penalty to bring the score back to 10-19. But, by then, it was too late – we were already chasing the game.

We were missing ROG for the game because he'd injured his knee a couple of weeks previously in a game against the Dragons. Paul Burke came in for him and did a very capable job, but we missed ROG hugely against Biarritz. That season had been flat all along but, even when we were struggling, ROG was good for a few points and his kicking game had got us out of trouble on more than one occasion. In a hostile situation like the match with Biarritz, ROG's experience, his tempo and his temperament would have been useful.

After the loss, I was disappointed and angry. I'd given away penalties but it wasn't as though I was being kamikaze, jumping around the place and getting involved with people. Unfortunately, I just got caught in close-in situations and was punished for it. No one said anything to me after the game, but I knew that Alan was frustrated with me and disappointed with our penalty count in the first half. I felt really low after the game, I could have accepted losing but the penalties really upset me.

That match against Biarritz was Alan's last Heineken Cup game, he left at the end of the season after we won the Celtic Cup. Jim Williams left then, too. It was nice to get our hands on some silverware, and great to send the lads off with a victory: I was also selected by Ireland for the tour in Japan but, overall, it was a disappointing season.

We had lost our focus a bit and we needed to change things around, try to get the hunger back in our game. At the same time, everyone else was getting better and we were no longer a shock to anyone. That 2004/2005 season was really the first season that other teams had taken notice of us, had begun trying to stop us playing, rather than just playing their own game against us.

But those challenges would be faced with a different coach at the helm. Alan Gaffney was returning home to coach his national team, Australia, which was a huge honour for him.

He hadn't been able to deliver the Holy Grail to Munster but he had left a big impression. He had been very passionate about Munster, to the point where it was really his life and, when he was down there in Limerick, the people loved him.

Alan and I had enjoyed a good relationship – although, because of injury, I had missed a full third of his tenure in the province. When he arrived he had made some key appointments, such as George Murray as video analyst and Sean Whitney as strength coach.

Wally and myself would have had issues with the management because we weren't being picked, but that's natural. It's very hard to keep everybody happy and when guys are not being picked they're not going to be happy with the coach.

I thought Alan was a good coach and I respected him. However, at times during that season, he showed his frustration and disappointment. When we performed badly, he'd go off on one and blast us. Funnily enough that was something I admired him for – it showed how much the whole thing meant to him. When he first arrived in Munster he was very calm, very quiet but, over time, he became grumpier and a bit stressed out on occasion. That's not Alan's natural demeanour – he's a really nice guy. I suppose we drove him a bit mad, I know I did.

Being down here meant a lot to him. I still think a piece of Munster is in his heart and always will be. But, as far as coaching is concerned, it doesn't get much better than being called back to your country to work with your national side.

The fall of the curtain on the 2004/05 season, and on Gaffer's reign as head coach, was significant for me. Deccie Kidney was on his way back to Munster – it was time for a new era, time for a fresh start.

I was already looking forward to another, perhaps final, push for the elusive Heineken Cup trophy. Next season, 2005/2006, would be our season. I was certain of it.

CHAPTER 16

BREAKDOWN AND BREAKTHROUGH

That's it. My career is over.

I was just about to sign a new two-year contract and now that's probably gone. Will this be okay? Will I get a new contract? Why did this have to happen to me now, just when things are going well?

I find out later that my cruciate is gone but, for now, I just look down at my knee to see it flapping about like a flag and every time I try to stand it buckles under me and sends me crashing to the ground. It doesn't hurt any more, but it just won't work. I sit on the grass and wait for help. Maybe it's not as bad as I think.

• • • • • • •

Our curtain-raiser in the 2006 Heineken Cup was always going to be a tough encounter. To play Sale away in England is never a pleasant prospect but it was especially daunting because they were going well at the time and intending to put down a marker, both for themselves and the rest of the pool.

About thirty minutes into the game, Gary Connolly passed me a ball and Mark Taylor, the Welsh International, tackled me. I almost managed to get clear of him but he grabbed me around the collar and flung himself across my body. I was running at the time and he threw himself across my two knees and basically tripped me with his body. All of his weight went on the side of my knee, which bent inwards, and my knee ligaments just snapped.

I was in sheer agony for around thirty seconds. Then the pain was gone. It was a strange feeling. The ball was lying on the ground and there was a load of bodies lying on top of me. When I tried to get up I found I couldn't, really, so I sat back down again and waited for our physio, Kirsty Peacock, and the Doc, Tadgh O'Sullivan, to check out my knee. I tried to stand again but the knee buckled under me and I fell back down on the ground. So, they took me off and brought me into to the dressing room.

My first thought was that this was lousy timing because I was in the middle of contract negotiations with the IRFU. The 2007 World Cup was coming up and the IRFU were anxious that any International players whose contract was up at the end of the season would be re-signed and sorted out as soon as possible. They'd already started talking to my agent, John Baker, and he was due to go in and chat to them after the Sale game. It had all been very positive, but now... I sat in the dressing room on the bed while Tadgh O'Sullivan checked my knee.

He was examining it from all angles but there was no stability in it at all. It was just flopping around. The severity of the injury began to dawn on me and I put huge pressure on Tadgh to be honest with me and tell me if my cruciate was gone. There'd been a lot of bad press in the past about cruciate injuries and it was the kind of potentially career-ending problem that every sports person dreaded. My heart began to sink as reality set in. My contract was up at the end of the season and it would take six or eight months to come back from a cruciate injury. This could be it, the show could be over, right here and now: I might not get a contract, my knee might never be right and I might never come back from it.

I was there in the changing room for about twenty minutes on my own, just thinking, fretting. But what could I do? Nothing. The knee was strapped so I got up, put on a jacket and hobbled out to watch the rest of the game. It was a miserable affair from start to finish. We lost the match and Frankie Sheehan came off with a serious neck injury. Frankie and I had made our Munster debuts together against Western Samoa in 1996 and we'd become close friends during our time in the red jersey. Now, the two of us were looking at a lengthy layoff. It was a bad night all round. We'd lost the game and two forwards had sustained serious injuries. I got pretty upset after the match in the dressing room but, eventually, I showered and hobbled away on crutches.

• • • • • • •

Most of the time, I try to hide my emotions and disappointments but I can't, really. My face always betrays me and people can read my emotions like a book.

After the Sale game, I just didn't really know what to do. At the airport I spoke to my Mum and Dad who were upset for me. I was quiet coming back on the plane. ROG brought me home to his house and I stayed with him that night because I had to have a scan done in Cork the following day. I'd been through serious injury before, particularly with my shoulder in the World Cup game against Argentina a couple of years previously. But you never think the worst, you always try to have hope. Before the scan I consoled myself that I might only have damaged my medial ligaments.

Deep down, though, I probably knew what to expect because, by the time we got off the plane in Ireland, I could see my knee was already starting to swell. But, suspecting it might be bad news didn't prepare me for the shock when Martin O'Driscoll, who took the scan, told me that not only my medial but also my cruciate ligament was completely gone. It was the worse case scenario.

Martin brought me into his office to show me the scans. He was a nice guy and knew us all, because he'd done so many scans for Munster players in the past. He wasn't the specialist, so he couldn't advise me further, but I wanted him to be honest with me about what he could see in the scans. He showed me the computer screen and pointed out where the knee was completely torn.

ROG had been good enough to drive me to the hospital – he was great, an absolute true friend who stayed with me and sympathised with me. But when I get upset like that I just want to be on my own. Right then, I felt no one could really help me, I just wanted to get home and be on my own. So, Munster organised a taxi to take me back to Limerick, and I had a lonely journey back home.

It was Saturday afternoon. There wasn't much food in the house and all my mates and neighbours seemed to be gone. I was starving with hunger so, eventually, I braved hobbling down to the local pub, Synott's. Between the pain of the severed ligaments, the pain of trying to walk and the pain of using crutches – my hands were hanging off me – I was in bits. But I ate some food and went home again, before Kirsty Peacock called out to check on me. Kirsty was fantastic, she took off the knee brace that I was wearing and strapped me up.

Two days later I was going to see the specialist in Dublin, but what the hell was I going to do until then? I certainly wasn't going to sit in and feel down and depressed. So, my mate, Arthur Ryan, collected me and we went for a few pints. Then my friends began to gather around me: On Sunday Johnny Lacey picked me up and brought me down to a match in Clanwilliam where we hooked up with Ian, Johnny O'Dwyer and Fergal Gallagher. It was a difficult time but at least I had friends to help me.

Probably the hardest thing was ringing my Mother during the taxi ride back from Cork and breaking the bad news to her and my family. I knew she'd be upset for me and would be worrying about me. It can be hard to break bad news to people and talk to your family about tough times, but I've always been lucky to have good family and friends and team-mates supporting me.

I was lucky enough to have huge support from a lot of people who were very reassuring about my chances of getting back. Denis Leamy had suffered the same injury and he told me to be positive – he'd made it back and so could I. The Munster and Irish team coaches, physios and doctors contacted me as well, offering their support, which was a real boost.

I was booked in to see Ray Moran, a knee specialist in Blackrock and, after examining me, he was optimistic but he didn't mince his words. The knee had to be repaired and he said he'd do his best to have me back in five or six months. The most immediate problem was the swelling and trauma to the knee, which would mean he'd have to wait four weeks before he could even operate. My long climb back to fitness would only begin then. Bloody hell, here I go again!

Ray's advice was for me to work to get the swelling out of the knee and then try to build up the muscles around the quad and calves so that, after surgery, I might be back quicker. So, I began the training process: I had to do leg weights, balance work and a lot of bike work to build up the strength in my knee before surgery. And it worked. I trained hard for four weeks and found that my knee had stabilised with the other muscles. I had to take care not to get a bang or a knock but, when the four weeks were over, I couldn't wait for the operation.

During this time, I also had the benefit of working with a rehab specialist called Brian Green. Brian had worked in the States with the Pittsburgh Steelers and had joined the Irish set-up to help with the rehab of injured players. He'd been assigned to get me back to fitness as soon as possible and he took his job seriously. He came down from Dublin and spent a huge amount of time working with me, even staying with me at times. He was an absolute rock for me and got so involved in my pre-surgery training that, by the end of the four weeks, he was actually invited by Ray Moran to watch the operation.

The aftermath of my shoulder surgery had been a terrible experience. The pain kept waking me up and, when I'd finally get back to sleep, it would wake me up again. It was different with the knee operation. When I came round my body was fine, overall – I could sit up, or lean over and look down. I was mad to meet Ray and find out how the surgery had gone, how quickly he thought I might be able to get back. He was there almost from the moment I woke up and told me the surgery had been a great success and the repair work had gone perfectly. The trick now was to rest, be careful with it.

The other massive worry for me had been my rugby contract with the IRFU. In the four-week build-up to my operation, my agent John Baker had been talking to the IRFU about my future. The Union told him that the most important thing was for me to have the operation and then we could sit down to have our discussions. I knew they weren't going to leave me in the lurch – they've a good record of looking after people – still, when you get injured just before contract renegotiation, you're always gong to be nervous. It had been playing on my mind from the moment I got injured but now I felt relieved.

The surgery had been a complete success so the only thought on my mind was that I could finally begin the fight to get my life back. My cousin, Ian, collected me from hospital and took me home.

Then Brian Green arrived down to Limerick to help me start the rehab process. Kirsty was there as well so, between the two of them, they were working non-stop on me literally teaching me how to walk again. Kirsty worked with me on Mondays and Fridays, while Brian would come on Monday evening and I'd train three times a day with him on Tuesdays, Wednesdays and Thursdays.

When you're out of action for a while, some muscles begin to fade away so, within a few days of the operation, I was back working on leg lifts. I also had to stand on one leg or lie on my back lifting my legs – improving balance – working on the glutes and on my core strength. From strength I progressed to agility training: walking up the stairs, jumping up the stairs, coming down the stairs, hopping, leg press, leg extensions, more leg weights.

Brian's big thing was just getting mobility back. He worked me really hard but, along the way, we had a lot of fun and a good bond developed between us. Compared to my shoulder rehab, the knee was a lot easier, but it was long haul so my rehab had to be progressive. There were days when I found the going really tough, when I didn't feel 100 per cent and Brian would spot it straightaway and call a halt. We'd head off and do something nice or get a bit of grub, just pull the plug and take a break. But slowly, week by week, it got better.

I had hit many brick walls while recovering from the shoulder injury – it was difficult to do anything – but within two or three weeks of knee surgery I was able to do my rehab. I had a schedule and was able to work on the bike or do upper body weights. I didn't need massage and I didn't have to go for physio – the exercise was the physio. Six weeks into the surgery I was back on my feet: I was stepping, doing high knees, doing all the basic exercises and starting to run again. One of the single, most important aspects of recovery is being positive. Every week after the knee injury I could see an improvement, I felt stronger and fitter. That encouraged me even more, propelled my recovery forward.

The operation had been in November and I knew Ireland were going to Lanzarote the last week in December. Incredibly, Eddie asked me to go with the team. I can still remember the excitement and elation of being asked to go. He wanted to spend a week doing some fitness work and relaxing before Christmas. The change of scenery was just what I needed and I felt it was a reward for the work I'd been doing. Eddie was looking forward to the World Cup in France and, by that stage in our relationship, we'd formed a much closer bond. I think he had a lot of faith in me and was very supportive of me. So, we went to Lanzarote and Brian Green videoed me doing a lot of stuff – I started to step and side step, do an odd shuffle to the ground and get back on my feet.

He brought the videos of me doing the exercises back to the IRFU's head of medical, Dr Conor McCarthy, who then gave the Union's Contracts Committee a progress report on my injury. It was all very positive. I was doing really well, progressing. I was on my feet, I'd suffered no relapses, nor had I developed any related injuries.

I underwent a full medical check in Lanzarote with the national team doctor, Gary O'Driscoll, who reported back that everything was going according to plan. We returned home before Christmas and, two weeks into January, I had a new two-year contract on the table. That was a fantastic relief: I was over the moon. I'd gone from worrying every day about my future to now feeling secure. I was now two months into recovery, I was making great progress and I had a new contract in the bag. It was a huge boost to me to know that, even in the midst of this injury, that the IRFU was prepared to give me this huge vote of confidence.

At the same time, Munster were turning the corner. They'd won every game in their pool, since losing that first fateful game to Sale. Then they played Sale at the end of January and walloped them, 31-9, in Thomond Park. The bonus point helped them top the group and set up a quarter-final against Perpignan in Lansdowne Road.

Suddenly, I was into 'what if?' territory. I started believing that Munster could go all the way, and I began analysing the calendar, working out the dates of potential semi-finals and finals, wondering if I could make it back for the end of the season. My knee was doing well so maybe I could play before the end of the season?

My focus had shifted, I had a contract and everybody was telling me how well my recovery was going. I knew that myself, I could feel it within me. "Right," I began to think, "let's start aiming to get back in case something happens before the end of the season". Brian thought the same way. "Let's keep going. Let's not do anything stupid but let's keep working as hard as we can."

•••••••

But life – death – overtook us all.

In the run-up to the Perpignan match there was a tragedy which touched the entire squad, when a former Munster team-mate, Conrad O'Sullivan, died.

Conrad was Mick O'Driscoll's first cousin and had known, and played with, most of the lads in the squad the previous season. His passing had a major impact on us. We all knew his parents – had met them many times – and Conrad would have been friends with us all. His death was a blow, which shocked and upset everyone. We were heart-broken, really. It reminded everyone what life can be like outside of rugby. Conrad was a lovely guy and a fine player. It was a difficult time, a loss from which we will never totally recover.

•••••••

We went on to beat Perpignan while Leinster beat Toulouse. It was game on between Munster and Leinster in the semi-final at Lansdowne Road for the honour of contesting the Heineken Cup final in Cardiff. The game took on all the trappings you'd expect of a major derby.

I was back doing a little bit of jogging and was depending on the lads to keep on winning as it might give me a chance to make it back before the end of the season.

I changed my focus a little. I was already training and rehabilitating really hard but I upped the ante a bit with the physios and started putting pressure on them to help me get back more quickly. I started pushing myself harder. When the lads beat Leinster 30-6 in the semi-final, I was ecstatic. I was feeling stronger than ever and my surgeon, Ray, gave me the thumbs-up to resume playing.

We still had two Magners League matches and Deccie named me on the bench for the game against the Ospreys. I came on for a desperately nervous last twenty minutes. It was only five and a half months after my operation and it was as much a mental challenge as a physical one to get through those twenty minutes. I avoided bangs and knocks and was euphoric at the end of it. I'd successfully made it through my first comeback match. The following Tuesday night I played the full second half against Llanelli.

Then Deccie asked Shannon's coach, Gallimh, if he could include me in their upcoming AIL final. The Shannon game was a week before the Heineken Cup final and, if I came through the AIL final, Deccie would be able to judge me on the strength of three matches to decide whether I was worth a punt on the bench. It was a difficult situation, for a number of reasons. If Shannon selected me, it would mean that Stephen Keogh and I would both be on the Shannon bench, but Stephen and I were also both vying for inclusion in the Munster squad for the Heineken Cup final.

The second complication was that, if Shannon selected me, it would mean Anton Meany, a guy who had been with Shannon all the way through the AIL competition, would miss out.

From a selfish point of view I was happy because it would strengthen my case for being included on the Munster squad a week later, but I was disappointed for Anton.

In the end, I was selected for the AIL final and both Stephen and myself came on against Clontarf to help Shannon win the trophy. It was great to be involved with Shannon but I didn't really feel part of it. I didn't really feel I deserved to be on the field for this All Ireland League final.

After the game, I caught up with Anton who was dressed in his tracksuit. I commiserated with him but there wasn't much I could say, except apologise for what happened. He was great about it and said he understood. I gave him the AIL winner's medal – it was his victory, not mine. I didn't deserve it.

• • • • • • •

Suddenly, I was into the last week of a lead-up to another Heineken Cup final.

I trained fully with the lads but always, at the back of my mind, was the uncertainty of who would get the nod for the bench. The back row was going to be Denis Leamy, Axel and Wally with Micko the second-row sub. It would be either Stephen or myself for the other spot.

Deccie had never spoken to me about the situation. He just told me to train fully, play the matches and put myself in a position where I could be considered. After that, it'd be up to him to decide what was best for the team.

When we travelled to Cardiff on the Thursday evening, we still didn't know what the bench was going to look like. Then, in Cardiff, Deccie called down to my room and told me I was going to be on the bench. I was elated, over the moon. I knew that he would have already called in to Stephen to give him the bad news, which would have been a massive blow for him. I went to Stephen to try to commiserate with him, to say, "Look, I'm sorry for what has happened…" But it was very difficult. I didn't really know what to say: All I could do was apologise and tell him I was aware of what he was going through, that we were good friends before and I hoped we would continue to be good friends.

Sport is a tough profession. One person's joy is, inevitably, another person's tragedy. Although I felt bad for Stephen, I was over the moon that I was finally about to lay to rest the ghost of my six-month, career-threatening injury – and do it in another Heineken Cup final, even if it were only from the bench. I was probably the happiest sub in history. I was delighted to be part of the day and proud of how hard I'd worked to get myself back – how hard we'd all worked.

I will be forever in Declan's debt for picking me, for keeping faith with me.

In the hours before the match I thought about my knee, I realised I didn't have to protect it, but I was massively nervous. I knew my fitness and power were less than I would have liked. I knew I couldn't last eighty minutes. But Mick O'Dricsoll was on the bench and could play in the back row as well, which meant Deccie could include me as a sub.

So, I wasn't 100 per cent but the leg was well strapped. It was solid and secure and well rehabbed. All I needed now was a chance to prove it.

• • • • • • •

The match day was intense. Out of a crowd of more than 80,000 there were, perhaps, 6,000 Biarritz fans compared to about 65,000 Munster supporters – it was phenomenal. Travelling to the stadium through the streets was like sailing through a sea of red emotion. It felt great to be back in Cardiff's Millennium Stadium.

There was an air of 'third time lucky' about the squad, that this time around it was going to happen for us. Deccie was back with us and Jim Williams had stepped up as a coach, helping Brian Hickey with the forwards.

The game itself passed me by. I was so excited to be there, I was more like a supporter cheering on the lads than an actual sub. From the off, the boys were on fire, despite an early Biarritz try. They played solid, intensive rugby and there was a will to win, a desire about the team that day that was just amazing.

Their scrum-half, Yachvili, is a great kicker and as the game progressed it became a tit-for-tat affair with both Yachvili and ROG exchanging penalty after penalty. Trevor Halstead went over for a try in the first half, but the significant score in the match came when Peter Stringer broke off the side of the scrum and caught Serge Betsen napping and scored a brilliant try.

Viewing the game from my vantage point on the bench, Strings' try was the turning point in the game, especially when ROG followed it up with a couple of penalties. At the seventy-minute mark, I was warming up behind the posts. All of the subs were warming up, just in case… I heard someone calling my name and looked at the clock: seventy-three minutes gone. Then I was being called to the sideline – I don't think I have ever been so nervous. My entire body was shaking at the thought of running out onto the pitch.

My entire season, this painful season, had led up to this point. I don't know why Declan decided to put me into the game. Maybe he felt that I deserved it after all the hard work I had put in and the heartache I'd gone through – I hope it was because he knew I could do a job for him. I don't know, I never asked him but I remember thinking, "Christ, I owe him so much".

I also knew how much I owed my physios, Kirsty Peacock and Brian Green. I considered the last six months of physical and mental pain they'd helped me overcome: How often Brian had trained with me. How often he had stayed over nights in my house so he could be closer to me in order to help me.

I took off my tracksuit bottoms and stood on the sideline. Jerry Holland patted me on the back: "Go out there and work hard. Be strong for the team. Keep the head".

I didn't touch the ball for the four minutes I was on, I just ran over and back like a blue-arsed fly and tried not to make any mistakes. And then it was over, my Cup final appearance was gone in a flash. We had a scrum which ended in Biarritz conceding a penalty. Strings asked the ref how much time was left and the official replied that when the ball goes dead … it's over. Strings' boot duly sent the ball spinning into the crowd.

In the end, the emotion and the joy on everyone's faces told its own story. We'd been on such a long journey together – the players, the subs, the coaches, the Munster staff, the fans – and, finally, we'd reached our destination. I've always believed that, despite the downs I've experienced, I've been lucky to have so many good things happen to me. The wheel of fortune keeps on turning and that's what keeps me going – as hard as some things are to take, you have to believe in change and that good things will come. Standing on the pitch in the Millennium Stadium, having just won a Heineken Cup final with Munster, was proof of that. My season had started dismally but, only six months or so later, here I was celebrating with my team-mates – the people with whom I'd been through hell and back – our first Heineken Cup victory.

The first person I thanked when I came off that pitch was Brian Green. He was in the States, so I phoned him and told him I'd been brought on for the final four minutes of the game and had been there when the final whistle sounded our victory.

I was upset, I was happy, I don't know what I was, full of raw emotion. I just remember thanking Brian and getting upset. I'd come through something that could have been a total disaster, and Brian had shown me there was light at the end of a very dark tunnel.

Deccie? Well, I didn't say much to Deccie when we met. I just said, "Thank you," and we just hugged each other. He knew and I knew. That was enough. I was delighted for him, for myself, for everyone. I thought about Claw and Gallimh, about Jim Williams, John Langford, Dominic Crotty, Killian Keane – I was sorry they'd never experienced this, despite the service they'd given Munster over the years. They, and many other unsung Munster heroes, had all played their part in this day and the victory was theirs, too.

• • • • • • •

Rugby has become a lot tougher since I started playing. These days, the players are bigger and stronger. The game is a lot more physically demanding and you can feel pretty sore after a game, even the younger guys. I'm forever asking the younger players in Munster how they feel after a game, hoping they feel as sore as me. After a big game it probably takes two or three days to recover from the stiffness and the muscle soreness.

As players, we owe a lot to our fitness coaches, people like Paul Darbyshire, Tom Cummins, Joey Gallanagh and Aidan O'Connell. These guys go above and beyond the call of duty to have players in the best possible condition which, in turn, makes our recovery after games speedier. We go into recovery the day after a game – we go swimming, we get stretched and massaged – and that makes a massive difference. Basically, you've got to flush out the lactic acid. Over time, your body and your mind toughen up and you get conditioned to the bangs and knocks the more games you play.

I've always found it tougher to take a tackle than to make one. Taking a tackle means you're getting banged and bruised, getting hit across your head, shoulders and back. Usually you end up falling or being hauled down, and then you've got the prospect of a bunch of big heavy lads falling on top of you. Making a tackle is easier but, obviously, trying to tackle a big strong guy running at full-steam straight at you, can be detrimental to your health.

When you pick up a serious injury, your recovery is as much a mental battle as it is a physical one. My knee injury came at the end of a good pre-season. I was still getting a lot of my strength back after the shoulder injury so, when it happened, I could only roll my eyes up to heaven and demand to know, "Why me?"

Looking back on that tackle against Sale, which temporarily destroyed my knee, I try to be philosophical. I was upset about the tackle: I'm sure he didn't mean to do it but I was a bit angry that he had made no effort to see how I was afterwards.

I can live with a lot on the pitch. I've learned to take the rough with the smooth over the years. I've been raked with studs, even punched in the jaw and I've scars all over my head, back and legs. But, if someone is man enough to come up at the end of the game and put their hand out to be shaken, then it's finished. It's left on the pitch.

CHAPTER 17

March 30, 2007
Heineken Cup Quarter-Final
v Llanelli (Stradey Park)
Lost: 15-24

After the triumphs of the previous year, we entered the 2006-2007 season determined to defend the title and win back-to-back Heineken Cups.

We didn't underestimate how tough that would be. We knew we were in for a difficult ride. When you win a major trophy, you become a target for everyone else. Every team you play raises their game because they want to measure themselves against the Heineken Cup champions. But we began the season in great form, winning away at Leicester in a group which also featured Bourgoin and Cardiff. Winning at Leicester was the perfect start, especially as ROG had fired up the English lads by giving an interview in the *Guardian* newspaper beforehand, in which he labelled the English Premiership as "over-hyped". The reaction in certain quarters of English rugby was predictably hostile and the rest of us warned ROG that he'd be taking the blame if we lost but, in the end, we came through the test. In fact, with Paulie as the new Munster captain, we won our first four games in the pool, including back-to-back victories over Cardiff just before Christmas.

The downside for me in the Thomond Park game against the Welsh was being cited for stamping on a Cardiff player. It was a massive setback – I'd just come back, having missed the previous season because of my knee injury. I was back in the team and playing well, so to blow that was disappointing.

The incident was stupid really, born out of frustration. We were pushing for a bonus point: We'd scored three tries and were mauling up the field when Mark Lewis pulled down the maul. They'd been doing all game long and I stamped on his calf as he was pulling it down, hoping he'd let go. It seemed like a pretty innocuous incident, but was picked up on camera and I was cited – and rightly so. The result was a six-week suspension, which meant I would miss the game after Christmas, away against Bourgoin. I would also miss the Leicester game, which was shaping up to be the decider for the top the group. All in all, I had a really frustrating few weeks, watching from the sidelines.

By the time we came to face Leicester in Thomond Park, we'd won our first five pool games. Thomond Park was soon to be redeveloped, so there was a lot of history tied up in the Leicester game, a lot of pressure. We wanted to preserve our unbeaten record in Heineken Cup games in the old Thomond Park.

Six days before the game, Munster had survived a real scare away against Bourgoin. We'd failed to get a bonus point, which meant we were only three points ahead of Leicester going into our match. In the end, Leicester brought a very strong team to Ireland and beat us by seven points. It was a massive blow to the team. We'd been in such a strong position after the first five games but, after losing to Leicester, we were faced with the prospect of a tough away quarter-final against Llanelli Scarlets.

Worse than that, we had lost our home record at Thomond Park. That dented our confidence and our pride, plus the last two performances against Bourgoin and Leicester were worrying – there was sloppiness and mistakes were creeping into our game. We had a niggling feeling that, mentally, we weren't right, we weren't up for the games.

Going to Stradey Park as Heineken Cup champions to play against Scarlets was always going to be a tough proposition. We had a good record against them in the Magners League but that particular season they were playing some great rugby and had topped their group. On top of that, we had to contend with the news that Paulie had to pull out of the game. He was a huge loss to us – not only is he captain in name, he's our captain and leader in spirit and in action. We were still confident, though. After all, we had players like Mick O'Driscoll coming in as a replacement for Paulie and

Mick's a great player. We believed we could do the job.

However, things didn't turn out that way, we really let ourselves down on the night and it was a game that, for me personally, showed just how much we were off the pace. Lots of things went wrong for us in the game. We made numerous mistakes and errors and Scarlets came out at the start of the game with all guns blazing. They got off to a great start and scored an early penalty and try. Suddenly, we were 10-0 down, which is a bit of a hammer blow in a quarter-final.

Things got worse when they scored another try and converted to go ahead by seventeen points. That's a big deficit for any team to come back from and, worse, Scarlets' confidence was growing by the minute. In the end, it came down to which team wanted it more and that night it was Llanelli Scarlets.

We had massive support there backing us, the fans were amazing, but we let ourselves and our supporters down with the performance. We tried hard to turn things around. Just before half time we actually managed a try and a penalty, and the score at the break was 17-8, which gave us a bit of hope. Back in the dressing room, Deccie was furious with us and with the way we were playing.

We went back out, determined to fight hard for our crown. But, though our performance improved and we gave it everything we had in the second half, the scoreline difference was just too big a mountain to climb.

The Welsh scored another try with twenty minutes to go and effectively killed off the game. We scored again but, ultimately, we left Wales on the wrong end of a 24-15 scoreline. The whole thing just felt wrong, it felt lousy. To go out in that fashion in a quarter-final left a sick feeling in the pit of everyone's stomach.

We just didn't seem to have enough desire, intensity and aggression on the night. On the other hand, it was obvious Scarlets really wanted the win. Their crowd was fantastic for them and their players repaid the great support with a great display.

Maybe the hardest thing to take about surrendering the Heineken Cup crown, and giving up the dream of winning back-to-back titles, was the fact that we felt we hadn't been beaten by a better team – we'd been beaten by a team that played better on the night. They had heart, we didn't. That's not Munster, and it's not the way you win Heineken Cups. We walked out of Stradey Park that night with a lot of questions and very few answers.

We had to confront the reality that something wasn't right in the squad since the loss to Leicester. We had to go back to the drawing board and effectively learn how to cope with the pressure of the Heineken Cup.

One of the biggest mistakes we had made that season was that we hadn't adapted to being Heineken Cup champions. The nature of rugby had changed and Munster had moved with the times becoming much more professional than anyone could ever have foreseen. We trained harder than before, looked after ourselves and prepared better than ever before. We watched DVDs of the opposition before the game and DVDs of the match afterwards. We looked for weaknesses on the other team, tried to anticipate their game plan and find ways to negate it.

Perhaps the biggest lesson we would take away that night was that other teams were obviously doing the same thing. That night in Stradey Park, the Scarlets came prepared: They had a game plan. They'd done their analysis of Munster and found a way of stopping us performing.

And we knew it. The changing room after the game was deathly quiet. The Llanelli players were on a high, but we were deflated, shocked. At the post-game meal, you could see how delighted they were. It was a massive thing for them to beat us, to beat the Heineken Cup champions. There was also a huge prize at stake – a Heineken Cup semi-final and the opportunity to stay in the hunt for the ultimate trophy. We had lost that opportunity.

The challenge for Munster after the Scarlets game was in how we would react. Deccie and the management were as disappointed as the players but we all knew, deep down, that things had to change at the end of that season. We sat down as a team and dissected every part of that year accepting individual and collective responsibility for what had gone wrong the season. It culminated in a day-long meeting at the Radisson hotel in Limerick, with Killian Keane acting as facilitator. We went through whatever problems we had had – our fitness, our preparation, the way we played – and looked at ways of improving. There was a lot of frank, open discussion and a lot of straight talking. In the end, it kept coming back to our performance against Scarlets.

It wasn't as though we didn't know what it was to be beaten. We'd been defeated by better teams before, and we'd also played well in games that we'd lost. But Llanelli was different. No disrespect to the Llanelli lads, but the loss that day said more about Munster than it did about Scarlets. At least, it did for us.

The Llanelli game had thrown down a gauntlet to all of us. Players had to embrace change but so did management. One of our back-room team departed and Deccie stepped back from being attack coach to concentrate on his own strengths – managing players and coaches: Pulling the whole thing together, pulling the strings.

In the end, we decided to draw a line under Llanelli and the 2006-2007 season. We had lost the chance to defend our title, we had lost our chance at winning back-to-back Heineken Cups. The other teams were raising their game when they played us. They were adapting and evolving and we had to do the same thing, and quickly.

As the season drew to a close, we were out of the Heineken Cup and off the pace in the Magners League. Our job, now, was to start building towards the following year. We won our last four games and started laying the foundations to go out and reclaim the Heineken Cup.

CHAPTER 18

There's only one thing worse than a Munster man with a chip on his shoulder and that's the entire Province of Munster with a chip on its shoulder. But that's what happened in the run-up to the 1999 World Cup. The Ireland manager, Warren Gatland, had selected a squad which was very light on Munster players – maybe only four or five lads.

I wasn't among them. I'd been invited on to the Ireland scene back in 1997 by Brian Ashton and had played a few games with the Ireland 'A's but, when Brian was replaced by Warren, I slipped out of the reckoning and missed the 1998 tour to South Africa.

Back then I don't think Warren had a lot of time for me – he thought I was far from the complete rugby player and, with experienced players like Dion O'Cuinneagain, Andy Ward, Victor Costello, Trevor Brennan, Axel Foley, David Wallace, and David Corkery to pick from, I wasn't on his selection radar.

But, by the time the 1999 World Cup came around, I figured I was worth a slot in the Ireland set-up and I wasn't alone. There were a number of Munster lads who felt aggrieved at Gatty's squad choices.

It wasn't just the players – Munster people have a very proud rugby tradition and there was a bit of bitterness about the Ireland selection. Warren had picked a lot of overseas players and, while there was no personal animosity towards the individual players, it seemed to us in Munster as though the Irish management had decided that overseas players were playing a higher grade of rugby than provincial players back home.

So, when it was revealed that the Ireland team would play the provinces as part of their World Cup warm-up, we felt it was a perfect opportunity to put down a marker. All of Munster seemed to feel the same way because the massive crowd which turned out was almost as highly motivated as the players. When Gallimh gave us our dressing room pep talk, it was with tears streaming down his face.

The game itself was a tight affair. We led in the second half but we were beginning to tire. If things had continued the way they were, we might have been overtaken but, instead, the Irish management miscalculated badly by deciding to bring on some of their big guns like Woody, Dion – who was captain – and Andy Ward to try and put us away.

The sight of them bringing on their big-game players gave us a major boost and we saw out the game, beating them 26-19. It was a strange experience seeing the Munster fans shouting against Ireland – the same team that they would be supporting in the World Cup a few weeks later.

Ireland faced Connacht in another of the provincial warm-ups and Wally and I were called up to play with Connacht because we were on World Cup standby and they had a lot of injuries. It was almost a repeat of the Munster game but, this time when Ireland brought on its big guns in the second half, they managed to pull away and win. We were robbed of the euphoria which followed the Munster match but it was still a great game to be part of.

A couple of weeks later, we were in Connemara with Munster on a team-building exercise. Wally and I had picked up a couple of small knocks, so neither of us were taking part in the activities, though we accompanied the lads as they climbed fences and poles and ran up and down the hills around Leenane in Co Mayo.

Then Deccie got a call from the Ireland camp: David Corkery was out of the squad and Eric Miller had injured his hamstring – myself and Wally were both required to make our way to Dublin.

As the Munster lads remember it, Wally and I had hobbled up the hills like two crippled old men but, once we got our World Cup phone call, we were miraculously able to sprint back down again, jump into our cars and drive straight to Dublin.

The pair of us were as nervous as kittens, excited to get the call but worried that our rush to Dublin might be in vain if David and Eric recovered.

In the end, it was case of joy for me and heartache for Wally. David was definitely out, which meant I was going to the World Cup, but Eric recovered so Wally faced a lonely trip home. Worse still, we were sharing a room in Dublin while we waited for final word on our fates so, when I was chosen, Wally had to watch as my Ireland gear arrived. It must have been an absolute sickener for him but Wally, like the man he is, got through it and went on to an incredible International career.

Two days later I came off the bench in Lansdowne Road to win my first cap against Romania in the World Cup. By rights the new caps, which included Gordon D'Arcy and Angus McKeen, should have gone on the lash that evening but there was no time. We were leaving the next day for France where we would face Argentina in the battle for a quarter-final berth.

People expected us to win the Argentina game but things are never that straightforward. There was a deep rivalry between the two teams and we didn't enjoy the best run-up to the game. We didn't have our own chef with us and the hotel food at our French base was just horrendous. We decided the McDonalds joint nearby was a better dining option so it wasn't unusual to see Ireland players wandering around with Big Macs, fries and onion rings.

Meanwhile, I had other things to worry about – I was rooming with Claw who had decided to make me his slave. He made me order room service for him, go to McDonalds for him, get him extra pillows and fetch fags for him. Claw – full name, Claw the Law – had a very definite view of how his rugby life should be ordered and no one, certainly not some youngster from Tipperary, was going to question his right to be waited on hand and foot.

Mind you, I was happy to be his slave. I was just excited to be there, to be part of it all and, anyway, Claw was great craic and, despite enslaving me, he looked after me in my first World Cup.

Neither Claw nor myself had made the twenty-two for the Argentina encounter – Claw was injured and I wasn't selected. It was probably just as well, because I was exhausted from my exertions doubling as Claw's minion!

Back then, it was tradition for the Dirt-trackers – the guys not in the twenty-two – to have a few drinks before a match. So, as tradition demanded, the night before the Argentina game we went for a meal and a few beers. A few became many and, before long, the Claw was leading the festivities which centred on drinking games and a Tervor Brennan inspired sing-song.

It all seemed great craic at the time but not so clever the next morning, when the Dirt-trackers were summoned from their sick beds for an early morning fitness session. The only one to miss the punishing session was Claw, who was excused exercise duty on account of the same back injury which had ruled him out of the Argentina game. So, while Trevor, myself and the other unfortunates sweated and struggled our way through an hour of pain and physical misery on the pitch, Claw was tucked up in his bed, having a snooze and awaiting the return of his personal slave whom he could send to Mickey D's to fetch his lunch.

• • • • • • •

The history books record our loss to Argentina but not the personal heartache of that defeat. The Ireland dressing room afterwards was one of the worst places I've ever been. The reality – and the significance – of what had just happened was beginning to sink in. We were out of the World Cup and already the vultures were beginning to circle with a lot of negative things being said about the future of Irish rugby and about the players.

In the midst of all the gloom there was one reason to be optimistic about the future: Brian O'Driscoll was only starting out on his Ireland career but it was already obvious that he was a special talent. The morning after the Argentinean defeat, Drico and I were talking in his room when he gave me the Argentina jersey he'd swapped the night before. It was an unusual thing to do – maybe Drico wanted to try and banish the memory of the previous night's game – but I was happy to take the jersey because, deep down, I knew that in years to come, this guy would become an iconic figure in the game. That Argentina match holds only bad memories for Irish rugby, but I still treasure Drico's jersey from that night – one day I'll pass it on to my son, AJ, and tell him the story behind it.

The World Cup ended my involvement with Ireland for a while. I was in the midst of a disappointing season with Munster, which ended in that heart-to-heart with Deccie in Cork and a realisation that I needed to change my attitude.

Things began to turn around for me, first with Munster and then with Ireland. I won my second International cap in 2001, when we beat Italy in Rome, and I was part of the starting team that defeated France in Dublin. I was due to start the next game against Wales as well, but the Foot and Mouth crisis intervened and the Six Nations was suspended. It was a disaster for the country but it also spelt doom for me because, when the competition resumed the following Autumn, I was again on the outside of Gatty's plans.

But, change was coming. Supposedly, Warren wasn't seeing eye-to-eye with the rugby powers that be and, in a run-off between him and his assistant Eddie O'Sullivan for the Ireland job, Warren lost out. I didn't really get to know Warren too well. His attitude was that this was International rugby and he wasn't going to start molly-coddling players – he told them what was required and then expected them to get on with it.

He did some work with the forwards but he wasn't a hands-on coach – he had other coaches around him to do that. He was a laid-back, quiet kind of bloke – there wasn't much roaring or shouting with him – but people still respected him.

The most notable part of Eddie's elevation was the appointment of Munster's Deccie Kidney and Niall O'Donovan to the Ireland staff. They were obviously two guys who were very familiar with me: I watched and waited.

• • • • • • •

After the Munster run to the Heineken Cup final in 2002, I found myself selected for the Ireland tour to New Zealand. I was nervous about the prospect of facing the mighty All Blacks but, when we got down there, Keith Wood took me aside and asked me if I was prepared to step up to the

You can take the boy out of the country, occasionally, but I will never forget the great family and people in Tipperary who helped me to make a career in the professional game.

After Clanwilliam, Shannon became my home from home, where men like Axel Foley and Mick Galwey became team-mates and friends.

Growing into the arms of Munster in 1999, with Axel Foley and David Wallace.

Playing with Shannon and Clanwilliam (above) provided me with the perfect platform to progress my career.

A man will do anything for his country, but I am not exactly sure how this happened in the early days of my Ireland career.

World Cup, Australia, 2003: Malcolm O'Kelly, Peter Stringer and I link for the national anthem.

That World Cup in Australia brought ecstasy and agony in my direction, but was scoring the vital try against Argentina, which kept our tournament alive, worth every ounce of pain?

(Above) in Australia in 2003 the guys and I try a new lineout formation, but (right) they left me to find my way to Tokyo on the Shinkansen Bullet Train in 2005.

When the Ireland squad got together, all of the rivalry between Leinster and Munster was left aside though, on this occasion. John Hayes (behind me) is not letting Shane Horgan off lightly as we all queue up for our official photos.

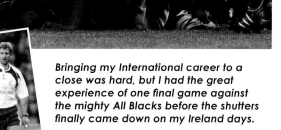

Bringing my International career to a close was hard, but I had the great experience of one final game against the mighty All Blacks before the shutters finally came down on my Ireland days.

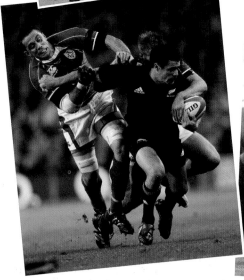

Winning our first Heineken Cup title in 2006 was special after so much heartbreak and so many near-misses by a magnificent group of players and management, so we were definitely in the mood for celebration. (Above) me with Donncha O'Callaghan and Mick O'Driscoll, (below) myself and Shaun Payne pay homage to Ronan O'Gara.

Our second Heineken Cup title in 2008 confirmed for us all that Munster had become the most respected, and sometimes feared, team in European rugby. I celebrate with Donncha and Paul O'Connell (right) and kiss that precious piece of metal (below)...

... then I take time to celebrate with my friend, John Hartnett and my Mum, Mary.

I never imagined my amazing journey with Munster would take me to 200 caps, but I had the great honour of running out for that historic total in September 2010.

Mick 'Gallimh' Galwey and Peter 'Claw' Clohessey, two of the greatest players ever to have worn the red of Munster and green of Ireland. I am proud to call them team-mates and friends.

Shortly after I was announced on the 2009 Lions squad for the South African tour by Welsh great Gerald Davies (right), my dream came tumbling down around me.

In the wake of the Heineken Cup semi-final defeat to Leinster, I was cited for the Leo Cullen incident and, following an ERC disciplinary panel hearing, I lost my Lions place.

Some of the great and very patient coaches and managers I have worked with during my career include Brian O'Brien and Warren Gatland (top), Alan Gaffney (right), and Eddie O'Sullivan.

(Above) Declan Kidney and I went through every emotion together as player and coach, but I also shared my ups and downs with Niall O'Donovan (left), Jerry Holland pictured here with Paul O'Connell (below left) after our 2008 Heineken Cup win, and (below) Munster's current coach Tony McGahan.

Would I have enjoyed such a memorable career with Munster without the help of great friends in the pack? I doubt it somehow! Here are just some of them (clockwise) David Wallace, Marcus Horan, Fla, John Hayes, Denis Leamy and Eddie Halvey.

plate for my country?

Woody was a legend in the game. He was Ireland captain and close to Eddie so, after chatting to him, I started to believe I could play a major part in this Tour. But, a week before the first Test, I damaged my knee ligaments in a game against a divisional side and ended up missing the first game when the boys nearly beat the All Blacks in Dunedin.

I worried that my tour was over but, by the time the second Test came around, I was back on the bench with my knee strapped up. It felt great to be recalled despite having not trained for so long: I felt wanted by the team and by the management.

When Keith Gleeson came off at 8-20 down with twenty-five minutes left on the clock I was raring to go. But I wasn't on the pitch sixty seconds when I got yellow carded for a moment of absolute stupidity. Norm Maxwell came on the wrong side of our ruck and stopped our ball coming back – I reacted by rucking him out of it but was immediately yellow-carded for stamping by the referee and sent to the sin-bin for ten minutes. It was a nightmare scenario for the team and for the management ... and for me. It was probably the first time that I got myself into trouble on the International stage but that was no excuse.

I trudged back to the sideline where ROG, who had been substituted earlier, was waiting. He took one look at my sorry face and started laughing at me. I was fit to be tied – here I was, in the horrors and going off my head about what I'd done to my team and to my career, and all he could do was laugh at me. I failed to see the funny side of it at the time. But we lost 8-40 and I had more to worry about than ROG laughing at me.

There wasn't a word said to me after the game but I knew Eddie was fuming. I just kept my head down, showered and got on the bus for the reception with the New Zealanders. As we got off the bus, Eddie called me over and basically told me what a bloody idiot I was and how livid he was with me – he didn't hold back. I didn't know him well at that stage and had no real defence to offer: All I could do was say sorry.

But I was gutted. I looked so genuinely miserable that evening that the lads took me out and got me absolutely hammered. At one point in the evening I was sitting in the nightclub looking the very picture of dejection, when Eddie came over and sat down beside me. He told me to cheer up, that it was only rugby and not the end of the world.

He was very decent on the night, but he hadn't forgiven me. Deep down he had marked me as a wild young buck who needed to be taught a lesson.

I drank a lot that night, whiskey and tequila shots – anything to try and numb the pain and the disappointment. I stumbled back to my room, got sick and my room-mate, the great John O'Neill, put me to bed.

When I finally got back to Ireland I expected some sympathy from my friends but, instead, I got an unmerciful slagging and, courtesy of Paddy O'Callaghan, a new nickname, 'Nicolas Cage' – from the movie, 'Gone in Sixty Seconds'. It took me a while but, eventually, even I could laugh about it.

By the time Ireland faced Romania the following September in Thomond Park, I was trying to put the All Black tour behind me and hoping that Eddie might be in a similar mood to forgive and forget. I was called in to the squad but any hopes of International redemption were dashed when Eddie gave me another dressing down for the stamping incident and dropped me as a punishment.

From that point on his whole demeanour spoke only of his anger and frustration with me. In training – in everything – he was hard on me: He spoke to me through Niall O'Donovan, and it was Niallo who briefed me on game plans and the need to watch my discipline. I was okay with that because I got on well with Niallo and, anyway, I figured Eddie had a right to be hacked off with me. I knew I'd have to prove myself to him all over again.

•••••••

In the run-up to the following year's tour Down Under, I started to get under his skin again.

Eddie was a very good coach – a very technical coach with a great vision and understanding of the game, and some great game plans which he was trying to impart to us. He wanted to designate the ball carriers to be senior players like Woody or Axel, but I wanted to do my own thing. I failed to follow orders and was a bit too much of a free spirit, which landed me in hot water – Niallo would come back to me after training and tell me that the boss was getting sick of me.

The trip Down Under was more of the same. I played against Australia but, later in the tour, Niallo took me aside and warned me that Eddie was getting annoyed with my attitude in training and my inability to stick to the game plan.

When I got sick the morning of the Samoa game, there were few words of comfort for me from the coach. He bluntly told me that I was too sick to play and if I didn't make the decision to pull out of the game, he would make it for me.

Even after the tour ended, I still managed to attract Eddie's ire. He got wind of the fact that myself and Shane 'Munch' Byrne had argued over lineouts in Australia, and then again during a subsequent team trip to Poland. Munch and I got on well but we sparked off each other: We both had strong opinions on rugby matters and weren't afraid to air them.

But Eddie decided to take us to task during a training camp in Athlone. He called us up to his room where he duly let rip. He warned us that if we didn't sort out our differences, there and then, we wouldn't be going to the World Cup.

I put my two hands up: "Fair enough, we'll just sort it out and it won't happen again." But, in typical Munch fashion, Shane said he didn't know what Eddie was on about. He didn't agree with anything Eddie had just said – we weren't fighting or arguing at all. What the hell was Eddie on about?

I waited for the eruption but Eddie just told me to leave and wait outside the door. I couldn't hear anything after that but when Munch appeared he said we were to pack our bags – Eddie's solution was to make us room together. What could we do? We laughed, we felt like two school kids who had just had been told off. From that point on, there were no more arguments over lineouts.

That was a common thread in my relationship with Eddie – I kept coming up in front of him like a bold pupil. Eddie wanted to be in control and avoided becoming overly friendly with the players. He wanted to keep his distance and if we met in the lift he wouldn't say much. That didn't really trouble me – if he didn't want to have breakfast with me or salute me in the corridor, I wasn't too bothered. Any encounter with Eddie, which didn't end in me getting bawled out of it, was a good one.

• • • • • • •

As I've said, it was the World Cup game against Argentina in 2003, which changed everything between Eddie and me.

Before I left to go home he sat down with me and thanked me for my contribution. It was the first serious conversation I'd ever had with him and he surprised me. We spoke openly about our relationship, or lack of one, and from that moment on our dynamic changed, although I still wasn't able to cement my starting position.

After the World Cup, Eddie selected me for almost every squad for the next couple of years, but I did feel as though I was being picked because I was a good tourist and a positive team influence, rather than being selected purely for my rugby ability.

By the time the 2007 World Cup came around I was getting very little game time. The team was doing well, they were winning Triple Crowns and enjoying a lot of success and it's always difficult to break into a winning side. Neil Best, Simon Easterby, Denis Leamy and Wally were ahead of me so, in the end, I was just happy to be picked to go to France.

Expectations were high going into the 2007 World Cup. No Irish team had ever made it past the quarter-finals and, though we were in a tough group with France and Argentina, there was a huge anticipation that we could do well.

It never happened – our performances were poor from the outset. There are a lot of theories as to why that was the case – maybe we had over-trained, maybe there was a lack of freshness. But it's easy to talk like that with hindsight, in the run-up to the competition none of us saw any of that.

There was an air of negativity after the opener against Namibia and morale plummeted after we scraped past Georgia. Everyone expected Eddie to make changes for the France game but it didn't happen. Before that match, he spoke to those of us not on the bench and said that, basically, he felt the boys in the twenty-two could go out and do the job. That was hard to take after watching the previous games, but I didn't question him, he was the coach and it was his call.

When he didn't throw caution to the wind for the game against Argentina and introduce new faces, I figured that was it, the World Cup was over for me before it ever began.

I'd always known it was going to be tough to get game time and, since our arrival in Bordeaux, I'd been hitting the gym with Mike McGurn. I figured that I'd leave France with something, even if it was only with an improved fitness level. Every time Eddie declined to include me in the twenty-two, I trained harder and, despite the frustration, I stayed positive and tried to help the lads as best I could.

I wound up spending a lot of time with our bag man, Paddy 'Rala' Reilly, and fellow un-used squad member, Brian Carney. The highlight of each day was heading up to Rala's room to watch DVDs of the Western TV series, 'Lonesome Dove'. The three of us were addicted to it and managed to get through two series' during that World Cup. Brian used to bring in Milka chocolate and Coke which he knew Rala and I couldn't resist. After a few nights of Milka and Coke, Rala and I realised we were on the wrong path, but Carns kept on pushing his confectionary – though, funnily enough, he never seemed to eat much of it himself. By the time I came home, I'd put on four kilos, despite all my extra training with Mike.

• • • • • • •

In the end, Eddie made his decision and it back-fired on him with him losing his job. Maybe if he'd made a few more changes, he mightn't have taken all the blame for what happened. I thought he was wrong not make changes and there was a feeling amongst the players that it was harder to get into the team than get out of it, but I didn't really have any axe to grind with him.

There was a lot of external pressure around that competition, a lot of stories about dissension in the camp that had little basis in reality. The main issue we had was about location – we were basically stuck in a hotel in an industrial estate in Bordeaux and were bored out of our minds.

But, when things started to go wrong, Eddie got a bit paranoid about the press. It was hard not to have sympathy for him – the vultures in the media, particularly the ones who didn't see eye-to-eye with Eddie, were looking for any angle to attack him, especially after he got a new four-year contract before the World Cup had even begun. They were sharpening the knives and wanted nothing less than to get his head on the chopping block, so he was worried about players talking to the press.

Eddie had always been a strong character but, during that World Cup, I began to see a lot of chinks in his armour – some of the stories going round were unreal and it must have been hard not be effected by that kind of pressure.

In the end, the World Cup was a total disaster. We'd gone out there with so much expectation but it came to nothing and, in its wake, we were all subjected to the Genesis Report. By the time the report came to its conclusions, I was back focusing on Munster and paid little heed to it. At the meeting where we discussed its findings, Eddie stood up and acknowledged he had made mistakes and could have done things differently. He accepted there had been communication problems and pledged to take the criticism on board. But, while Eddie admitted his flaws, the players had to take responsibility also – at the end of the day the players were the ones on the pitch. It wasn't as though we were short on talent – this was the same group that had delivered so much success in the Six Nations previously.

When Eddie got the sack I felt bad for him. He had his flaws, like us all, but he was a good coach and had worked hard for the team: He brought a lot of success to Ireland. At the end, though, it was probably time for a change. He might not have lost the players but he had lost the fans and the media and, without them, it would have been very tough to carry on.

• • • • • • •

Deccie's installation as Ireland coach in 2008 gave me an opportunity to stake my claim for an Ireland jersey once more.

He selected me for the Autumn Internationals against Canada and the All Blacks. I was delighted to get the chance to play against the All Blacks though I wasn't 100 per cent coming into the game as I was returning after a groin injury. Still, I was so anxious to get back to the International scene that I put all thoughts of injury to the back of my mind, and focused on doing the job at hand.

As things turned out, it wasn't the injury I needed to worry about. Once again, I got myself into a scrape and was suspended for three weeks for stamping. It was hard to take in: I was only just back in the Ireland set-up and had immediately managed to shoot myself in the foot.

I ended up slipping back down the pecking order. Denis Leamy was coming back from injury so, suddenly, there was him, David Wallace, Jamie Heaslip and Stephen Ferris ahead of me. I was in the squad for the Six Nations but didn't play any games – I was the twenty-third man in a squad in which there were no injuries – I was close again, but not close enough. Still, I couldn't have any real complaints. Deccie had already explained to me that I wasn't going to be in the twenty-two because the boys who were ahead of me were playing well and he was going to go with them. I still felt there was a chance that things might change and I might get an opportunity, but it didn't happen. The boys played fantastically the whole way through and won the Grand Slam without me – it was great for Ireland but it was tough watching from the stands.

That game against the All Blacks in the autumn of 2008, was my final game in an Ireland shirt. The following year, Deccie sat down with me and outlined my International prospects. I wasn't going to make the twenty-two for the 2009 November Internationals or for the Six Nations, so he didn't see any point in picking me for the wider squad either. At that stage in my career, there wasn't much point in me holding tackle pads for a couple of weeks. I was fine with that, and I promised to be there for him if he needed me, if there were any injuries.

The conversation seemed to sum up my Ireland career which brought me twenty-seven International caps and many great memories – not least of which was being hailed for a time, even in jest, as 'The Man Who Saved Irish Rugby'. I intend to dine out on that story for years to come!

CHAPTER 19

May 24, 2008
Heineken Cup Final
v Toulouse (Millennium Stadium)
Won: 16-13

It's the morning of our departure for the Heineken Cup quarter final against Gloucester and Paul O'Connell is outside in his car, waiting to give me a lift to the airport for our flight.

I knew he was coming and had left the front door open for him. But he's not coming in – he's sitting in the car, looking at me through the open door, watching me crawling on the floor of the kitchen, calling for the family cat, Lulu.

It'd be funny – just the thing for a good slag in the dressing room – except I'm not crawling, and I'm not talking to Lulu. Instead, I'm lying there on the ground, moaning and groaning after coming round from a sudden collapse.

I'd been getting my gear ready for Paulie's arrival and, after leaving the door open for him, I'd momentarily gone back into the kitchen to mix up a protein drink. Trouble was that the previous frosty night had left the water freezing cold and as soon as I started drinking the mixture, the freezing water caused my oesophagus to contract which cut off the oxygen supply.

I blacked out and lay comatose on the kitchen floor for a few seconds and was coming round again just as Paulie arrived. Not the ideal preparation for a Heineken Cup semi-final against the likes of Gloucester, admittedly, but at least it gave the lads less of a reason to slag me than if I'd really been crawling on all fours looking for my cat.

• • • • • • •

We've been on a march for much of the season, ever since we lost to Wasps 23-24 in our opening game. After that, we beat Clermont Auvergne 36-13 at Thomond Park, and then faced the team that had outplayed and outfought us the season before – Llanelli Scarlets.

That loss to Llanelli had had a much bigger impact on us than perhaps even Llanelli imagined. The defeat had triggered some major soul-searching in the Munster camp, and we'd made a lot of progress in, effectively, re-imagining ourselves. So, to return to the scene of the previous year's crime was packed with just too much symbolism for us to ignore. If we had changed, if we had improved, then this was the perfect time and place to measure that change.

I was out of the game, the result of dislocating my thumb two weeks before against the Dragons in the Magners League. The weather on the day was appalling but even that seemed appropriate. Stradey Park had been the scene of our last nightmare, so the howling wind and lashing rain seemed fitting somehow. In the event, the team turned in the kind of gritty, aggressive performance that resulted in a 29-16 victory.

But it was the manner of the victory as much as the scoreline that really counted and, when Llanelli came to Thomond Park a week later for the return fixture, we turned in another tough performance and ground out a 22-13 win.

Despite the wins against Llanelli we still had to face Clermont Auvergne in France and Wasps at home in a pool that was living up to its billing as 'The Group of Death'. That point was driven home to us when Clermont beat us 19-26 at the Michelin Stadium.

The match was memorable for a few reasons, not least because, in the lead-up to it, Axel had blasted us out of it in a team meeting at UL. That season was Axel's last before he retired and he was determined not to let it slip by quietly. And he wasn't the only one to question our hunger and our attitude. The day before the game, Deccie warned us that we were one bad result away from being out of the competition. He told us that, perhaps, one Heineken Cup, a Celtic Cup and Celtic League were enough for us, and left us under no illusion that we were at another crossroads: We needed to rekindle our desire if we were going to make any further progress in the competition.

The Clermont game was a rough affair with no fewer than three Clermont Auvergne players sin-binned, and ROG was left bloodied and bandaged after someone stood on the side of his head.

But, even though Clermont had a 23-6 lead with three quarters of the game gone, we battled back to claim a bonus point. Lifeimi Mafi went over for a try, ROG converted and then scored a penalty, and suddenly we were only seven behind. We traded penalties at the end, but the bonus point we secured was enough to keep us in the hunt.

Our final pool game was against the defending champions, Wasps. They were three points ahead of us but, as long as we won by more than a point, we would go through. There were various permutations but the message boiled down to one fact: We had to win and stop them scoring tries.

It was another night of bad weather and the foul conditions were matched by the temperaments of the two packs but, ultimately, winning was all we cared about and when Denis Leamy went over with only seven minutes to go, we were safe.

My preparation immediately before the quarter-final against Gloucester was probably not the best – blacking out because of oxygen starvation and banging your head off the kitchen floor on the morning of your flight to England, is not a course of action I would recommend to up-and-coming players.

Deccie had made a couple of major calls going into the Gloucester game, bringing in Denis Hurley for Shaun Payne and Tomas O'Leary for Peter Stringer. As things turned out, Tomas had a great game and, in its aftermath, has gone on to play a huge role in our success.

Other changes were forced on us by circumstance and the build-up to the match was far from ideal. ROG played, despite feeling sick, but Marcus Horan hurt his back during the pre-match warm-up, meaning Tony Buckley was in the team and Feddie Pucciariello was called on to the bench. The problem was no one had any idea where Feddie or his gear was.

The scramble to find Feddie resulted in him being tracked down at the back of the stands eating a burger, while a motorcycle cop was dispatched to locate the team bus which had Feddie's gear stowed safely away. The effort was worth it, though, because the game wasn't too old when he was brought on to shore up the scrum.

Gloucester put us under a lot of pressure early on but their Scottish wing, Chris Patterson, missed three first-half penalties, which meant that pressure was never reflected on the scoreboard. Even so, the game was tight and tense – trips to play Gloucester at Kingsholm are never pleasant affairs – but an Ian Dowling try just before half time swung the momentum our way.

The second half was easier, you could sense that Gloucester doubted themselves. A great chip by Denis Hurley put Dougie Howlett through for another try and ROG added another penalty to leave the final score 16-3 in our favour.

Roll on the semi-s.

• • • • • • •

The value of Paul O'Connell to Munster – to Ireland and the Lions – is hard to describe. He's an inspirational man to have at your shoulder in any game. He's big, strong and tough and has a rare ability to lead players.

His private nickname is 'Psycho', which has everything to do with Paulie's competitive nature – and the fact that ROG and I had to give him the nickname before he could give it to us.

He's one of the most competitive people I've ever known – not just about his rugby but about everything else. He can barely cook for you – or let you cook for him – without looking over your shoulder to see what you're doing, or see if he can do it better. Like me, he has a young son and would think nothing of coming into the dressing room before training and cranking up the rivalry. He'd shout across the dressing room that his little guy, Paddy, was walking or talking or whatever and then say, "Hey, Quinny, that's a lot sooner than your AJ started doing it, isn't it?"

There's another side to him, though. He lives around the corner from me and he's always popping round for a chat or a cuppa. Whenever I was injured, or when I've felt down after a game, Paulie has always been one of the people who would drop in to see how I was doing or offer support. He might not look as though he's got a soft side, but he has. In fact, when Ruth and I saw how attached Paulie had become to our cat, Lulu, during his visits we decided to present him with one of his own. So now his days feature feeding Frank.

But on the pitch, whether it's in training or during games, Paul doesn't shy away from telling players what he expects from them. In the run-up to the semi-final against Saracens in the Ricoh Arena, Paulie was determined that we would play to the very best of our abilities, and beyond. Saracens were a tough, tough team with a great tradition and we knew they weren't going to take kindly to anyone coming onto their patch, trying to turn them over. The reward if we beat them would be huge – a return to the Millennium Stadium, a fourth Heineken Cup final, and the prospect of a second title in two years. So, the lead-in to the semi-final was a nervy time and at one point Paulie and Denis Leamy had a crack off each other in training.

Denis is a hard guy in his own right, never willing to back down or give an inch, and his nickname – 'Rock' – has as much to do with his physical stature as it has to do with the fact he's from Cashel. So, when the two of them have a real cut at each other, the rest of us know to stand back.

Not that anyone was particularly worried – going at it tough and hard in training is the way we do things. I've been as guilty as anyone of being overly competitive in training. It's earned me more than a few slaps over the years and a few heated rows with the likes of ROG and Marcus. But, at the end of it all, that tension stays on the training pitch and isn't allowed to carry over into matches or into our personal lives.

And when Paulie stood up to inspire us later in the week, he made sure that his speech pointed out that Denis was the man he wanted on his shoulder when he goes into battle. That was the right thing to do and say, and Paulie has never backed down from doing the right thing, or the thing that was best for Munster.

The first half against Saracens went according to plan, even allowing for them scoring a try right at the start of the game. It was a blistering start by Saracens, but ROG pulled back a penalty and then scored a great dummy try to leave the score at 10-7 to us. After that the game settled down into a tight affair. We weren't playing great, but we always felt we had enough in the tank to get through.

Right at the death of the first half, Dougie Howlett made a great run to their 22 before he was caught, and I arrived at just the right moment to pick up the ball and make it across the line.

With a half-time lead of 15-7, we were confident about the forty minutes still to come. But the second half began badly and, by the time the third quarter had come around, we were stuttering badly and Saracens had pulled back to within two points of us, ensuring the last ten minutes were going to be tense.

We traded penalties with them then dug in and waited for the clock to run down. At the end it was an ugly win, but a win nonetheless. The dressing room atmosphere had more of an air of defeat than victory about it. People were down about the performance, about the fact that we had let Saracens get close to us in a game which we should have controlled.

I was happy having scored a try, but the day ended on a sour note when Deccie vented his frustration at me and a couple of the other lads who had swapped jerseys with our opposite numbers – in my case, Richard Hill. Despite what we'd achieved and what we'd won, we still weren't allowed to swap jerseys. I was pissed off and angry, but what can you do? It was time to shower and get changed and get out of there. Leave it behind.

●●●●●●●

So, here we were again. Back in the Heineken Cup final.

It's the place every player wants to be in. We'd had our fair share of turns in the spotlight but, despite winning in 2006, it was impossible to forget that we'd twice let the prize slip through our fingers.

For me this was a personal watershed. I already had one Heineken Cup winner's medal, but that had been in 2006 when I'd spent most of the season injured and only appeared at the end of the final for a few minutes. But, now, here I was in a Heineken Cup final after having a good year, playing all season and reaching the final the way I wanted to, on my own terms.

The quarter-final win over Gloucester had been great, the win over Saracens in the semi-finals less so because we nearly lost the game right at the death. Our form was still patchy when we played Glasgow a couple of weeks later in Musgrave Park in the Magners, and we wound up losing that game. The worrying thing about the loss to Glasgow was that we had practically all our first-choice team playing, with the exception of Donnacha and Denis. Despite the air of confidence surrounding the upcoming final against Toulouse, we still managed to take our eye off the ball against Glasgow, and it cost us the game.

Still, if there was a positive to be taken from that loss, it was that there was no panic after the game, no sense of implosion or impending doom against Toulouse. We knew all about the Frenchmen. They were a fantastic club and had an unbelievable record in the Heineken Cup. But so had we, and we wanted to taste that success again. Going back to the Millennium Stadium was special for us, after what had happened there in 2006 in front of amazing support. I could feel the hairs rising on the back of my neck in anticipation of a repeat of that amazing, fanatical support.

We were all up for it, and the two weeks leading up to the final were like torture, they seemed to last for an eternity. One bit of light relief arrived in the form of my stag party. Because of our schedule, opportunities to hold my bachelor party were scarce so, one week before the final, we found ourselves in Killaloe on the Limerick/Tipperary border.

We had a great time: There was a barbeque and a few drinks before we headed back to Claw's nightclub, The Sin Bin. But, it was a strange night for me because I wasn't drinking – not a drop. I must have been the only stag in history to wind up driving all his friends home at four in the morning from his own bash!

It was impossible to push the game from my mind. I just wanted to get on with it. We left for Wales on the Friday morning and the send-off the team got from the fans at Shannon Airport was unbelievable. When we arrived in Cardiff we went straight to the Millennium Stadium to have a bit of a walk-through. It felt like déjà vu to be back there for a third final.

Standing there in the stadium, we were confident that we had a great team and we knew we were capable of winning, but that confidence was the very thing that made us nervous. We tried to remain calm, and Deccie worked hard to prepare us mentally for what lay ahead and to make sure we kept our feet on the ground.

So, we headed back to our hotel in the Vale of Glamorgan, where ROG and I spent our time chatting in the bedroom. I was a bag of nerves and so was ROG. At one point he reckoned he was going to have a nervous breakdown and when I woke up on the Saturday morning, I found myself in a worse state than I had been the night before. The morning of a final is about taking control of your emotions, mastering your nerves.

After what had happened in 2007, we were determined not to slip up again. We could still remember the taste of success from two years previously, and we wanted to experience that sensation again, more than ever. We knew we'd spluttered and coughed in the semi-final, but that was in the past. We were in the present, and that meant facing Toulouse in the final. That Saturday morning stretched on and on. We just wanted to get to the stadium, soak up the atmosphere. Get out of the traps, get going.

Deccie spoke to us in the hotel. He spoke quietly about taking the opportunity at hand. About living in the here and now, about doing it for ourselves. It was important to be reminded of that, of personal ambition. As a team we often forgot about that – in a place like Munster, it's easy to get swept up into the emotion and ambition of wanting to win for everyone else – the organisation, the supporters and our families. He reminded us how hard we had worked, about the sacrifices and the efforts we'd made in order to get to this point, to get to within striking distance of achieving the ultimate goal of winning the Heineken Cup, especially against a European rugby powerhouse like Toulouse whose budget and playing squad far exceeded ours.

But we had an unbelievable squad, too – though the season had seen gut-wrenching changes to our line-up. John Kelly had left at Christmas when he turned down a short-term extension to his contract. Every player was sorry to see John depart, he'd been an integral part of our team and had been a massive part of the Munster journey and had scored so many memorable tries for us in crucial games.

But he left, as we all do in the end, and in through the door walked Dougie Howlett. Howlett added a new dimension to Munster, and, together with Rua Tipoki and Mafi, was the third Kiwi in our line-up that year. The three lads had helped us change our back-line play that season so that we were able to vary our game. Despite the money that Toulouse had, we knew that we were a match for anybody.

All those changes could be traced back to the quarter-final loss against Llanelli in the previous year's quarter-final. That game, the disappointing, heartless, passive performance we put in against the Welshmen, had brought our problems to a head and caused us to sit down and honestly confront the issues facing us. In the intervening months since Llanelli, we'd developed our game to a new level and we wanted to put that more expansive game into operation – we were never going to play a tight game in that final. Sure, we were going to stop Toulouse and face up to the powerful men in their team, but we were going to play an open game of rugby.

Going into the game, we knew they had a very effective maul, they'd scored a lot of tries from it, so one of our main goals was to negate it – make sure we had a good set-piece, a good lineout and a good scrum. We would stop Toulouse from dominating in those areas.

When Deccie talked to us in the hotel, he spoke about the need to keep our emotions in check and not to let the occasion overcome our need to focus. That was vitally important because, climbing onto the bus bound for the stadium, everything felt like '06 again except, now, it seemed there were twice as many Munster people on the streets. The place was absolutely jammed, with Munster supporters everywhere. Hanging out of windows, pubs, off walls. It gave us all a huge boost, took our minds off our nerves and got us thinking about the task ahead, but it's also easy to get lost in that welter of emotion, to lose track of the reason you're there, and forget that you need to concentrate.

• • • • • • •

In the first few minutes of the game there are no more nerves. I didn't have time for them, none of us did.

The game kicked off at one hundred miles an hour, and Toulouse put us under serious pressure for the first twenty-five minutes. We had a game plan, which was to dictate the tempo from the start. It was a good plan, we just didn't get the chance to try it out. Instead, they came at us with everything they had. But Elissalde missed a couple of dropped goal attempts so all they had to show for twenty-five minutes of dominance was three points from a penalty.

It was a good return for us, considering we hadn't had a chance to start. We began to claw our way back. Denis Leamy had a try ruled out by the Television Match Official, but the turning point for me came when Toulouse had a scrum defending their own five-yard line.

They put in, but we pushed them off the scrum and, in the midst of the massive pressure we were putting them under, their No. 8 knocked the ball on at the back of the scrum. I was behind Marcus and we got a great angle up on the scrum and put pressure on them, and turned them over. That meant a second scrum but our put in. Denis Leamy picked off the base of the scrum and, after a few pick and go-s, eventually got over the line. It was a great score for us on two fronts: it boosted our confidence but, more importantly, it was a massive psychological blow for Toulouse, considering the dominance they'd earlier enjoyed.

Denis's try laid down a marker to Toulouse that they were playing against a different team that day, a team that was determined to fight and die for each other. We showed that the whole way through. After being battered a bit for the opening twenty minutes, we could have dropped our heads and gone into our shells a bit.

But we held on, soaked up their pressure and didn't panic and finally we were rewarded with a great try. By the time we arrived back in the dressing room at half-time, our confidence was growing. They'd dominated the beginning of the game but finished the first half behind by four points. No one underestimated the task ahead, but we were delighted with where we were in the game: 10-6 up. A lot of people spoke: Deccie again tried to reassure us; we needed to stay calm. Paulie stepped up and tried to get us going again but there was already a feeling in the room that today was going to be our day. We weren't going to lose this one, we weren't going to be robbed and we weren't going to throw it away, no matter what. Toulouse were there for the taking and we knew it.

Toulouse came at us at the start of the second half and charged ROG down a couple of times. Then, fifteen minutes into the game, came one of the most bizarre encounters of my career. The ref gave a scrum on the ten-yard line and their scrum-half was a great New Zealand player, Byron Kelleher. He's a player I'd have great respect for but, that day, I was given free reign to try and frustrate him and get at him. He was a very influential player for Toulouse and we felt it would benefit us if we put a bit of pressure on him because he might be a guy who would lose the head a little bit. So, all match long, I did my thing and had a bit of chit-chat with him, trying to put pressure on him, trying to psyche him out.

We had the scum but the ref that day was Nigel Owens, who could be a bit strict, and he decided to reset the scrum. Kelleher started roaring at the referee that Munster were up to something illegal and I decided to give him a bit of banter back. So, I just walked over to him at the side of the scrum and told him to shut up.

It was only a bit of banter, really, just mind games. But Fabien Pelous – who is an absolute legend of the game and someone who I'd have massive respect for because of his years in the Toulouse and French teams – decided to get involved. He pushed me away, so I pushed him back which caused him to give me a kick up the arse. It was a move which, by now, just about the whole world has seen and I've taken plenty of stick about it. But getting a boot up the backside from Pelous also won us a penalty and got him sin-binned.

Pelous getting sin-binned wasn't something I wanted to happen, but it was his own fault. He raised his leg to me and, while it wasn't the most painful thing in the world, I certainly felt it. It had all happened in a split second. I just tried to stand my ground and not be intimidated by him or Byron Kelleher. Looking back on it afterwards, it was something that I would have preferred had not happened. Then again, throughout my career those kinds of decisions have often been against me – I was always getting penalised for doing silly stuff. Now, in the middle of the Heineken Cup final, a decision was finally going my way. ROG stepped up and kicked the penalty and put us 13-7 ahead with about twenty-five minutes to go.

But, Toulouse aren't considered the best club in Europe for nothing. They were always going to strike back. Tomas O'Leary cleared the ball from a scrum but their winger, Cedric Heymans, caught the ball in touch, took a quick throw and chipped over our defensive line; Jauzion toe-poked it on and Donguy beat ROG to the punch and touched down.

Elissalde converted and suddenly we'd been hauled in: 13-13. The score was a blow to us and gave them huge confidence. The game hung in the balance. But we'd been here before. Our work rate was second to none, and we knew that we had to keep going – if we were to win the game, there could be no let-up. This was about pressure, intensity, desire.

After the try, they came at us again. They put a lot of pressure on us and, at one stage, they had an overlap inside their own half and decided to kick the ball across field. Marcus Horan was out in the wing and was able to get back to the goal line and touch the ball down. It was fortunate, because, if he hadn't been there, Toulouse would have been in for a try.

I remember shouting at Marcus for him to pass the ball to me because I wanted to take a quick 22 – there was no one on the 22-yard line and Marcus passed the ball. Looking back on it now, it was a crazy decision, really. It worked out okay for me because I got a penalty, but I was very fortunate that decision went in my favour because, at 13-all, what we needed was to slow the game down a little bit, not have me taking a quick 22. We just needed to get the ball to ROG so he could take the 22 and kick it long down the field, but I risked it all. I'm eternally grateful I got away with it, and won the penalty.

With eight minutes left, ROG put us 16-13 ahead. At that point we stopped playing, retreated into our shells and decided to hold on and rely on our work rate.

Our defence had been amazing the whole game and during that time, we'd only conceded one try, which came from that individual piece of Heymans brilliance. Generally speaking, our defence had been incredible all day and, with about seven minutes to go, we decided to keep the ball tight.

We ended up playing seventeen or eighteen phases of pick and go. It wasn't planned. We were just trying to run the clock down and shut Toulouse out, but we didn't realise there was so much time left in the game. We did everything in our power to see the game out and nearly managed it but we were penalised with only two minutes to go. At that stage we were just hanging on, hoping for the final whistle, barely able to wait.

Then Toulouse cleared their lines and came down field, but they lost their lineout and we were back on the front foot again. With thirty seconds left on the clock we had the option of either kicking a goal or holding onto the ball. The referee had told ROG there was another play after the kick so ROG and Paulie started debating the best thing to do. We were only three points ahead and a goal would have left us only six points up – within reach of a converted try.

I was further back down the field, wondering to myself, "What the hell are we doing?" We didn't seem to know what we were doing. There was confusion over whether to kick, run, run the penalty or just try and hold onto the ball. I was in the back-field at this stage because I thought we were going to kick the ball at goal. I saw ROG tap it and then I saw Toulouse swarming all over Paulie: "Here we go again," I thought. "We're going to screw this up."

But then, the referee's whistle blew...

• • • • • • •

When you're a youngster, winning a medal is amazing. It's the best thing in the world. All that time and effort, all the sacrifice and the long nights training – winning is the only thing that makes it all worthwhile. Truly worthwhile.

Winning a Heineken isn't much different, in many ways. Standing on the pitch that day in the Millennium Stadium, the feelings rushing through my body were all premised on the same emotion: Joy. When the whistle sounded I dropped to my knees. It was hard to look at the Toulouse players and not feel their pain – they were shell-shocked. We knew how they felt, we'd been through it twice before. But this was our day and we were ecstatic to get our hands on the Heineken Cup again.

I even managed to win the Man of the Match award. I'd like to be able to say that I felt the award vindicated me – that after all the ups and downs of my career, that Man of the Match award was my crowning moment – but, being honest, that's not how I felt at all. I was just relieved to get through the game, happy to be a winner and happy to be part of another magnificent day with Munster. This victory had been very different to 2006's win: I'd played a full eighty minutes of it and felt the day belonged to me as much as to anyone else.

By the time Sky Sports interviewed me on the side of the pitch I felt like I was in a dreamland. I kept searching the crowd for Ruth. She was at the game and all I wanted to do was hug her. I knew the general area she was in and made a beeline across the pitch towards her part of the crowd. When I finally managed to reach her I just hugged her and cried.

I just wanted to share that moment with her. After all we had been through with my rugby career, it was just special that she was there with me.

I went back out onto the pitch and just started jumping around and hugging the players. It was hard to believe – it took a while to sink in really. We lapped the pitch and then climbed the steps to the podium. Watching ROG and Paul raise the Heineken Cup was a memory and a half. The atmosphere, the excitement, the adrenaline rush – we were on the ultimate high. We couldn't wait to get back to Limerick, get back to Shannon.

But nothing ever runs smoothly and, at some point in the game, I had picked up a scratch in my eye. I think during the game someone's finger went into my eye and I had a bit of irritation in it. Soon after leaving the stadium my eye began to get more and more irritated and, by the time we got to Cardiff airport, I was in a lot of discomfort. The partying and celebrations that night mostly passed me by and I wound up having to use eye drops for a few days and wear an eye patch and sunglasses.

Still, there was a lot more celebrating to be done and, over the course of that week, Limerick's citizens showed their joy and gratitude at what the team had accomplished. We had a reception in the Mayor's Office and took an open top bus tour around the city before thousands of people cheered us onto a stage in O'Connell Street.

It was something to savour – I was thirty-three years old and had been a professional rugby player for twelve years. In that time, I'd been part of an amazing journey with Munster's players, its management and its fans. But I'd been on an amazing personal odyssey as well. I'd enjoyed incredible highs and deep lows. I'd found great friends along the way and discovered, when I went looking for answers to the problems that confronted me, sometimes I needed to look no further than myself.

In the struggles to overcome the career-threatening, physical injuries and the mental barriers confronting me, I'd found a way to prevail – I'd gone over, under, through, around … whatever it took.

Sitting back in 2008, savouring our Heineken Cup win, it was hard to see how life could get any better. But my life to that point had only been preparation for the months to come. Within twelve months of being named Man of the Match in Munster's Heineken Cup win over the tournament's greatest club, I would be propelled, professionally and personally, towards an entirely new experience. I would achieve heights I never thought possible but, in that very moment, I would plummet to depths I didn't know existed.

Right now, though, all that was in the future. Right now, there was only joy in the embrace of my team, my province, my family and Ruth – what a wonderful life.

CHAPTER 20

THE LION KING

Picture the scene – twenty-five or thirty of Munster rugby's biggest, strongest, toughest sportsmen are jam-packed into a room at Thomond Park.

We're in the middle of our build-up for the 1999 Heineken Cup away game against Saracens. Deccie has called us all in for a chat ahead of the game and no one quite knows what to expect – either we're going to get a pep-talk or we're going to get a bollicking. Most likely the latter.

The room is quiet when Deccie wheels in a TV monitor and video machine. The lads look at each other: What the hell is going on? Are we going over tapes of the opposition?

"I want you to watch this lads," says Deccie. "Just watch."

So, for the next couple of hours, the entire Munster squad, a team supposedly in search of their first Heineken Cup trophy and ravenous for another big-name scalp, sit back in their seats and watch fluffy little bundles of golden fur romp across the screen as we view 'The Lion King'. Tempting though it might have been to make a joke or say something smart, no one utters a word – this is a Deccie Kidney production, so everyone is concentrating hard on exactly what kind of message Simba, Timon and Pumba are delivering.

Any little kid knows the story of 'The Lion King': The dad gets killed and his young son escapes into exile but, eventually, comes back to rescue his family and claim his title. But Deccie wasn't trying to entertain us, he was trying to impress upon us that bad things happen: Life and sport will knock you down and maybe even knock you out, but you can come back from the worst of blows and still achieve great things.

Deccie was obviously a bit nervous about how it might go down – he and Niallo asked a few people afterwards what they thought: "Was that crazy or what? How did that come across?" Everyone said it was great.

But that ability to try new things has always been one of his greatest strengths. His main priority has always been to get the best out of his team and he doesn't mind what new tricks he has to learn to achieve that.

In the end, he called it exactly right showing us the movie, because we beat Saracens on their home ground in a tough encounter. I think they'd have been mortified if they'd known that Munster's secret weapon had been 'The Lion King'.

"Hacuna Matata," – this quote from 'The Lion King' means, "No Worries," and, while, it might not have become the philosophy of Munster, dusting yourself off after taking a beating and getting back in the hunt for the title was right up our street!

• • • • • • •

It's been hard for other teams, other nations, to figure Munster out. They haven't got the foggiest when it comes to working out exactly why Munster have been so successful over the last decade.

"Sure, you've got some good individual players, but not that many," they say. "So, how have you managed to achieve everything you have? You're not that good."

Maybe that's true. Maybe, on paper, our team-sheet doesn't look like a who's who of the rugby world. But then, Munster has never really been the story of an individual. Instead, it's been about motivation and determination, about fighting for the men in the red jerseys to your right and your left. In the end, that's what it comes down to – we're the sum of all our parts, a team.

In his two terms with us, Deccie Kidney understood that. He knew that winning was about a team, an organisation, pulling together, pushing each other to achieve new heights. He expected Munster, its players, coaches, management and back-room staff to sacrifice their individual needs for the good of the team.

But he didn't ask them to do something he wasn't prepared to do himself. He wasn't everyone's cup of tea, and he didn't do everything right, but one of his best qualities has always been his willingness to change himself, to progress and develop.

In the early years of professionalism the game of rugby wasn't very technical – certainly not as complicated as it is now – and Deccie wasn't what you'd describe as a tactical genius.

Back then, Deccie was more of a hands-on coach and he was excellent at it but, as the seasons went by, he moved away from that function. He took on the role of head coach, playing to his strengths of leading, organising and keeping the squad together and happy. People like Jerry Holland and Niall O'Donovan, and later Brian O'Brien, helped him. They were very experienced, successful, guys in their own right, so they knew what was expected.

In the transition period that brought us all from amateur to professional status, the team around Deccie guided him and, in the very early days, tried to get the schoolteacher out of him and help him to treat the players as adults.

However, Deccie was the main man and he had his own way of doing things. His big thing was that the players needed to have a life away from rugby, a different outlook, whether it be college or a part-time job. He always encouraged guys to have something outside of their rugby career.

At the start of Johnny Lacey's playing career with Munster, Deccie called him in after one training session and asked him, "Do you read at all, Johnny?"

"Sure, I read the papers for the sport," replied Johnny. When questioned further by his coach he admitted that he didn't read many books.

"I'd like you to go to the library tonight, or to the bookshop," Deccie instructed him, "get a book, take it home and read it."

"What book?" asked Johnny.

"Oh, any book," replied Deccie.

So, off went Johnny to the bookshop and went straight to the sports section where he spied a biography of George Best. He duly bought it and read it over the next couple days before going back to Deccie and taking great pleasure in telling him all about Best's drinking and womanising during his playing career.

Deccie may not have been impressed by the subject matter but he laughed at Johnny's depiction of Best's life – it wasn't really about the book, Deccie was just happy that Johnny was doing something outside the world of rugby.

He believed that rugby wasn't rocket science and didn't want the thing to be too complicated. He reckoned you could have this game plan and that game plan, but if you got your attitude right and got yourself as fit as you could and you applied yourself properly, then everything would follow on from that.

He was constantly breaking new ground with us. We started working with a sports psychologist and setting goals. I hadn't a clue what the hell 'goal setting' was, but we gave ourselves targets to aim for and, all of a sudden, we were hitting those targets. Each year the target would get higher and higher and we would achieve more and more.

Deccie would trawl through books on sports psychology for inspirational and motivational quotes or pieces of wisdom he could use on us. He'd find stuff from across the world, bring it along and read it out or put it on the projector.

Sometimes he used unusual motivational tools such as 'The Lion King' movie but, at other times, he used material from much deeper sources than Disney.

A favourite was Marianne Williamson's 'Return to Love, Reflections on the Principles of "A Course in Miracles"' [Harper Paperbacks (1996)]: *Our deepest fear is not that we are inadequate. Our deepest fear is that we are powerful beyond measure. It is our light, not our darkness, that most frightens us. We ask ourselves, Who am I to be brilliant, gorgeous, talented, fabulous? Actually, who are you not to be? You are a child of God. Your playing small does not serve the world. There's nothing enlightened about shrinking so that other people won't feel insecure around you. We are all meant to shine, as children do. We were born to make manifest the glory of God that is within us. It's not just in some of us; it's in everyone. And as we let our own light shine, we unconsciously give other people permission to do the same. As we're liberated from our own fear, our presence automatically liberates others.*

Inspiration like that was hugely important for us a team because, at that stage, we didn't really believe in ourselves and we didn't think that we could be great.

Deccie set about changing that mindset. People started to sit up and say, "Well, why can't we do it? Who's to say we can't do it? We can do anything we want. We can be in control of our own destiny".

We were used to the idea that we could claim a big scalp here or there, but that was the limit of our dreams.

When 'Quins came to Thomond Park in the last of the 1997/98 Heineken Cup pool games, it was already clear we couldn't make the quarter-finals but we were up for the game and we beat them. The place was packed out, and the atmosphere was electric, everyone was thrilled with us beating a big-name English team. It was seen as another historic night for Munster rugby but, really, what had we achieved? Nothing – at the end of the day we were still out of the Cup.

We needed to lift ourselves and our vision beyond that typical kind of moral victory bullshit which was preventing us from moving to the next level. And that's what Deccie gave us – the ability to believe in ourselves. Second best was nothing – we needed to start achieving things, making knock-out stages, topping groups. We weren't always happy with him – you're never going to be happy with your coach unless he picks you all the time – and we didn't always agree with him, but we respected him.

Nothing in Munster rugby was left unchallenged, not even the provincial set-up, which was based on club loyalty. After lining out for Munster, players would return to their own clubs – places like Shannon, Young Munster and Garryowen, which had proud histories of their own. When you lined out in a Shannon jersey, you didn't give a tuppenny damn about Munster – your real team-mates were the lads wearing the Shannon shirts, and everyone else could go to hell. That attitude had to change and, slowly but surely, Deccie, Niallo, Jerry, Brian and everyone else working with Munster slowly began to change it into a full-time affair. The introduction of competitions like the Magners League helped and players began to realise that the lads wearing the red of Munster were their team-mates now. These were the guys that, for the next few years, we'd be training with, relying on, cursing about, loving and bleeding for. We were no longer a group of misfits from a wide range of clubs. We were a club ourselves – the club of Munster, the team of Munster.

Under Deccie's direction we started to evolve, first as a team and then as a squad. We began to realise that we had the players to compete with the best in Europe – good, strong characters who were improving each year. We brought in quality players from outside and we became stronger mentally and physically. We wanted to win and we believed we could win: Then we started to win.

Something else happened. As our performances became consistently good, our fans started to sense something special was happening, that rugby's planets were starting to align. Everything began to meld together into what became know as the Munster Journey, though I don't think that description accurately reflected what we were about – it was more than just a journey. Somewhere along the line, we became a movement – a cause – and there's nothing harder to beat in the world than a cause.

• • • • • • •

I've had a lot of great coaches in my time in a red jersey and the Munster story could never be about one man, nor even about the role of coach – Munster's success has been built on the shoulders of many people.

Following Deccie's first departure from Munster, just after we lost the 2001/02 Heineken Cup Final in the Millennium Stadium to Leicester, Alan Gaffney took charge. At the time we were being labelled with the tag of 'The Nearly Men' who, in the space of a few short years, had reached two Heineken Cup finals but lost both.

Alan did a great a job with us. He encouraged us to play more expansive rugby, and we won a Magners League title in his last season in charge, but the Heineken trophy eluded him and he swapped the Munster job for the national coaching post with Australia.

Following Deccie's second departure, in the wake of our second

Heineken Cup win in 2008, Tony McGahan took charge.

Tony was well-known to us as he'd been our defensive and skills coach for the previous couple of years so, when it was clear that Deccie was leaving, the players gave their full backing to Tony's elevation to the role of head coach.

He'd done a brilliant job with us up to that point and we reckoned the top post was an honour he deserved. Tony appointed fellow Aussie, and former Brumbies coach, Laurie Fisher, as forwards coach and Axel as the assistant forwards coach. Dutchy Holland, the man who'd scored so many tries for us as a player, was named backs coach.

Tony's been one of the best coaches I've played under. We've had our differences but he's done a tremendous job since taking over as head coach and he's allowed me a lot of time and space, particularly over the last couple of seasons.

He's also managed to challenge and reinvigorate me, remind me that I'm a professional rugby player with the best job in the world and that I should be constantly striving to improve, even at this stage of my career. His work ethic and desire to see Munster succeed are second to none and have inspired me, and the other players, to train harder and push harder.

It's not just the coaches who have propelled us along this last decade and a half. Garrett Fitzgerald, Munster's Chief Executive, has played a huge role in what we've achieved. It was, largely, his job to oversee the transition of the province from amateur status to professional operation. Our successes in the Heineken Cup, and our ability to attract top coaches and players, as well as investing in local talent, are outward signs of the kind of approach he brought to the role. But they don't tell the whole story – along the way, Garrett also juggled the personalities, expectations, egos and dreams of a lot of players and coaches. Munster owes him a great debt. All of us – the players and the management – owe a huge debt of gratitude to the people working furiously behind the scenes to ensure the wheels of the Munster machine are well oiled. People like Brian Murphy, our operations chief, play an incredible role ensuring that we players can concentrate on playing rugby.

And Pat Geraghty, our PR guru. Pat has gone beyond the call of duty for many years on behalf of the players, and his passion for Munster knows no bounds. On one memorable occasion before a Heineken Cup quarter-final against Stade Français, in France, Pat challenged some shady character who was hanging around one of our private training sessions with his mobile phone. Words were exchanged and there was a bit of pushing and shoving before the stranger finally understood that he and his mobile phone weren't welcome. It's impossible to watch exchanges like that – seeing how passionate and protective people are of the Munster idea – and not be inspired.

• • • • • • •

I think the wheel came full circle in my relationship with Deccie in 2008 when we beat Toulouse in the Heineken Cup final and I won the Man of the Match award.

The honour could have been given to any one of our team after that display but, when it came my way, I did feel that I'd repaid Deccie just a little bit for all the faith he'd shown in me down through the years. Our relationship had been rocky in the early years but, in the end, I think we'd become friends who understood each other.

Still, when we met on the pitch after the final whistle, Deccie didn't talk to me – he didn't have to say anything. We didn't have to get in deep about the whole thing: He just hugged me. And I hugged him back.

CHAPTER 21

May 2, 2009
Heineken Cup Semi-final
v Leinster (Croke Park)
Lost: 25-6

"You bollox. What the fuck are you at?"

My hand is slapped away. I'm looking at Leo Cullen but I'm not paying much attention to him or what he's shouting. Somebody's always shouting in the middle of a game like this. It's another way of saying "Hello sir, how are you today? Would you like a bang on the ear or a kick in the arse to go with your double moccachino?"

I should know. I've been slapped, raked, thumped, kicked, pulled, yanked, and stamped on enough times to understand how this game is played.

Bad language is a helluva nicer way to be insulted than most rugby alternatives.

So, Leo Cullen calling me names or bawling me out in the middle of a Munster Leinster Heineken Cup semi-final in Croke Park isn't something that's going to stop me in my tracks.

Besides, he can talk. He's just come barrelling through our maul, trying to pull it down moments after I lifted Paulie in the lineout.

I know Leo because Leo's like me – he's disruptive and very competitive in close combat. He has his job to do. I have my mine.

This is what Munster pay me to do. This is what the Munster fans demand I do. They don't expect me to go weak at the knees at the sight of one of 'Les Blues' coming through the middle. This is it. This is what I do. I am the reinforcements.

He has Paul around the neck, so I grab him and pull him backwards. I want to pull him sideways. But what can I do? I'm a strong man, and so is he, and he has momentum on his side.

I need to get him out of here. We need this maul. We need to seize the initiative. We need to put pressure on them. We need to stir our fans. We need to score. We need to get back in the game. We need to win. We need, we need, we need…

I need to stop Leo so I reach across for his shirt and he swipes my hand and curses at me. So what? What do you expect him to say? "Hi, Quinny. Tough old game, what? Best of luck there, old boy." Hardly.

So, I don't pay much heed. You often get grabbed around the neck or pulled or obstructed. There's always somebody shouting at you. Or you're doing the shouting yourself. So, I'm thinking, screw it.

I know I made contact with his face, but there wasn't much in it. After all, I know what was in my own mind, what my intentions had been. I hadn't intended to hurt him or damage him around the face, so I don't expect any big deal to be made of it.

But I know I made contact, so I tell myself, "Just be careful, like". Nobody likes to get their face pulled at or touched in a game. I'm the same, so I wouldn't do something like that.

Why would I start doing that at this stage in my career? Going for somebody's eyes. Why would I do that? I'm thirty-four. I'm in the last couple of years of my career.

I have a tough reputation and I catch a lot of flak for being mouthy and for giving away stupid penalties but I'm not a dirty player.

In the days, weeks, months and year ahead, people would ask me about this moment: "What was in your mind? What were you thinking?" What was I thinking? I'll tell you what I was thinking. I was thinking: "Leo you bollox, you're going to illegally pull down the maul and I'm going to stop you".

Did I think: "Now, if I angle my fingers just right, I might be able to gouge Leo's eyeballs, cause him a serious, long-term injury, possibly put him out of work, but I need to be careful because the ref is nearby and the TV cameras might pick it up?"

Did I think that? No.

There was no plan to grab for his face. It was just grab anywhere. Careless, but not malicious.

When it happened, you know, I kind of knew my hand shouldn't have been there but I wasn't even in aggressive form. It was just a case of, "There could have been something in that".

But right there, in the moment, in the heat of battle, I didn't have time to dwell on that.

I don't think I did anything nasty.

Leo doesn't think I did anything nasty.

The ref doesn't think I did anything nasty.

Play away.

• • • • • • •

Games don't come much bigger than playing Leinster in the semi-final of the Heineken Cup in Croke Park.

Over the years, Munster has built a reputation for itself – we pride ourselves on being different. But it wasn't always like this. Historically, Munster has always played catch-up with Leinster and Ulster, ever since rugby was set up in the late 1800s. We always felt we were the poor cousins.

There were heroic moments like beating the All Blacks 12-0 on October 31, 1978; drawing 12-12 with The Pumas of Argentina in 1973; or beating Bob Dwyer's Australia in 1992. But, overall, Ulster and Leinster were much stronger: Ulster dominated Irish rugby from the mid-1980s until 1992, and was the first Irish side to lift the Heineken Cup.

Munster, meanwhile, was the typical Irish team: win a few games, take the odd massive scalp but then settle back into happy anonymity, glad just to have a few pints and a few slaps on the back: "You didn't win the cup but, Jaysus, you sure gave it a right lash!"

That all changed with Deccie Kidney, Niall O'Donovan and Jerry Holland. Deccie taught us to think differently. He taught us to stop settling for second best. He made us watch 'The Lion King'. So, now things are different for Munster. We've won two Heineken Cups and played in other finals, we have the top players and leaders in the country. Right now, we are in the ascendancy.

With the retirement of David Humphreys, Ulster struggled for a while but are now looking strong again, while Connacht are still trying to capture the third Irish spot in the Heineken Cup.

Meanwhile, our biggest rivals, Leinster, are in danger of seeing their 'golden generation' of players – Brian O'Driscoll et al – depart the provincial scene without ever getting their hands on Europe's premier trophy. Unthinkable. The pressure on them must be immense.

In the papers they're being labelled 'ladyboys' and their fans are being ridiculed for singing "Allez, les Bleues," in the heat of battle when their team needs them most.

It's a mad world.

Now, it's time for us to step up and hammer another nail into the coffin of Les Bleues. Maybe bury them once and for all.

They've got great players, perhaps brilliant players, and are a fantastic team – on paper, at least. But we've already beaten them this season. Twice. The first time, we embarrassed them 18-0 on their home patch in the RDS, and later in the season we thumped them 21-7 in Thomond Park. The victories weren't easy because they never are against Leinster. But they were victories, and rugby teams and rugby players thrive on victory. At this level, winning is about mental strength above all else, and mental strength comes with confidence and with winning.

We're not going up to Dublin so we can hand the initiative back to Leinster. We're going up there to take their scalp. Again.

There's a massive buzz about this game, you can feel it everywhere in Munster. The teams, the fans, the entire province is on an absolute roll.

We performed really well against the Ospreys, playing some great rugby and, in his first season as head coach, Tony has us peaking, we think, at just the right time. Right now, the only people standing in the way of us claiming our rightful spot in another final is a team which must be short on confidence and which has already been soundly beaten by us this season.

Everything about the build-up to this game has been exciting. For a lot of the lads, this will be their first time playing in Croke Park, so it's going to be a massive occasion for them and there's a great mood building in the camp.

• • • • • • •

On the Friday before the semi, we met the Cork lads at Limerick Junction. Before the train departed for Dublin I was greeted by my Dad, which was a special moment for me – my father wishing me good luck on the same platform where, years before, my brothers and I had ridden our bikes and spent hours playing. If I had written a script for the lead-up to the match against Leinster, I couldn't have made it more personally special.

The only thing missing was the Leinster scalp, but that would come soon enough.

Everybody – the fans, the media – was making us hot favourites and, while we were long enough in the tooth to know that life doesn't work that way, we all hoped to beat Les Bleues.

Deep down, we all figured this was Leinster's last chance, not just for that season, but maybe the last chance for the team they had assembled.

They had a lot of big game players, great players, but they hadn't delivered, hadn't broken through yet, and everyone knew they were running out of time.

In the back of our minds we knew this was Leinster's last chance to do something and that they would be doubly dangerous because of it. The senior players discussed it a lot with Tony, we said they'd throw everything at us, they'd throw the kitchen sink at us. There was no danger of us under-estimating them, but we still believed we were worth the favourites' tag and expected to win.

Personally, I was quite calm in the build-up to the match, which was important because these games can be aggressive affairs. They can get fairly hot. Players know each other, fans know each other and things can get out of hand. People get fired up and things can happen. Munster-Leinster games are niggling games at best and, before the game, I spoke to

Paulie and Leamy. My advice was, "Let's be careful, and watch our distance with them – don't get bothered." Ahead of the Leinster showdown, we were all very aware of watching our discipline and of not getting involved in anything.

Little did I know that within a few hours I'd be thinking, "My own advice was like the kiss of death for me".

•••••••

At the time, I didn't see anything wrong with how we approached the game but, looking back now, I'm not so sure. With hindsight I think maybe we were missing something. As a team, we talked the game up and down and tried to ensure we weren't underestimating them. But, looking back, I think we were missing that bit of nervous tension in our build-up.

I wonder, now, if we were a little too comfortable. Not that we were cocky – we anticipated Leinster being tough opponents – but I wonder if we paid too much attention to the fact that the match was going to be a great occasion. Maybe we got a little too comfortable with our own star billing.

Travelling back from Croker after our Captain's Run, we were stuck in traffic for ages, so we had time to think about the occasion. Being in Croke Park had been great: The stadium was fabulous and the pitch was great and we were all looking forward to the game.

The only real doubt came on Saturday morning at the hotel, in the unlikely shape of a good friend and a Tipperary hurling legend, Nicky English. He lives close by to the Radisson Hotel we always stay in when we travel to Dublin and he has developed a habit, on the day of a game in Dublin, of dropping over to the hotel to see ROG and myself and have a cup of tea and a chat. He's always very welcome: I've been there in the stands on many a big day for Tipp and I have a huge amount of respect for Nicky and what he's achieved.

I remember him making a comment to me, after meeting a few of the lads that day and just being around us, that he felt there was something not right about the team or that we just looked a bit too calm. As an athlete who's achieved a lot, he'd seen something as an outsider that we hadn't, it was obviously something small but it was there, nonetheless.

I didn't really pay much heed to it but I've often wondered about it since, about what it was he picked up on: About whether or not there was something out of sync in the team and whether or not that was the difference between winning and losing that weekend in Dublin.

But, back then, on the morning of the Leinster game, I didn't think about it. I didn't have time.

The team gathered together, knowing this was a massive opportunity. If we beat Leinster again, we'd be in the running for another Heineken trophy and we'd do what no other Irish team had ever done – win two Heineken Cups in a row. We spoke about how much the day meant to us and how we would remember that game and that day for the rest of our lives.

• • • • • • •

Post-game, I'm in a dressing room beneath Croke Park. Even down here, it's impossible to hide from the bitterness of defeat.

We've lost to Leinster in a Heineken Cup semi-final. Our semi-final. The one we were supposed to win. The one that was supposed to be a prelude to winning our second Heineken Cup in a row – the only Irish team to do so. It was to be a Munster first. We were going to write Munster history, Irish history.

It was a funny kind of game; stop-start with massive intensity to it. We started well, but a lot of things began to go wrong for us and we began to make mistakes. We didn't have a lot of opportunities and the Leinster lads were in our faces a lot. I remember trying to play, but it was hard and I didn't get much time on the ball. I was trying to put myself about and be physical and not take any crap.

But they outsmarted us and outfoxed us and were more physical than us: they out-Munstered us. That was unexpected and put us off our own game a little. They got ahead and then sat back, soaked up the pressure and just waited for our errors to arrive – they executed their game plan perfectly.

It wasn't as though we didn't expect a tough game, even though this was a team we had just beaten twice in a season. They were never going to lie down, but we knew that and were well prepared for it.

But something was off with us. It only needs to be a small mental thing – maybe we're 99 per cent of the way there, mentally, and just one per cent off. Against a team like Leinster and in a Heineken Cup semi-final one per cent off is enough to tip the balance.

In the end, Leinster beat us comfortably. They played very well and we played poorly. It was hard to take, to be honest.

So, all around me in this dressing room, there are shattered dreams and broken bodies. Paulie, ROG, The Bull, Tomas – everyone is devastated. As for me, it's impossible to describe: Losing is a bad experience for me.

But, in the space of few minutes, I came to understand something I never knew before: There are things that are worse than defeat.

Tony McGahan, our coach, approached me and told me there had been an incident.

Incident? What kind of an incident? What's it got to do with me?

Then one of the fitness lads came up to me and said something was definitely going on, they had got wind of it while they were still on the sideline. The Sky Sports team had got some sort of footage. They were playing it again and again and it didn't look good.

"What doesn't look good?" I asked.

"It's about you, Quinny. They say it doesn't look great.

Somebody said it was the Leo Cullen incident. Bullshit. There was nothing in that. Even when it happened the Leinster crowd didn't react much. My mind began to race: What about Leo? He didn't react much beyond a bit of language. Does his reaction count for nothing. What about the ref? He was right there, he saw nothing, he gave nothing.

My stomach started to heave. Jesus, this could be bad.

Something very big, something very bad was building up a head of steam and it was headed straight for me. There I was, still gutted by the result, still trying to come to terms with losing everything I'd worked for this season. But something else was at play. Something that would make this heart-wrenching semi-final loss seem pointless by comparison.

Slowly, the penny began to drop.

● ● ● ● ● ● ●

It's a funny experience being in the public eye. People think they own you, that you are public property.

At the very least they think that they're entitled to ask you questions about one of the most vitally important moments in your life. They don't consider that they are asking you about the very thing that has plunged you into an abyss, in which you're struggling to breathe.

In the midst of it all, they want to dwell on tiny points, which they think prove that I did or didn't deliberately gouge Leo Cullen. One of their favourite questions is why I apologised to Leo after the game. As if, saying sorry to him was proof that I felt guilty about it all myself and was blatantly trying to smooth things over ahead of a possible citing investigation.

But that wasn't the case at all, and I don't think Leo thought that way either.

I apologised to Leo, because that's what I do. I just said to him that if there was anything in it, it wasn't intentional. I said, "Look, Jesus, I'm sorry for pulling your face there, I didn't mean anything". We shook hands and I wished him well in the final. It's in my nature to say sorry.

Over the years with both Munster and Ireland, the boys are always slagging me that I say, "I'm sorry, I'm sorry, I'm sorry, I'm sorry". If I bumped off you in gym training, I'd probably come up to you and tell you ten times, "I'm sorry, I'm sorry about that". Usually the response is delivered with a laugh: "Never worry, Quinny, don't worry about it". So, saying sorry to Leo wasn't unusual.

I just told him, "Jesus, if I grabbed you in any awkward way there, that was unintended. Sorry about that and best of luck in the final". Leo didn't even remember what I was going on about. He made no reference to it.

Later, after I was cited, Leo wrote in his letter to the ERC Hearing that his reaction on the pitch was because my hand went across his face and that no player likes that in a game.

He didn't think I put my fingers in his eyes or touched his eyes.

Leo was brilliant about it and he's a tough guy, he's a tough player. He's taken plenty of swats and boots and kicks down through the years, he's a good player and I respect him. So, his reaction on the pitch didn't surprise me, and I respected him a lot for how he acted and how he spoke afterwards. It was good that he wasn't putting the boot in or telling the media that it had been deliberate or malicious. For me, personally, there was some comfort in what he said and how he acted – he didn't point the finger.

But that didn't surprise me – I'd have done the same thing. For me, what happens on the field should stay on the field. I've always shaken hands after the game, no matter what went on.

• • • • • • •

In the early days after it happened, when the pressure on me was almost unbearable, I went back over that moment, time and time again, in my own mind.

Everyone watches the TV replay and thinks they know what happened. They think that they can interpret my state of mind and guess my thoughts by watching an action replay.

It might be what the pundits get paid for, but it's bullshit. How could they know? How could they ever hope to know what was in my mind, when, honestly, I wasn't sure myself?

I thought I knew. I thought I knew that there was absolutely nothing in it. But when everyone in the world is questioning you, you start to question yourself. And when everyone in the world is condemning you, the temptation is to condemn yourself.

So, in the minutes, hours, days, weeks and months that came after the Leo Cullen incident, I replayed it all in my mind. Again and again.

I'd watch the TV replay and know it didn't look good. But, really, the TV shots didn't mean anything to me. I wanted to know my own mind. I wanted to confirm to myself that I hadn't tried to gouge Leo.

I wanted to be honest with people but, first, I wanted to be honest with myself: To say to myself, "Is there some part of me – some one per cent of me that actually did this by instinct or half meant to do it?" I wanted to know.

So, I've replayed the moment hundreds, maybe thousands, of times in my mind and the answer is always the same.

No.

There was no intent in what I did, no malice. It was just a reaction to him, to what he was doing. It wasn't a conscious decision, I just grabbed anything I could.

The act was brief but the consequences were almost a life sentence for me. In the 0.4 of a second it took for my hand to travel across Leo's face, I had no idea the impact it would have on my life, on my family's life.

Within minutes of the game ending, my entire world plunged into darkness.

I was about to lose my place on the Lions Tour; I was about to be vilified in the press; I was about to damned as a dirty player by a lot of people. But having my reputation ruined wasn't the worst of it.

I've always had a love-hate relationship with rugby and I've always been very aware that the game dictates my moods and my mental state. Win and life is the best. Lose and life is the worst. But what happened after the Leo incident was something different.

Within hours of the disappointment of losing a Heineken Cup semi-final to Leinster, I was battling something much deeper and much darker. I sank into a depression which took me months to get out of and, by the end, I knew how lucky I was to have come up for air again.

It engulfed me. It subsumed me. It frightened me.

CHAPTER 22

IN MY DEFENCE

I wouldn't say I'm over the Lions. I don't think I'll ever be over it. I think back over the last year a lot and wonder about how it might have been, of how it could have been.

But back on that day of the Leinster defeat, sitting there in the dressing room in Croke Park, I knew even then that things weren't going to work out for me. I felt empty, unbelievably empty. Watching that video in the dressing room, watching myself – my hand – in slow motion … it's hard to describe how I felt. I just had this empty feeling in the pit of my stomach which was being filled with blind panic and nervousness.

George, our video analyst, had put on the tape and I watched it with Axel, though he'd already seen it. It didn't look good. In fact, in slow motion it looked awful. The video showed my hand didn't go directly on to his face, my fingers had caught Leo's jersey initially before going across his face so that was positive. But in slow motion…

It was clear, early on, that the incident was going to snowball. At the post-game press conference the first few questions to Leo and Drico were about the incident: Leo said he didn't recall it and didn't have anything to say about it. But talk of the incident was spreading like wildfire and the footage kept being repeated on TV. It didn't look good on the screen and I knew I was in trouble.

I showered and dressed and trudged on to the bus back to the Guinness Brewery where the team was due to have some food with friends and partners before getting the train back home.

I waited outside for Ruth to arrive, but it was terrible standing there, afraid to look at the phone or talk to anyone or even ring my friends. Ruth arrived and we went upstairs but it was incredibly hard because I just wanted the ground to open up and swallow me.

Some part of me was just hoping the entire thing was a bad dream from which I would wake up. I just wanted it all to go away. But it wasn't a dream it was a reality in which every minute seemed to last an hour. I couldn't relax, couldn't enjoy anything. I was still hopeful that things would work out: I wouldn't get suspended and I wouldn't miss the Lions Tour, that people would understand I didn't mean it, it wasn't intentional.

But, deep down, when I really thought about it, I knew I was in trouble. People were telling me, "Hey, it's not the end of the world," and offering every other comforting cliché they could but, inside, I had a sinking feeling.

It was impossible, at that point, to explain to people what the selection for the Lions had meant to me. All my rugby life I've had ups and downs – my triumphs on the pitch have been matched by injuries, heartbreaks and disappointments. But with the Lions selection, it felt as though the wheel had come full circle. My rugby career was coming to an end and the Lions achievement would have been a massive reward for having stuck with rugby down through the years.

So as I sat in the dressing room that afternoon watching my team-mates trying to come to terms with the bitter disappointment of losing the semi-final, I wished more than anything else in the world that I was just like them, that I was only trying to deal with losing a Heineken Cup semi to our biggest rivals. I looked at my beaten friends and I was envious of them, wishing I were reaching that stage of being disappointed and pissed off at losing a massive game.

But I was ten levels below the pain they were feeling. At the Guinness Brewery reception, I couldn't eat, couldn't drink and things didn't improve after that. At home, I tried to sleep but couldn't, I was up for most of the night. I got out of bed and went to lie on the couch – I was exhausted but when Ruth came to check on me in the middle of the night, she found me lying there, on the sofa, with my eyes wide open, staring at the ceiling.

I tried to distract myself, to get out of the house and find things to do. On the Sunday we went down to our friends, the Laceys, for their young son Evan's birthday and, on Monday, I took AJ out in the buggy. We ended up in Monaleen Church, where I lit a few candles: I held AJ in my arms and prayed that the storm would pass and things would work out. But things didn't work out. As I drove over to Dundrum House later that day for a round of golf, the Munster manager, Shaun Payne, phoned me to confirm that I'd been cited. The Hearing would be the following Wednesday, which meant I had to suffer for at least nine more days before learning my fate. It's a strange feeling knowing you're going to get lynched but also knowing you've got to wait nine days for the mob to get the rope.

My moods swung uncontrollably. At times, I was sobbing and crying, I wasn't able to stop myself, but at other times I'd get bursts of energy and would inwardly vow to fight the citing tooth and nail.

"It's not going to happen," I'd say to myself. "They won't take away my Lions Tour… It's not that bad, it just looks bad in slow motion… I didn't mean it and they'll understand that."

Then I'd think, "I'm screwed". No matter how many times the pendulum swung back and forwards, I always came to the conclusion, "I'm screwed".

In some ways, it seems crazy to look back now and remember how it affected me. Nobody had died and no one was sick, so maybe I was over-reacting but, at the time, that kind of objectivity just wasn't possible. All I knew was that I'd gone from the greatest moment in my career to the worst, and that the journey was scary and frightening. I was physically shattered. It just wasn't possible to sleep – I was trying to grab an hour here or an hour there, but it wouldn't come and I was becoming exhausted and more stressed.

The fatigue and the anxiety were difficult to deal with, and I just couldn't muster enough energy even to eat, so I went to see the Munster team doctor. It was obvious I was going through a tough time but he could also see that, with the sleep deprivation on top of everything, I was getting panicky so he gave me some medication to help me calm down and get some rest.

It worked and I began to get a little sleep but, when I woke up, the first thing I'd think about was the citing. The pain wouldn't go away – it was like living in a nightmare.

I focused on my family, on Ruth, on our son, AJ. He had been a dream come true for me when he was born and to have him there at that difficult time was a big part of what got me through. He was only five months old but he'll never know just how big a help he was to me, just being around him helped me put things into perspective. A few cracks began to appear in the grey cloud which had enveloped me as I realised that I wasn't facing the end of the world, I had a wonderful son and wife and I had family and friends, and thousands of people in Limerick, in Munster and in Ireland who cared about what happened to me.

Every day, more letters arrived in support. These fans had been with Munster and with me through thick and thin, now here they were in my darkest moment, standing shoulder to shoulder with me, offering their support. It was a humbling experience. Little by little things were improving. My energy levels began to rise and I got a bit more enthusiastic about trying to defend myself, about trying to be proactive and put together my defence.

● ● ● ● ● ● ●

The evening after Shaun's phone call, Young Munster held a celebration dinner in the Strand Hotel to honour Paulie's elevation to Lions captain. It was mainly a Young Munster thing but they'd generously invited the other Limerick players who'd been selected for the Lions, and their clubs. I didn't want to go but Ruth persuaded me that I needed to get out and not hide myself away. It was important, she argued, that I go along and honour Paul and show people that I was staying strong and that I would get through this thing.

But it was a difficult and very emotional evening for me. My former clubs, Clanwilliam and Shannon, had both been invited, so, many of my old friends and colleagues had come along to honour me for making the Lions Tour. But the effort they made to show their support just made me feel even more wretched – they were all so proud but I had no idea whether or not I would now make the Tour.

There was a voice in my head telling me that I wasn't going on the Lions Tour and that I was there that night under false pretences, accepting their congratulations.

Seeing those people in the audience really brought home the enormity of what was happening. I was embarrassed, I felt I had let everybody down. But no one mentioned the citing. They just put their hand out to me and let me know that they were there for me. A lot of people did that – they didn't know what to say to me, but they felt for me and they supported me. It was wonderful to see how many people cared, to see how affected these genuine Munster people were at my situation, how sympathetic they were towards me.

I was called up on stage where the TV presenter, Hector O hEochagain, was doing the honours. Hector asked me a few questions – he was great – but I choked up a little. I felt like a fish out of water standing up there, I felt like a fraud, but I had to try to convince myself to stop being a victim and not ruin the night for any one else.

I wanted to be there for Paulie. He's always been a wonderful, close friend to me and to be named captain of the Lions was an incredible honour for him, for Limerick, for Munster and for Ireland.

But, more than that, deep down I knew that Paulie would have pushed my case for my inclusion on the Lions. At some point, he would have been asked for his opinion about the Lions selection and he clearly backed me. So, I figured I owed it to him to be there that night, no matter how I felt personally.

And, hard as it was that night, I am glad I went along. I was grateful that Ruth persuaded me to go – it was the right thing to do.

I still have Young Munster's presentation, a trophy and a rugby ball, at home in the attic with my other stuff. I still can't bring myself to take it down and look at it.

• • • • • • •

By the end of that week I'd met with my solicitor, Donal Spring, to start planning my case for the ERC Disciplinary Panel Hearing. Another friend, John Power and his sister, Una Heffernan – both solicitors – also volunteered to help and began to research other, similar cases.

I tormented the team manager, Shaun Payne, for any information he could give me and yet another friend, John O'Connor from Cashel, contacted a video analyst in London who had participated in the high-profile case of the Arsenal soccer player, Eduardo, who had been suspended from playing on the basis of video footage.

The video analyst and his company were able to break the footage down into milliseconds and show that my hand had initially made contact with Leo's jersey, that my intent was clearly to try and pull him backwards. Their analysis demonstrated that the main contact by my hand was with Leo's jersey and had only lasted 0.4 of a second.

It was great to be able to throw myself into the case. The last few days had been torture: I'd felt like a criminal but, finally, I was able to focus on defending myself and clearing my name. Of course there was the suspicion that it might all be a lost cause, but I had to try.

People continued to phone me with their support. Deccie Kidney and Tony McGahan both contacted me to wish me all the best, but there wasn't much anyone could do: I just had to go through the process.

The night before the Hearing Ruth and I stayed with her sister Gillian, who's married to Mal O'Kelly. They were great but, by the time, I woke up the next morning I was already sick with nerves – I got dressed, met my agent, John Baker, for a cup of tea and then walked down to the ERC offices with Donal.

We didn't kid ourselves about how hard the Hearing would be. The incident looked bad on TV – that was the reality of it. But everything else was in our favour: Leinster and Leo had been very helpful, with Leo lodging a statement saying he felt there was nothing in it. Paul O'Connell had given evidence in support of me and then there was the fact that there'd been no injury, no marks and no remonstration with either the referee or the touch judge.

Against all that, there was one piece of evidence not in my favour – the TV footage…

When we got in there, the room was pretty sparse with one big table. We, and the prosecution team, including Roger O'Connor and Max

Duthie, sat on one side and the ERC Disciplinary Panel sat on the other. Introductions done, we got on with it. It was a rough experience, very adversarial and I was upset to see just how hard they were pushing the accusation that what had happened was intentional, that I'd deliberately gouged Leo.

We gave our side of the story and we brought in a top eye specialist to define the eye area and to confirm that, in his view, I wasn't in that eye area. There were lots of reasons why it wasn't intentional. We showed the slow-motion footage of how I had tried to grab his jersey, how my finger was hooked on his shirt and how my hand slipped up off his jersey.

Then the other side put their case.

They questioned the Eye Specialist and challenged his opinions. Still, everything was going well until the TV footage and, suddenly, we were hurting again. They went through various camera angles and shots and put a different interpretation on the TV footage.

It felt like we'd taken five steps forward only to immediately be forced six steps back. The whole affair was like that – two hours of to-ing and fro-ing. It was a terrible experience.

It was difficult not to see the prosecutors as the enemy. In your heart of hearts you know there's nothing personal in what they're doing, that it's only their job, but when you hear someone stating their firm belief that the incident was deliberate, then it's very, very hard to take.

I was sick to my stomach during the Hearing. I just wanted to stand up and shout, "That's not bloody true, that's not what happened".

I wanted to convince them, have them see things from my, rugby, point of view, have them believe me. I knew it was a long shot but I still felt, deep down, I might have a chance if I could get my point of view across. They would see that I just wanted to be honest and straight with them.

When my turn came to speak I talked about everything, about the pain I'd been through since the incident and about what was at stake – the offer of a lifetime, my only opportunity to play with the Lions, my first and last chance to do that.

It was emotionally draining. I could feel my eyes watering at the time and I choked a bit but I managed to hold it together – I needed them to see, to understand, to believe.

To be fair to the Panel, I did feel that they listened and believed me and that they felt for me. But I also think the media attention left them with few options and, of course, there was the video. Everyone who had seen the video felt that it had damned me.

Then, after almost seven hours, it was over. The Panel shook hands with me and I felt there was genuine sorrow from them that I was in this unfortunate position. Even the prosecutor shook hands, something that I found hard to reciprocate. But I guess they were only doing their job. I couldn't blame them, or anyone else.

We sat outside again and waited. It was a long hour, very long. We hoped the wait might be a good sign that, maybe, even if I wasn't completely exonerated, I might only receive a short suspension which would let me travel with the Lions.

Then we were called back in.

It was an unbelievably tense moment, like being back at school and waiting for your exam results – you feel your entire world rests on the next few moments.

But then it happened. The Chairman read out his findings and delivered his verdict. There were three levels: If they thought it accidental, there'd be no sanction; if it were careless, or intentional, then there would be sanctions.

Me? I was in the middle – careless. They believed it wasn't intentional, which was great, but I'd still be sanctioned. They imposed the minimum sanction, but that was still a twelve-week ban starting from the day of the match.

That was it, my Lions dream was over. Sixty seconds was all it took for the Chairman of the Panel to tear my world apart with his ruling, but there was nothing to be done, just get out of there as quickly as possible and start dealing with it.

I felt empty but I steadied myself, shook hands once more with the Panel, and left. Donal was disappointed with the result and we agreed to wait to see the Panel's full findings before discussing an appeal.

Ruth was there and, together, we walked outside into the glare of the

TV cameras and the hue and cry of the press corps.

The Hearing was massive news – that was clear from the number of photographers and reporters gathered outside the ERC building.

The English media was there in strength to see my fate – they reckoned that I had been controversially selected ahead of Tom Croft for the Lions in the first place, so they were anxious to see whether I would be out and Tom in.

I'd known all along that the majority of the press weren't on my side – I'd read some of the coverage in the newspapers soon after the match and a lot of it was very hard to take. There were pieces written by people who I thought I knew better, but who highlighted the incident in a way which was completely at odds with how it had actually happened. I knew, in my heart of hearts, that I hadn't intentionally tried to do what some commentators were suggesting, but it was still a shock to pick up a national newspaper and see their accusations.

The Lions aspect made my case high-profile and, I suppose, some of them were being paid to give an opinion but it was still hard to accept. Likewise, there had been a lot of speculation surrounding how long the ban should be. If I'd gotten six weeks I could still have made the Tour and the Lions' management team, Ian McGeechan and Gerald Davies, were being really supportive. They kept in contact with me and told me they hoped I'd make it, but the twelve-week suspension ended any chance of my involvement.

I was angry that, in the eyes of some media commentators, I was guilty before I ever had a chance to prove myself innocent. I didn't believe my case was trial by media but I did think that there was a lot of pressure placed on the people making the decisions.

• • • • • • •

The Saturday following the verdict, I went to Ibiza with Ruth and AJ: It was great for us to get out of the media spotlight for a few days and spend some time with our son.

We'd already decided to appeal the ERC decision and the new Hearing was set for the following Wednesday, in Glasgow. We had a new addition to the legal team, the well-known barrister Michael McGrath, who had reviewed the original Hearing and was trying hard to help us. Michael took on an incredible workload for the Appeal and I'll be forever indebted to him.

Still, the writing was on the wall. In Ibiza I confided in Ruth that I wasn't getting my hopes up – if something came of the Appeal then fine, but, if not, all I could do was draw a line under the episode and try to move on with my life.

In Glasgow my team argued on a number of grounds – such as, not enough weight had been given to the evidence of our original Eye Specialist, and that the incident was accidental. But there would be no eleventh-hour reprieve for me, no 'happily ever after' – the Appeal lasted only a few hours and upheld the original verdict.

It was difficult accepting that things hadn't worked out and I'd reached the end of the road – there would be no more hearings, no more appeals. By the time we arrived home from Glasgow, I was also beginning to feel relieved that the whole Lions controversy, and the media circus that went with it, was over. But, I was still on the emotional rollercoaster ride and, somehow, I had to come to terms with the fall-out of the past few days.

A perfect opportunity to get away came in the shape of the wedding of my cousin, David Quinlan, and his girlfriend, Alana. We'd originally planned to go to their Las Vegas wedding but it had clashed with the Lions trip to South Africa so we'd, reluctantly, declined the invitation. But now, in the wake of the ERC decision, our plans for the trip of a lifetime to South Africa – me playing for the Lions and Ruth and AJ travelling with the rest of the squad's wives and children – lay in shreds.

So, with Ruth's sister Gillian encouraging us, we decided to take in David's wedding and take AJ with us. My Mum, who'd also had to cancel her own South Africa trip, came with us to help look after AJ. She was delighted to help out because, although she would never admit it, she had been hugely upset by the Lions controversy.

If South Africa wasn't meant to be for us, then Vegas certainly was. Just travelling there was a morale booster as we were accompanied on the flight by around thirty-five cousins and friends all heading for David and Alana's big day. We planned to spend seven days there where, even in the full glare of the 'Bright Light City', I would only be one more, anonymous Irish tourist. So we switched off and pushed the Lions episode as far from our minds as possible. My Mum looked after AJ and Ruth and I were able to go out in the evenings – we even got the odd lie-in courtesy of my Mum who would get up early to take her grandson out so she could show him the sights and sounds of Las Vegas.

The lights, the casinos, the fun were just what we needed and, better still, we were with people we loved and trusted. Six of us – Ruth and I, my cousin Ian and his wife Brenda, and my other cousin Josephine and her husband Jack – took a helicopter trip over the Grand Canyon.

Poor Brenda didn't enjoy the trip much as she was terrified of the heli' flight – plus she had to put up with the rest of us ribbing her about it – but, for me, days like that were helping push thoughts of rugby further and further from my mind.

We lounged by the pool, splashed in the water, hired a cabana to shelter AJ from the sun – David's wedding was proving the perfect antidote for all of us, including Ruth.

She'd been through a rough time in which she'd had to put up with my dark moods. Ruth could see, in the first week after the Leinster game, I was simply numb with pain and when you're in that kind of a bad place it's difficult to have clarity of thought or be positive. She helped me to be proactive and try to clear my name and, when the ruling went against me, she helped me accept that I couldn't change things and had to start dealing with it.

In the past, I'd have crumpled up into a ball if I'd been faced with something like the Lions controversy, but she helped me get through it all. It didn't get rid of the pain but it certainly helped ease it and I'll always be grateful to her for that.

I didn't want to come back from Las Vegas, really – the Lions Tour of South Africa was starting and I didn't want to be plunged back into the media spotlight as the drama unfolded on the nation's television sets.

So, almost as soon as we returned to Ireland, we left again for a holiday in Portugal to celebrate our first wedding anniversary.

While in Portugal, I arranged to meet Arthur Ryan, an old friend, who was there on holidays, and together we went to a local Irish bar to watch one of the Lions matches. It was strange walking in there and having people look at me – it felt a little like living in a goldfish bowl. But I couldn't really object – what did I expect, walking into an Irish bar to watch the Lions? As ever, anyone who recognised me was very supportive – they came up to me and said, "Hard luck, you should be out there". I began to feel I was reaching a point where I could deal with the disappointment.

So, I sat back, had a couple of beers and watched the game. My initial reaction, after the first ten minutes, was that South Africa would be too strong for the Lions. Having been beaten by the Lions twelve years previously, the Springboks were always going to be up for that Tour. As things turned out, South Africa were lucky in the first Test. They got a good start but the Lions came back strongly.

There were a lot of Irish lads there and I was willing them to win but, still, it was a strange experience. I'd very mixed emotions watching the game, it was impossible not to visualise myself out there in a Lions jersey. I watched a second Lions game – the emerging Springboks game – in Portugal as well, with Arthur and another friend, Gar Prendergast. Watching the Tour was getting easier, the pain less acute, and the three of us got 'wellied' on pints.

By the time the second Test came around I was already back in Ireland. I caught the last twenty minutes of that game and then watched the final Test at home on my own. They should have won the third Test and my heart broke for ROG – he just got caught with the last penalty of the game and was so unlucky. I remember thinking that sport could be so cruel and, certainly, it was brutally cruel to him that day.

By that point, if the sharp pain of missing out on the Tour had dulled, the regret remained. I constantly replayed the "What if?" scenario in my mind. My replacement, Tom Croft, started for the Lions when Stephen Ferris got injured, and I couldn't help thinking, "What if things had been different? That should be me." It was a useless exercise – a pointless waste of energy and emotion, but I couldn't help myself.

I discussed the Tour with the lads when they came back, but not in too much depth. Suddenly, there was no more Lions coverage in the paper or on the TV – it was over and the end of the Tour gave me a chance to start putting everything behind me.

I started talking to people, with our team psychologist, Gerry Hussey, and with Tony McGahan, Deccie Kidney and Brian O'Brien, and with friends like Killian Keane, Keith Wood and Mick Galwey.

I wondered how I could ever get myself back up for rugby again after the heartbreak it had caused me. There were days when I struggled to get out of bed and then struggled again to get through the day.

My immediate priority was to get back into training and into a normal routine. I went back to training with a lot of the younger, Academy guys as the Lions and the Internationals were still on a break.

Training with the younger lads made me appreciate how much fun the sport is. It made me realise that I was lucky that I could still run on to the pitch as a professional rugby player. Sure, something awful had happened but I had to think of the future and of the good things that still might happen.

I made a conscious decision not to be a victim and tried not to blame anybody else, not to look for an easy way out or have a chip on my shoulder. In the past, I might have tried to justify my actions by placing the blame on other people but, by the end of that summer, I had accepted responsibility for my actions. I understood that, no matter how much moaning and groaning I did, I couldn't change the situation. I had only one option and that was to deal with it all. I was still getting anxious and stressed and I was still having good days and bad days but, slowly, I was beginning to realise that I couldn't live like that.

I'd always been the kind of closed person who got anxious and stressed but who couldn't talk to other people about my problems. For years I'd been bottling things up so, when the Lions incident occurred, it brought me to some pretty dark places – places which were so worrying that the fear of them finally made me seek aid.

The Lions disappointment proved to be a turning point for me, making me take a look at my life as a whole. My professional rugby life had brought with it a lot of pressure and I'd long since reached the stage where I was failing to appreciate the good things in life and was, instead, fixating on the stresses.

For years, I'd subconsciously heaped pressure and stress on myself and then refused to deal with it. I was all about independence, about being a strong person who could cope with everything and upon whom everyone could depend.

But the downside of that attitude was that I didn't know how to open up to anyone and so I let my pressures build and my troughs get deeper.

If there was a silver lining to the black cloud which settled on me that summer, it was the possibility that the Lions disappointment really had happened for a reason – it was the catalyst that made me reach out and ask for help.

CHAPTER 23

BATTLING MY DEMONS

Rugby has been my suit of armour. It has been a release, a haven in which I've been able to get away from the pressures of life. Sport has always been there for me; it's always given me a place to express myself and that's true of hurling, football, soccer and golf. Above all of them, though, is rugby. The professional game has given me a coping mechanism for life, provided me with a set of goals, which I could identify, reach for and achieve.

The problem is, it's been a double-edged sword: It's created as many demons as it has protected me from and my life, for so long, has been ruled by match day. Before the games I am edgy and wound-up and after the games my mood is entirely dependent on whether we've won or lost. Winning leaves me on top of the world while losing often plunges me down, down, down.

To say life as a professional sportsman has been a rollercoaster is an understatement. It really has been the best of times and the worst of times and beneath it all has run an undercurrent that I should feel lucky and privileged to lead this life. And that's true: I do feel lucky and very privileged. Rugby has given me much in my life, but there has been a price to pay along the way. Being in a pressurised environment for fourteen years now as a professional rugby player has added to my own personal pressures.

When I started playing for Munster and Shannon it was a dream come true. I'd worked for years as a mechanic in Tipperary and, suddenly, I was getting paid to play the game I loved. I was so happy, I was just living the dream. But lurking at the back of my mind, even in those early days, there was a tendency to stress about the smallest things and, around the age of twenty-four, I began feeling down.

I could see no reason for feeling that way because things were going great for me – I was in the Irish squad, about to make my debut, and I was playing really well with Munster. To the outside world I was this macho, jovial guy but, inside, I just wasn't feeling good about myself. I sensed something was not quite 100 per cent right and that I needed to do something about it.

So, I went to a doctor and told him I was feeling depressed. That was a huge step for me to take, though I probably didn't explain myself very well: I probably didn't know what the hell I wanted to say.

He responded by telling me that everyone feels down and a little stressed every now and again, and that I wasn't a depressed kind of person. He didn't brush me off but, at the same time, I felt there was no real grasp or consideration of what I was saying. I went away thinking, "Okay, that's that, I just have to get on with things and deal with this myself".

And that's how things stayed for the next decade, or so, of my career until the Lions episode in 2009 exploded my world and forced me to look for help in dealing with my worries, anxieties and my depressions. Looking back on it, I don't hold any grudges – the doctor involved was a wonderful medic and a great person. Like I said, I probably didn't express myself properly and, back then, feeling down or blue probably wasn't on anyone's radar – at least not for a professional rugby player who was living his dream.

But the reality of the situation was that, after that first attempt at seeking help, another decade passed before I broached the subject again. I wish I'd been taken more seriously. I do think that my rugby career, my life, could have been different if I had been taken more seriously back then.

• • • • • • •

I haven't had an unhappy life – in fact it's been wonderful. But I get down and stressed, finding it hard to relax as things crowd in on top of me.

The mental side of my life, and my control of it, is poor. I have good days and bad days in which I go from highs to lows, not just with rugby but with everything. It's not as though I sit there depressed for days on end – maybe it's just some mornings and evenings, or maybe a day, where I get overwhelmed.

I've developed a lot of bad habits over the years, stressing myself out, putting myself under too much pressure. I'm a hyper-stressed type of person – unbelievably well disciplined in some areas of my life, but highly-strung and wild in others.

I'm late for stuff and I'm always running and racing, always stressing. Wherever I am, or whatever I'm doing is never enough for me. I always want to be somewhere else and I'm always thinking about tomorrow or the day after, or next week – what I have to do, what jobs I have on.

That's had a massive impact on me over the years. At times, I've stopped enjoying myself, stopped living life with the enthusiasm that I should have been injecting into it. I don't want to do that any more, I don't want to be that kind of person any more. I'm at the stage now where I'm trying to find myself, get to know myself, understand myself but, for years, I was a very closed person.

That's something that people, my friends and my family, wouldn't recognise about me. People look at me as this strong, gregarious guy with a great will to achieve things and to do well. That's true, up to a point – I do have that will to win, a desire mixed with the discipline required to achieve it – but there's another side to me, a much softer side that's become more pronounced the older I've grown.

It's a dimension of me that I haven't been able to be open about, that has stopped me being vunerable with other people. Instead, I denied I had any issues, and I persuaded myself I could handle everything on my own.

Not all of the anxiety I feel is rooted in professional sport. I've always felt that other pressures were at work within me, since I was a youngster. I've always felt that I tried to grow up much too quickly, though it was no-one's fault but my own.

I had an idyllic childhood with loving parents who were great to me and who worked hard all their lives to do their best for their kids. But there was something in me from the age of twelve or thirteen years old, whereby I put myself under a lot of pressure to go out and start working. I made a conscious decision at that age that I wanted to carve out my own path. I was always worrying about the future: "How am I going to get through school? What am I going to do when I finish school? What job am I going to get? How am I going to get a house? And where am I going to live? How will I get a future for myself?"

At that age, I should have been worrying about my classwork, but this constant obsession about what the future held for me stopped me concentrating on those things. If I'd spoken to my Mum and Dad they would have told me not to worry about that sort of thing so early in life, but I didn't want to open up to anyone, I felt I could deal with it all myself. In the end, I wound up putting myself under pressure during my teenage years by working my way through my holiday time, until I left school at sixteen and immersed myself in full-time employment.

I don't know why I did that and, looking back now, that was a huge mistake. I treated growing up like a job instead of letting it happen and just enjoying it. It's not as though I was doing something unique – lots of people started working at a young age. Many of them will wonder what the hell I'm talking about – people like my father who was running his own farm as a youngster – but it has affected me through the years. I'm very nostalgic about going home and I crave my childhood years. For as long as I can remember, I've been like that.

●●●●●●●

When people talk about me, they often point to my indiscipline and speak of how 'the red mist would descend' on me during a match, at which point I would do something overly aggressive and stupid and get sin-binned or give away a penalty. But that's wrong, I never felt as though a mist suddenly descended on me. My mind was clouded – that's the best way I have of describing it – and when my mind clouded over, it would, sometimes, be followed by irrational behaviour. It's a part of my game that's always been there. I'm very, very competitive – I want to win every game I play – and I'm also very confrontational on the pitch because I'm at the coalface of the game, on the edge and close to the ball.

In most ways I'm a very controlled person. I don't get into trouble away from the game and I don't fight in nightclubs or pubs or brawl and argue with people away from the pitch. I couldn't have played professional rugby for thirteen or fourteen years if I was out of control or completely lacking discipline on and off the field.

But it's always been a battle to try and keep myself on the straight and narrow, to contain my emotions. Those moments on the pitch when my mind clouded over and led me to do something stupid usually resulted in anger first of all but, soon enough, the anger would dissipate and I'd be left with a darker void inside, feeling only sad.

Often, before we run out onto the pitch, I say a few prayers that, after the game, I'll be able to come back in and sit in the dressing room and not be disappointed and frustrated with myself that I messed up. I suppose I'm being a bit of a coward, praying to God not to screw up individually, but I can't help it – it's happened to me too often for me not to worry about it. The suspension in 2009 and losing out on the Lions tour was a light bulb moment for me – an emotional trauma. I was consumed with the thought, "Why does this stuff happen to me?"

I've been hard on myself all my life, always knocking myself, never giving myself a pat on the back for the good things I've done in my life. The Lions incident was just the latest step in a downward spiral – selection for the South Africa tour had been something brilliant and meant the world to me. It was vindication, redemption for everything I'd gone through in rugby.

But what happened? What did I do with my moment of redemption? I screwed it up, I pressed the self-destruct button. Of course I did – that's typical of me and was true of not just the Lions but of rugby and life in general.

I was furious with myself and kept questioning myself over and over: "Why the hell am I doing this? I can do such good things on one hand and make such a mess of things on the other. Maybe, I'm this person who just keeps pressing the self-destruct button."

In the immediate aftermath of the suspension and the loss of the Lions opportunity I couldn't see a way to open myself up to anyone. All I knew was that bad things seemed to keep happening to me and I was just mad at myself, really mad. It brought me very low and I had suicidal thoughts. I wasn't suicidal – I would never have followed those thoughts through – but that's how I felt at the time. I was so upset, stressed out, tired and unhappy that, at times, I just wished that the pain would go away.

My parents, my friends, people reading this book will think, "I didn't know any of this – why didn't he talk to us?" Other people will look at me and question how I could ever think that way. They'll say, "But he's got everything going for him".

And they're right, on one level at least. But they don't understand that, when you haven't got control of the anxieties in your life, it's difficult to concentrate on the good things.

Back in the summer and autumn of 2009, I was in the middle of an emotional Catch 22 entirely of my own making, but that kind of self-awareness was beyond me. All I knew back then was that the Lions disappointment had brought me down to breaking point: I'd never felt so low in my life.

But the episode also triggered a deluge of self-analysis. At the same time as I reached that lowest ebb, I also reached the realisation that there was more at play here than just the heartbreak of missing out on the Lions tour, and that I needed to delve deeper.

The affair was an eye-opener and, when I finally opened my eyes, I discovered that I was at the bottom of the barrel and there was only one way to go. I thought, "I've never felt this bad in my life – it's time to start coming out of this blackness and get back up".

Somewhere, there had to be a pattern to my behaviour, something that would show how and why I've managed to press the self-destruct button on so many occasions down through the years. If I could find the pattern then maybe I could stop this kind of thing happening? I needed to learn about myself, understand myself and try to become a better person, a stronger person.

I went to the Munster team doctor, Mick Shinkwin and told him how upset I was, and that I didn't know where to turn. I knew I could trust Mick – he was the man all of us players would go to if we broke down physically during the season and I felt sure he could help me now.

He listened to me, understood and cared about what I confided in him, and helped me. When he stepped down from his position with Munster at the end of that summer, I was devastated, because I was thinking selfishly about who would help me now. Fortunately, he was replaced by a young doctor from Limerick called JP O'Donohue. I knew nothing about JP, but as soon as we spoke together I had an instant connection with him. He understood where I was coming from when I told him that, "This isn't just about the Lions, there's other stuff going on in my head. I'm feeling down – I don't know where I'm at – but, at times, I'm feeling suicidal. I'm trying to cope, but I can't. I want to go and talk to someone".

I had been on some medication, nothing much, just something to help me relax, help me sleep. But I wanted to do more than take medication, I wanted to talk to someone professional, someone who could give me real advice on how to cope with what I was feeling. I needed to talk to a psychologist but even getting to that point was difficult for me: I had to convince myself that there was no shame in taking that first step.

There would have been a time that I'd have felt ashamed to admit to having to go and see a shrink – I was aware of the stigma attached to that. But not any more, there are too many men in this country who are afraid to talk about their problems, afraid to go and speak to someone who might be able to help them. There's no shame in talking to someone who might be able to tell you what's going on in your own head.

I sought out the former All Blacks winger, John Kirwan, during one of our trips to Treviso. John is the current Japan coach but, as a former Italy coach, he still lives in Italy and I knew he would be at the game so I made a point of seeking him out, just to have a chat.

His battles with depression are well documented and he's never been afraid to talk about how much he has suffered because of it. I wanted to talk to someone who I knew had gone through it all as a player, someone who knew how I felt. John was very decent to me, he told me there was no shame in opening up which gave me the confidence to see someone.

I finally went for my first meeting with the psychologist in late September and had around six sessions before Christmas. It was a revelation – it didn't feel like counselling at all. I'd been nervous about speaking to a stranger but the psychologist turned out to be very warm and kind, and made me feel relaxed and comfortable. For the hour I was there, we chatted, and he helped me put things clearly in my mind, he made me understand that things weren't going to change in a day.

I opened up to him and told him I just wanted to enjoy my life, be a better person, a more honest person. For the first time in my life I was opening up to someone, talking about my inner-self and about how I was feeling. It was wonderful to be able to talk to a professional like that, someone with no agenda, someone who just listened and gave their professional opinion.

I found that, when you stand back and look at the issue of mental health with some perspective, you come to the realisation that dealing with it is fairly straightforward – or at least it should be.

After all, if you've got a physical problem, a broken finger or a cut, then you go and get it fixed. It should be the same if you've got a mental health problem; there should be no stigma about getting help to fix your problem, no shame attached. It's simply about talking to someone, trying to get to know yourself and understanding where you're at.

• • • • • • •

At the same time as working privately with the psychologist I was also working closely with Munster's sports psychologist Gerry Hussey. The Leinster game had taught me that there's no guarantee that things won't go wrong, so you have to try and work the percentages. You have to try and prepare mentally and look at the positive side of things and then you go out and play the game of rugby you want to play.

So, now, ahead of games, I work through the negative thoughts in my head with Gerry. For the last year, since the 2009 semi-final disaster and the Lions mess, he has been making me prepare properly with notes and positive affirmations. It's all about the stuff that goes through my head. It's hard for me to do but I need to control the 'control-ables' in my head and avoid thinking in negative terms.

I use Gerry's physical prompts to help me stay focused: The prompts are just little slips of paper that carry reminders of what I'm doing, what I should be doing. They literally say, 'Control the control-ables. Focus,' and tell me I can rule what's ahead if I concentrate on my job and on good discipline: Be competitive, but be positive. If the outside world or thoughts of the Leinster nightmare or just general negative thoughts crowd in around me, I take the prompts from my pocket, have a read, relax, think about what they're telling me and they help me loosen up again and feel positive.

My work with Gerry has shown me that to live life properly – which will, in turn, help me to play consistently high-class rugby – I need to be able to focus properly at the right time. He's enabled me to say: "Right, I'm not super-human but here's what I can do, here are the things that I bring to the game. These are my strengths. These are my qualities. Focus on what I bring to the team."

At the end of it all, I know that I'm a good rugby player and, on my day, I can turn a game, I can win a game for Munster. But, importantly, I've learned that I can control what I do, make my tackles, make my runs, avoid the negative. I can do something about what's in front of me, but I can't do anything about what's in the past, what's behind me. I can control my work rate and my attitude, my preparation.

I wonder, sometimes, if people question my commitment because of the Lions thing. I wonder if they say to themselves, "Does he still have it or did he have the crap knocked out of him last year after the Cullen incident? Will he still be the same hard-as-nails Quinny?"

They're entitled to ask – I asked the same question of myself. In the immediate aftermath of the Lions fiasco, I spent all summer thinking about whether I had lost my appetite for the game, whether I could ever go out and compete again. How could I come back after that?

The controversy weighed heavily on me and I was aware that there were people around who viewed me as a dirty player, who ran around a rugby pitch trying to tear people's eyes out.

But, once I got onto the pitch, any doubts subsided: I found my will to win hadn't diminished, nor had my determination. That was a massive relief for me because, if I had been that way, then I would have walked away from the game. If I couldn't perform the job that Munster and my team-mates need me to do – play on the edge, be in the opposition's face, be at my most committed – then it'd be time to leave it all behind.

• • • • • • •

No doubt, people will think this is all proof that I really am a bit mad but I don't mind that so much. I've given my whole life over to professional rugby and, unless you live in that environment, it's impossible to understand the pressures that are brought to bear on you.

I've already explained that, for years, rugby was the barometer by which the rest of my life was lived. The pressures of professional rugby dictated, off the pitch, whether I'd be happy or sad while, on the pitch, they controlled whether I'd be focused or whether I'd cloud over.

But you can't live your whole life that way. The last twelve months have helped to clear the clouds from my mind and I am getting a better outlook on life. I'm beginning to understand and enjoy life more, I've begun to enjoy my rugby again. I've told myself to calm down and enjoy the game and, as a result, I've lost a lot of the stress and nervousness I used to feel. Ruth tells me to enjoy it: "Do the best you can. Just try and play with a smile."

I'm not trying to be an all-new, touchy-feely sensitive Alan Quinlan, but I'm no longer getting so wound up that I find myself getting penalised, which is a disaster for me and my team.

But that progress has its roots in all the work away from the pitch. In rugby, I've always been surrounded by great players and, in the last year, I've had the benefit of having another team of great people around me, and this time they weren't wearing red shirts.

The medical staff at Munster, the psychologists and professionals who worked with me in the world outside rugby, have all helped, as have my friends and family. And, of course, Ruth: Throughout that bleakest of periods, she was a huge help and a huge support to me, always offering me a true perspective on life and encouraging me to get back up again.

These days I'm less anxious, less afraid that lurking in the background is the self-destruct button. Opening up has been a major part of that: Talking about the darkest aspects of my life, about how I wasn't coping with every challenge in my life, has been a revelation.

I mustn't get too cocky over the progress that I've made. At times, in the last few months, I've felt myself slipping backwards as the pressures build and the darkness threatens to envelope me once more. But I continue to battle to ensure that the progress I've fought so hard to make doesn't disappear. Getting to know myself, identifying the triggers which cause my pressures and stresses and lead to depression, has been a huge step forward and I've learned to extend my hand if I need help.

I know I'm not alone. Everyone in the world has problems and issues, and lots of bad things happen to good people. But I'm trying to learn to enjoy life and appreciate it and I'm proud of the fact that I'm doing something about it.

These days, when I play golf at Dundrum House in Tipperary with two friends, Willie Crowe and Joe Hayes, Willie always informs the pair of us, after watching us duke it out for a couple of hours on a golf course, that golf – and sport – is all a battle of the beautiful minds. Willie is right.

But whatever battle comes my way next week or next month, well, I'll deal with that when it happens.

April 24, 2010

Magners League

v Ospreys (Thomond Park)

Lost: 11-15

Everyone's down. Losing to the Ospreys was disappointing – we wanted a good feeling going into the upcoming Heineken Cup semi-final against Biarritz. A positive win against the Ospreys would have cemented our place in the semi-finals of the Magners League but, now, we have the complication of knowing that, a week after playing Biarritz, we will travel to Cardiff needing a win on the road.

We lost the game to a strong Ospreys team who came to Thomond Park highly motivated, who played as though their lives depended on it. They'd been knocked out of the Heineken Cup in the quarter-finals and there was a certain amount of pressure coming from within their squad – and from their owners, coaches and supporters – to try to deliver a trophy.

All they had left was the Magners League so they came highly determined, and beat us. It was a strange match. We never reached a point where we thought it was beyond us and they never looked like scoring a try against us but they had pressure on us and our discipline was poor. We gave away too many penalties. They had a lot of possession so we were making a lot of tackles. It was 6-3 at half time and we wanted to come out in the second half and try and get a score or try and knock over a few penalties to get ahead.

But the opposite happened. They got a couple of penalties to go ahead, 9-3, 12-3 and 15-3. At that stage, we were twelve points down and stalling just twenty minutes into the second half. They're a good defensive team and little errors started to creep into our game, so we had to start chasing.

When you're chasing the game then everything starts to build against you. When you're chasing the game – forcing things, trying to get tries, trying to get into the game against quality teams – it's not easy. Teams can shut up shop, defend, be patient, do the simple things well. The Ospreys did that against us.

We got a penalty to bring the score back to 15-6 and followed up with a try to bring it to 15-11, but then Ronan missed a few kicks. He held up his hands after the match, stood up and told the rest of us that he "kicked shit".

That's the measure of the guy, telling us he kicked badly and apologising to the group, but you can't blame a kicker for something like that. Certainly, if someone's discipline is brutal or they get sent off, or they do something crazy that costs the team then, maybe, you can be pissed off or angry with them, but that wasn't the case with ROG. There's a massive amount of pressure on him every time he walks out onto a pitch and, the reality is, his kicking has won games for us over the years so you can never hold him accountable for one bad night.

The reason we lost the game was because we were poor. Even if Ronan had kicked his penalties – which, in fairness, weren't easy kicks – we wouldn't have deserved to win. We lost because we were poor in many areas: Our scrum was poor, our lineouts were poor, our maul was poor. And they're the kind of things that had been cropping up all season which, in previous years, were strengths of ours. All season, teams have been targeting us in those weak spots. It's been bloody frustrating.

• • • • • • •

Going into the Ospreys game, I took a look around the dressing room and around the pitch at the players, all of us. You have to question everything. Whether individuals are letting the side down, whether I'm letting the side down, whether everybody is giving their best but our best just isn't good enough any more?

As you look around the team, as you look around the dressing room, you wonder, Is everyone here still 100 per cent up for it, 200 per cent up for it? I ask these questions of myself. About my desire and hunger. We've been there so often that we tend to take it for granted a bit now – I don't mean we take winning for granted, I mean we take our desire and hunger for granted – we think those things will just come naturally to us.

But, this season, that hasn't been the case. This season our hunger and desire weren't up to the level required. In previous years you might have got away with that but not now that the competition has become so strong. We certainly haven't been as focused for games as we should have been – and I include myself in that.

The coaches are probably the same. We all need to look back at the season and dissect it to try to figure out what went wrong, collectively and individually. I believe that's the only way we'll intensify that desire, that hunger to win.

•••••••

After the Ospreys game, we just try to bin the result. We take heart from the experience of the previous few weeks when we had lost in the Magners just a week before playing and beating Northampton in the Heineken Cup. The lads talk about that saying, "Look, it's not good but let's just concentrate on what's in our control and that's Biarritz". We know we have to carry the day against Biarritz and then take it through the following week and beat Cardiff but we know we've made it difficult for ourselves. On top of that Paulie, Dougie Howlett, Ian Dowling and Keith Earls are all doubts.

And Paul Warwick's newborn baby is ill. His wife gave birth to Eire Jean Hickie the week of the Ospreys game and, in the week leading up to Biarritz, Paul has missed training. Everyone is aware of the situation with his baby daughter and everyone understands, wishes his family the very best.

So, we just get on with it. The coaches present their analysis and lay out how they want us to play against Biarritz and we start to prepare for the semi-final. Shaking the Ospreys loss isn't easy, though. We were very poor against them. We could have won the game and, afterwards, I just sat back and found the whole thing very disappointing. In previous years, these were the games we always won. But the whole season has been inconsistent and losing that night to the Ospreys in Thomond Park kind of sums up the way our season is going for us.

Now we know that, if we are going to do anything in the Magners, we'll have to go to Cardiff and really dig in and get a minimum of a bonus point to qualify for the League semi-finals. We are facing a game against Biarritz with an unnecessary burden.

It is time to put the Ospreys thing to bed and look forward, to concentrate on Biarritz and do some analysis of their players. The best thing about the Ospreys match is that it had been a Sunday game so we had Monday off. It's been great to have a break and spend a little bit of time with AJ, away from the game. Still, the Biarritz match is always on my mind. It's hard to get away from the fact that we have a Heineken Cup semi-final on Sunday.

•••••••

Bad news for the Biarritz match – we've now got the massive disappointment of knowing that Paul O'Connell won't be available, though at least we're lucky to have a replacement of the caliber of Mick O'Driscoll

I kind of knew this was coming as Paulie's been out for a while. Being realistic, we knew going into the Ospreys game that it was very unlikely that he was going to recover. Problem is, we don't really know for sure what the problem is with Paul. He had a groin problem and he got a cortisone injection into his groin but then seemed to pick up an infection. Paul's house is right behind mine so I spent a lot of time with him that week, and it was hugely frustrating for him not knowing the full extent of what was wrong or what was really going on.

Injuries that aren't getting any better are massively infuriating and groins can be like that. It's right in your midriff, which is an area subject to a lot of daily stress and strain. Even just walking and running are problematic with that kind of an injury, certainly for a rugby player.

With this kind of a problem it was always unlikely that Paulie would be available but it's a major blow. Everyone knows how good a player he is and what kind of leader he is, so just to be without him is going to make our job difficult. We've been inconsistent all season and what we need most of all now are leaders who will dominate the opposition. When you're getting hit on the field, and when your back is against the wall, you want a fighter, and Paul is a fighter.

We'll also be without Denis Leamy and Donnacha Ryan. They're long-term absentees so we've always known that they weren't going to be around, but this week has been a disaster in terms of injury worries putting everyone on edge. We're training without knowing what the exact team is going to be. At the beginning of a week like this, leading up to Biarritz, you want everyone available and you want to be able to name your team and work together as a team for the whole week.

●●●●●●●

This whole week is typical of our entire season. Patchy, hit and miss, frustrating. We've been trying to put our finger on the problem all year long without any success. I think we've just been inconsistent this year and performed poorly. We're still making the same kind of stupid mistakes that we were making in the early part of the season. You just can't continually repeat errors and expect to escape unpunished.

Every team we play raises their game by 10 or 15 per cent just because they're playing Munster. I suppose it's a mark of respect that no one underestimates us but it means that we don't get any easy games. There's no point in whining about it because if you want to be a great team, then you need to raise your own levels 10 or 15 per cent and beat everyone else. One of our problems this year has been disruption. The lads were away with the Lions, then they were away with Ireland and, in the meantime, we've been unlucky with injuries. Combine that with playing poorly and other teams getting better and playing harder, and that sums up our season. It's difficult to know but, perhaps, the hunger just isn't there. You can't see what's going on inside other players' heads, but maybe this year we weren't as hungry as we have been in previous years.

Everybody's wondering what's different this year, what's gone wrong? But it's not just the fans and the bloody media wondering what's up with Munster, it's us as well. Maybe, the simple truth is, we didn't want it as much and we got caught on the hop trying to address the problem mid-season. Maybe, by that stage, it was just too late to get back. I don't know. The standard we've set ourselves as a team is pretty high. Most teams would be pretty pleased to get to the knock-out stages of two major competitions and get to a semi-final. To be in the last four in the Heineken Cup in Europe is still a great achievement. For most teams reaching the semi-s would be a success, a victory in its own right, and we understand that not every season can be a smooth ride to triumph.

Still, no one in Munster can kid themselves that any of us would be happy with a semi-final appearance. Long ago, at the start of the whole adventure, we gave up the right to wallow in moral victories. We all agreed that Munster was about winning trophies. In years gone by, in the early days, we encountered disappointments but the same pressure to perform wasn't there. That's not the case any more, and hasn't been for a long time. Now, we all take ownership of the performances and the results. At this point, even before the end of the season, we're probably all – players and coaches – reflecting, and wondering which Munster team will turn up to play the Frenchmen.

Do we need a couple of new players, a couple of younger players to step up and force a few changes in the team? Probably.

CHAPTER 25

2009/2010 Season
C'EST LA VIE!

April 24, 2010
Magners League
v Ospreys (Thomond Park)
Lost: 11-15

Biarritz in the semi-final. Bloody hell.

This is going to be tough for everyone but no one else is carrying the same burden into this game as me. Twelve months ago we were heading into another Heineken Cup semi-final – against Leinster – and expectations were high.

We were a tough, talented team with two wins against Leinster already under our belt that season, and no one really thought we would lose to them. The press was calling them 'ladyboys' and, while we knew that wasn't the case, we didn't countenance them beating us. But, they outthought, outfought, outplayed and out-Munstered us. We lost the game and I lost the Lions.

Now, this week, in the build-up to the semi-final against Biarritz, it's hard not to spend every waking moment remembering the horrors of last year and sweating about this year. There's lots of negative stuff going through my head that I'm trying hard to shake off. I'm having lots of conversations with myself. Telling myself, "Now, Quinlan, don't screw this up". But, the last time I was here I came out of it really pissed off, upset, disappointed and hurt. I have to work hard to avoid the demons, even now, even after all I've been through in the year since the Lions disappointment.

But my work with Gerry Hussey over the course of the last season has been an immense help. It's enabled me to loosen up and remember that I'm playing rugby with great players and with friends. In some ways, I've enjoyed this last season. I've avoided getting injured and I've avoided on-field confrontations with refs – I've tried hard and played well in the last couple of months.

But now, the moment of truth is approaching for us all. All the planning in the world can't prepare you for a Heineken Cup semi-final in France.

Biarritz in the semi-final. Bloody hell.

• • • • • • •

Obviously Biarritz's forwards are going to be very strong and they're going to target us in the scrum, lineout and maul. We've been here before – they're very strong but we see all kinds of opportunities in the backs.

If we can get good possession to our backs, then we know that our backs pose a great threat to them, because Biarritz's set-up has defensive frailties. The Ospreys had lots of line breaks against them and we just want to build phases against them and try to move them around a bit.

But, the reality is, we have to perform up front. That's our primary focus going into the game: Get our set pieces right and we can expose them a bit if we can get good possession to our backs.

Our biggest problem is the injury list: We know what our forward line-up will be but we don't yet know our wingers or our full-back. Keith Earls has a groin injury so he hasn't trained much, while Dougie Howlett and Ian Dowling are both carrying injuries from the Northampton game – Dougie has a hamstring setback and Ian has medial ligament problems in his knee. Dougie had a fitness test before we trained on Friday but it was no good and though Ian tried to train he wasn't right, so we're down two wingers. It's a blow, but now it's down to the other lads with, Lefeimi Mafi and Denis Hurley coming in, two quality guys.

The Friday training session was held in Thomond Park and, afterwards, I spoke to ROG. The session was good and we felt sharp and pretty pleased with the way things are progressing ahead of the semi-final. ROG was excited because he reckons there are opportunities to attack Biarritz in the back line with the likes of Maffs, Earlsy and Denis Hurley.

We chatted about the injuries but ROG, rightly, believes there's no point in any of the boys playing if they're not 100 per cent, because the match is going to be on a soccer pitch in the San Sebastian heat. We need to raise the tempo of the game and try to put Biarritz on the back foot, so it's not the kind of game for anyone who's not fully fit.

We know they have a lot of threats: They have Takzidzwa Ngwenya, the African sprinter, out on the wing and he's a guy who would be at home in the Olympics. Damian Traille, their French centre, broke his hand last week so he'll be a loss to them. But, even though their influential No. 8, Harinordiquy, has broken his nose, he's still going to play.

So, we know what we're up against and the excitement is beginning to build. Training's been good and, notwithstanding the injuries to the team, everybody's beginning to remember that this is a Heineken Cup semi-final. Motivation won't be a problem. The Heineken Cup is what we built the foundation of this Munster team on, so there's always an unbelievable buzz for the competition. Still, at the back of my mind, there's something about the Biarritz game, a nervousness that I can't define – is it worry or nerves? Looking back at the rocky season we've had, I probably have every reason to feel uncertain. Nonetheless, we've had as many good days as bad and it's useful to remember the results and the performances against Northampton and Perpignan. Those results are proof that, if we get things right, we can beat anyone so let's hope we get it together on Sunday in San Sebastian.

We all met up for our last night in Ireland before flying out. The Cork players were in the Radisson hotel so, after our last session, we had the usual steak, chicken and salad dinner. Then the Limerick lads went home while the rest stayed over and chilled out before the flight.

Thank goodness we flew. A week ago it looked like we might get caught by the volcanic ash cloud from Iceland and have to go by coach, which would have been hell. When we landed in Biarritz we went straight to the stadium. I played there in 2005 against Biarritz in the quarter-finals and we lost. I have particularly bad memories of that match because I got caught for a few penalties – three or four of them – and their kicker was deadly.

This time, when I run out into that stadium, I just want to do the best I can and not get too stressed or worried about what happened in the past.

People feel we can do a job against Biarritz and you can sense the confidence building. Screw it – what's gone on this season has gone on and we're missing the players that we're missing. But we still have a team that's good enough to beat Biarritz.

The night before the game I went for a walk with ROG and Micko and talked about the game. I spoke to Micko about our set pieces having to be really focused, especially our lineout –Biarritz have a very strong lineout.

We know we have a challenge on our hands and we'll have to compete hard against them and be physical if we're to win. It's strange playing a French team in a Spanish stadium but this is all Biarritz country, and we're under no illusions about how the crowd and the atmosphere will be: Hostile.

They'll have a lot more supporters than us and they're familiar with the ground and set-up. This is going to be a big challenge for us, but we've been through this scenario before. Munster has always been blessed with an ability to produce the right core of players for days like this – players who will step up to the mark away from home.

• • • • • • •

I'm rooming with ROG the night before the game and there's always a nice bit of slagging between the two of us. We've become very close over the years. We have a good rapport with each other and chat a lot. My Mother thinks he walks on water and will happily tell everyone that getting a kiss from ROG is like being kissed by the sun.

It's funny between us. At times, if you saw us on the training pitch, you'd wonder if we were team-mates at all. We bitch and moan at each other and we have more than a few cuts off each other. All of that comes down to the competitive spirit in us. We want to be the best and we want Munster to be the best.

Lately, I've been slagging him off a lot because I think he's a bit too quiet. He's not as talkative since the kids came along and he's mad for sleeping – I have to remind him, regularly, that he's a grumpy sod. We always said Axel was the grouchy one, and that you'd have to be careful about speaking to the grouchy one of the squad. But things have changed: I keep telling ROG he's the new Axel, the new grump-meister. But he just grunts back at me in the bedroom when I'm trying to ask him questions or make conversation.

The night before Biarritz, I was a little late getting up to the room and when I walked in I expected a bit of an old chat. But grumpy drawers was already in bed and all I got was a raspy, "Eleven o'clock now, lights out". That was that.

I suppose there's a familiarity there with ROG, which has grown into the two of us getting on well. We've been together on the good days and the bad and I think we know that we just have to get on with it. I can't honestly tell you why we room together, it just happened. A few years back we were getting on well, having a good laugh together, and just asked if we could room together. That's how it started and it's just stayed that way.

The thing about Ronan is that there's a misconception amongst some in the media and the general public that he's very defensive and a bit grouchy. In truth, he's a very, very honest person and a really respectful one. He's the kind of person you can lean on or talk to if you need advice or help. And he's a straight talker. He's not a bullshitter. He doesn't flannel people and I think that may be why he's perceived by some as being a bit bad-tempered. But he just says what's on his mind and speaks the truth, I admire and respect him for that. In some ways I wish I were a bit more like that. He believes that if he has something to say then he should go ahead and say it.

You have to remember that he's constantly in the spotlight. He's at the forefront of all the teams that he's played with, one of the top guys, and, as a result, he's always in the public domain. Public property and that's a tough place to be.

ROG is always willing to dig out his teams, whether he's playing for his country or in Europe for Munster. But there's always a massive amount of attention focused on him, on his goal kicking and on his general play, because he's a big-game player and people are always looking for weaknesses and chinks in his armour.

I do know that he's a mentally strong guy and he's up for a challenge and he's been there to rescue Munster from some dire situations.

Within the Munster set-up I have a lot of great friends but, with ROG, there's a very close bond. He's a guy I ask for advice and I think he understands me, which isn't easy at times. He doesn't pull any punches with me and I value that. He challenges me and we tend to be the ones that will have it out together if there's an issue in training.

But it's just water off a duck's back. It doesn't even need apologies afterwards, we just get on with it. I need to be challenged and I need that kind of pressure on and ROG will do that for me.

In the hours before the Biarritz semi-final, before we got on the bus for the stadium, we chatted about what lay ahead. We both knew how great it would be to reach another final but we knew we had to go out and perform. We knew it was all there for the taking. We were quietly confident, but the nerves were building. The nerves are always there, the butterflies in the belly – we laugh about them. We always tell each other that we know many thousands of people would give their right hands to be in our position but, ahead of games like this, you find yourself thinking, "There must be easier ways of making a living".

The morning of the game was the normal lead-in: We had our breakfast and stayed in bed until half past ten. Tony spoke to all of us at the team meeting in the hotel and we tried to focus on the job in hand. The kick-off was four o'clock but the day went quickly and soon it was time to board the bus.

Off we went.

• • • • • • •

We had a good buzz going in the first twenty minutes. Biarritz had a lot of possession, threw it on us, but we tackled them aggressively. We didn't break our defensive line and we got a great try from Keith Earls. It had been a great break from Donnacha which led to the try and it was a massive boost to us because we'd been soaking up a bit of pressure. Suddenly, we were 7-0 up but, with ten minutes to go in the half, they got a penalty at the scrum.

I remember going down in the scrum thinking, if we can just hold them out here for this phase of play, then clear the lines, it's half-time and we're 7-0 up, that's a massive psychological boost. But, though it was our scrum, they pushed us back, won a penalty off it and took their three points. That was the type of game it was – they were just stronger than us on the day. I'm no technical expert in the front row stuff, but their targets were set and they turned us over in a couple and grew in confidence. The first two scrums worked out okay, but they felt more confident once they started to get a bit of a shove on. They were clearly dominant – you could feel their heave coming, knew you might get caught but there wasn't much you could do. I kept thinking that, if we refocus, maybe we'll be fine, maybe we just got caught once. But they kept coming and it kept getting worse and worse. It was tough, though you can't individualise the problem – we all have to take responsibility for what went on.

After the game I spoke to The Bull about it all. John was beating himself up over the scrum – he reckoned it was a disaster and he had to take ownership for that. I tried to tell him he didn't need to do that but, as well as being a close friend and someone I have huge respect for, John is a really honest guy and was really down about it all.

Of course, it wasn't just down to John, it was down to all of us. French teams put a massive emphasis on the scrum so they're very strong – on that day, Biarritz were stronger than us and we couldn't get any good ball off our scrum and lineout. They grew in confidence as the game went on and, in the end, the set pieces in San Sebastian cost us the game and a chance of being in the final. Sitting in the dressing room at half time I thought, we're 7-3 up but we should be 7-0 up.

We weren't playing well, we'd lost a few scrums, lost a few lineouts and it was hard not to think, "Hell, what would it be like if we started playing well?" We never got a chance to find out. Biarritz beat us by playing a very sensible kicking game and, once they got their noses ahead, their effort and their enthusiasm worked perfectly for them – their honesty was there.

They just kept plugging away, pinning us back with kicks and gaining in self-belief while we couldn't find a way back into it. We were trying our best but we were just flat in all aspects in the second half. In the end, the biggest disappointment of all was that we went out without a fight. That's not Munster, that's not us.

We caught some flak after the game for not walking around the field acknowledging our support. I guess that was wrong, but people should understand that we weren't trying to snub anyone or insult anyone. In years gone by, if we had lost a semi-final we would have gone round the pitch and thanked the supporters. But, after the Biarritz game, we were just sick to our stomachs. For all of us, it was just very, very difficult. I think there was a bit of shock mixed up with massive disappointment. We felt that we had let everyone down, ourselves, our friends, our families, our fans.

In previous years, getting to a semi-final was a great achievement for an Irish province and, at the end of a game, you were delighted to go and celebrate getting that far in a European competition, even if you lost.

But that day, after losing to Biarritz, we didn't see things that way. Defeat was a hammer blow. In the previous year, when we lost to Leinster, we felt that we had left a Heineken Cup behind us. Now, a year later, we felt we'd done the same thing again – left another trophy behind, and underachieved

• • • • • • •

It's difficult to sleep after a loss like that but, by the time I got home to Limerick that night, it was around two in the morning and I was disappointed and exhausted, so it didn't take me long to go over.

At around 8am, I was woken by a shower of missiles: AJ was standing up in his cot beside the bed, raining down teddy bears on my head and calling, "Dada, dada!" As tired and dejected as I was, the bombardment of Tigger, Mickey Mouse and Barney couldn't fail to put things into perspective.

I had to laugh. Life is good.

When Alan John Paul Quinlan – named for his father and his two grandads – arrived into this world just after 6pm on January 14, 2009, he was more than I ever expected. He made his mark on me almost immediately, promptly poo-ing on my arm when I picked him up for the first time! Handing him back to Ruth, I realised that this was the most important moment of my life – better than anything I'd ever achieved in my career, better than winning ten Heineken Cups.

Bringing him home that first night was an amazing feeling, to have this little bundle – this actual human being and extension of myself and Ruth – lying asleep on my chest, was incredible.

Within one day of his birth, Tony McGahan had announced to the rest of the squad at training that the Golden Child, AJ Quinlan, had arrived and I was duly given a round of applause and lots of useless advice on bringing up children. It was a nice feeling.

Ruth was a natural mother right from the start, but I had a lot to learn about looking after a new baby. At the beginning, I would change his nappy and his baby-grow as soon as he got wet. That meant I was waking him up every couple of hours to change him, which was crazy. Eventually, Ruth's mother, Rena, who stayed with us for a few weeks after the birth and was a huge help to us, advised me to let him sleep for a while and slow down on the nappy changing!

AJ is not quite two years old now and he's a great little boy. One of the great advantages of playing rugby is that my job is flexible, so there's always a day or a half-day somewhere that I can manoeuvre so I can hang out with AJ.

We've spent a lot of time together, trailing around the parks of Limerick, Tipperary and Dublin, AJ in the buggy with me pushing him along. I sometimes wonder what AJ will tell me when gets older – will he remember his old man taking him for long strolls and talking to him about life and rugby and missing out on the Lions?

Those buggy trips with AJ were some of the highlights of my life. He helped me get things into perspective, and just to see him smiling back up at me from the buggy was a tonic. In the early days I just couldn't stop staring at him and Ruth and I took him everywhere – to restaurants, to shops, on holiday to Ibiza, Portugal and Las Vegas. He's a well-travelled toddler.

He's also a kind, happy little boy, always smiling and cuddling and Ruth did an absolutely wonderful job with him, right from the beginning, getting him settled and into a routine. In return, AJ has settled both of us into a routine of his own – we've seen just about every episode of Mickey Mouse that's ever been made.

He has the benefit of a besotted extended family. Ruth's sisters, Stephanie, Karen and Gillian are, along with hubbies Mal and Peter, among his biggest fans, showering him with love and attention. Meanwhile, on the other side of the family, my sister Carol, her husband Phillip, and my brothers John and Andrew, who's married to Shona, can always be relied on to look after their nephew at a moment's notice.

Likewise, AJ has two sets of doting grandparents, John and Mary, and Paul and Rena: He's a lucky kid.

I don't have any massive aspirations for him and I won't push him into sport or into rugby. If sport becomes part of his life then, fine, but it'll be his choice. Sport has been a huge part of my life and it's given me a lot – career, friends, discipline – but everyone has to follow their own path.

Still, the way he kicks a ball about at the moment would seem to suggest he'll be a sporty person. He's not quite old enough for the hurley yet but he loves his rugby ball and his round ball so we'll have to wait and see what direction he goes in – golf might be a good option.

Undoubtedly, I'd like him to have lots of opportunities in life. I'll do the best I can for him, work hard to give him the opportunity to get a good education and not to have to rely on sport like I had to. I'll try to tell him about the mistakes I made in my life and advise about the small things I'd have done differently, given another chance.

But, whatever he does, I just want to be there for him, have him see me as someone he can always talk to. We're really close now and I want us to always be that way. I just want him to be happy, to enjoy life and to be open and honest and kind.

In March, 2009, three months after AJ was born, Ruth's sister, Gillian, and her husband, Peter Smyth, had their own son, Peter Paul. The two boys had a joint Christening in Dalkey, County Dublin before Peter's parents, Jimmy and Pamela, threw open their home and held a double celebration for the Griffins, the Smyths and the Quinlans. It was a great day.

Sadly, little Peter Paul had a genetic condition known as SMA, and he passed away the following November, aged just seven months old.

On the morning of his son's funeral, Peter Smith gave one of the most touching speeches I've ever witnessed, paying a wonderful tribute to his baby boy, which left me wondering at the tragedy he and Gillian were going through and marvelling at how they were coping with it.

During his short life, Peter and Gillian were amazing parents to Peter Paul and an inspiration to us all.

When AJ grows up, I want him to look back and remember his little cousin. They would have been great friends.

• • • • • • •

Ruth and I separated earlier this year after being married for two years and being together for six. She and AJ live in Dublin now and I travel up and down as often as I can to see them.

There's no point in saying that the separation hasn't been painful because that wouldn't be true. You can't be married to someone – be in love with someone – that long and part without hurting like hell. It's a source of regret to me that Ruth and I have split. I haven't stopped loving her and she's a major part of my life. I know it's been hard on her too. Then there's AJ. When I come home now from training, or from games, or from the shop, the house is empty.

So I am learning new things. I am learning how to adapt and, along with Ruth, I am learning how to do make the best of our new situation. We spend a lot of time together and have family days when we go out for meals and walks: I'm constantly talking on the phone with my son, listening to him try out his newest word.

• • • • • • •

Ruth and I met in 2004, just after John Hayes' wedding. Paul O'Connell, Peter Stringer and myself had been on holiday in Crete and Paulie and I came home early for The Bull's wedding. Strings stayed out there – he loves the sun and we couldn't have prised him out of his sun lounger with a crowbar.

John's wedding reception was great craic and I bumped into a friend of mine, Catherine Tiernan from O2, who invited me up to the K Club to watch the European Open. So, I travelled up with Gallimh and Johnny Lacey, intending to have a few drinks, watch the golf, enjoy ourselves and come home.

Although I'd no idea who she was at the time, Ruth was working at the event, meeting and greeting guests going in to the corporate box. As soon as I laid eyes on her, I thought she was beautiful – I kept making excuses to leave the corporate section just so I could come back in again to be met and greeted by her. But I was too shy to talk to her directly and, by the time we were in the car that evening going home, I was already cursing myself for not saying anything more to her than, "Hello … again," a couple of dozens times.

I hadn't tried to break the ice or get to know anything about her – not even her number. Fortunately, Gallimh was able to tell me that her sister, Stephanie, was going out with Ireland player, Malcolm O'Kelly.

I left it for a couple of days, but I was determined to get to know this mystery woman, and so I contacted Malcolm and Stephanie who asked Ruth, on my behalf, if I could ring her. Eventually the phone calls led to a dinner date in the Radisson hotel in Dublin and things just went from there. She was well-travelled, funny, charming, honest and really independent. That determination to succeed in life, to be her own person, was one of the things that most attracted me to her.

The travelling between her home in Dublin and mine in Limerick was a complication, but one which we were happy to put up with – I'd fallen madly in love with her, simple as that, and we went out together for four years before we married.

We tied the knot in St Michael's church in Tipperary town on June 19, 2008, in beautiful sunshine and it was one of the happiest days of my life. The wedding was celebrated by Fr James Egan and Ruth and I were surrounded by family and friends.

Ian was my best man, ably assisted by groomsmen Fergal Gallagher and Johnny Lacey – I'd already acted as best man for Ian, Johnny O'Dwyer and Fergal. Johnny Lacey still hasn't given us all a day out but we remain hopeful...

My other groomsman, Johnny O'Dwyer failed to make the day, as did Frankie Sheehan – both their wives were in labour. Johnny's wife, Sandra, later gave birth to little Aine while Frankie and his wife Norma introduced baby Callum to the world.

Like the stalwart friend he is, Johnny O'Dwyer actually made it to the wedding reception at Dundrum House in the evening, just in time to help the rest of us buy Pat Shortt a few shots of whiskey and persuade him to get up on stage and treat us all to a rendition of the 'Jumbo Breakfast Roll'. Unfortunately, Pat was a little the worse for wear and promptly forgot the words of the song, but the backing band's drummer was able to help out and Pat, professional to the very end, mimed his way through the entire thing.

●●●●●●●

When AJ arrived my life was complete. Watching Ruth for those nine months, as she carried our unborn child, was enough to make me admire women for the rest of my life: She was just so beautiful and elegant during her pregnancy.

We had our ups and downs in our marriage but what young couple doesn't? Certainly, it's difficult being married to a professional rugby player – there's a lot of travelling involved and, after games, I'd be physically drained, while winning, or losing, would have a huge impact on me.

Ruth wanted us to sit and talk, to be open and honest with each other, but I wasn't good at that stuff. I tried to make up for my shortcomings in other little, more practical, ways – I'd make Ruth breakfast or cook her dinner or put petrol in her car.

Gradually, we started to realise that something had to change in our dynamic: I grew to recognise what it is to be someone's soul mate.

But things didn't work out as we had hoped and, before the summer, we made the decision to take some time apart. Ruth moved back up to Dublin with AJ. I travel up and down a couple of times a week to spend as much time as possible with my son, and he and his mum regularly travel down to Limerick. It's not a perfect situation but Ruth and I are doing the best we can.

Looking back now, there are things that I would have liked to have done differently, there are times when I'd like to press the rewind button. I never thought I'd be one of those people whose marriages didn't work out. I never intended for that to happen, neither of us did – we started out with as much determination and optimism as any other young couple.

I know that my career with Munster is in its final years, perhaps months, and I am looking at where life takes me next. Perhaps I will move to Dublin to be closer to AJ, but I don't yet know. Who knows what the future holds for the three of us? But I am determined to be there for my son as much as I can and, at the moment, Ruth and I are concentrating on the best thing in both our lives – AJ.

He's a ray of sunshine for us both and, while tensions might surface in the future as to whether he will wear the red of Munster or the blue of Leinster, right now his mum and I are doing everything we can for him.
It is a source of regret to me that we were one of the marriages that didn't make it, but I don't regret our marriage for one second. We had wonderful times and how can I regret something that created AJ? Life doesn't always

work out the way you want it to and, if it has to be this way, then I'm content my son has the best mother in the world.

• • • • • • •

I've had my ups and downs in this game. I've been injured and I've been dropped from teams, I've been sin-binned and I've been suspended. But it has all been part of a journey and I like to think I've learned from the mistakes I've made along the way.

Who'd have thought I'd get this far? I was a wild young kid from Tipperary at the start of all this and I'm proud of how far I've come. In 2010, I was named Tipperary Man of the Year in one of finest honours I've had bestowed upon me. I've had a wonderful life and I'm very grateful to my parents, John and Mary, and my sister, Carol, and brothers John and Andrew and, of course, to Ruth and AJ. It would be a mistake to allow the turmoil to overshadow all of the positives.

There's not a lot I would change about my rugby life. Maybe – if I had the chance to go back – I'd wipe the slate clean of the Lions thing. Playing for the Lions would have been a fitting end to a journey that started all those years ago with Clanwilliam and which brought me to Shannon, Munster, Ireland and even the Barbarians. But it wasn't to be.

Still, it's hard to have regrets: The ups, the downs – they all helped to make me the player I am and maybe things happen for a reason. I've had the opportunity to play for my province and my country. I've enjoyed the support of the greatest fans in the world and I've been honoured to play with, and against, the greatest rugby players in the world.

There were many great, shared, moments – Claw's determination to enslave me while on International duty; Gallimh's unofficial press corps; my roommate ROG's failure, after a few pints, to be able to distinguish between my kit bag and the urinal – which still make me laugh out loud. So does the time when ROG blamed me for losing out on a free racehorse when we were invited by Kieran Fallon and Aidan O'Brien to Ballydoyle. ROG had convinced himself the lads were about to give him a horse – or maybe a leg of a horse – and when the offer never materialised, he was convinced that I'd somehow ruined the moment for him. I don't think he ever truly forgave me!

I played rugby for lots of reasons: I played for myself, my family, my community, for the fans. But I also played for the guys next to me, whether their jerseys were black and amber, blue, green, or red. My team-mates, past and present, made my journey extra special.

I'm not sure what the future holds. I'm thirty-six years old now and I'm on a one-year contract with the province that I have called home for almost a decade and a half. The hunger is still there and I want to achieve more – I'd like to stay here forever as a player.

But that cannot be. Like products on a supermarket shelf, professional sportsmen are a perishable commodity and my rugby best-before-date is getting closer and closer. At some point in the near future, I will sit down with Garrett Fitzgerald and Tony McGahan, to discuss when I end my career.

In the meantime, I train hard and I look after myself. I try not to drink too much, limit the cigarettes to an odd one here and there and I try to enjoy my rugby.

But it's hard to have a pint in peace these days. In one of life's true ironies, two of my mates, Johnny Lacey and Arthur Ryan, have opted to become rugby referees.

Their journey to the dark side of our sport means that, even when I walk off the pitch, I can't escape the attention of the men in black. Long after I eventually retire, I anticipate I'll still be subjected to the analysis, criticism and finger wagging that I have found to be the hallmark of this species of individual. God help me.

• • • • • • •

So, I am planning for the future – I've got the same fears and concerns that any professional sportsman has, but I'm not looking too far ahead. To do that would be to repeat the mistakes of the past, and that's not an option.

I intend to work closely with the Mental Health Association of Ireland, which has kindly asked me to become patron of their organisation. Over the course of the last decade, I've come a long way in understanding the issue of mental health and learning how important it is for people to be able to talk to someone about subjects like depression, anxiety, stress – issues I've struggled with throughout my own life.

It's a subject close to my heart, so I'd like to help bring awareness to people. The inability to open up and ask for help is a problem that is particularly prevalent amongst males in rural Ireland, where there's a stigma, almost a shame, attached to any attempt to break with the traditional, macho image.

If I can help one person to come forward, to understand that there are services just waiting to help them, then I will feel that I have played a small part in something positive.

I have other interests outside of rugby and I've been lucky enough to count some hard-working entrepreneurs among my past and present team-mates.

I'm involved in a wine importing business with Feddie Pucciariello, Paulie, ROG and Gary O'Donovan. Feddie was only in Munster for three or four years but he became a firm favourite in the dressing room and in the stands. The wine venture was his idea: His grandfather owns a vineyard in Argentina and we liked the idea of getting involved, too. Now, we import from the Languedoc region in the South of France and, while the company is still small at the moment, we have high hopes. Munster Wines is the firm's name and Thomond Reserve is the product – it's among Ireland's best and I can thoroughly recommend it for all weddings, Christenings and parties! ROG and I, along with Denis Leamy, Dougie Howlett and a few others, are also involved with Feddie in a bio-fuel business in Argentina.

In the past, I've covered rugby with RTÉ and the BBC and it's an interest I'd like to expand in the next few years. I really enjoy chatting to people about rugby and I've found the punditry a lot of fun over the last couple of years. It's strange to be on the other side of the microphone at times, but it also seems quite natural to me – maybe that's down to all those hours I spent at the Limerick Junction Racecourse as a youngster, pretending to commentate on the races.

I'm not sure about coaching, I'll finish my coaching courses but I'll need a few months away from the game to see if I have an appetite for it. In the meantime, I want to concentrate on the here and now because life can pass you by if you're not looking. When I eventually finish, I'd like to travel and look up some of my old Kiwi and Aussie friends. It'd be interesting to live life not having to worry about next week's game.

• • • • • • •

Dressing rooms can be lonely places but, on match days, they come alive with the buzz of players and back-room staff, full of the sights, sounds and smells of a team on the march.

The flags of the six counties of Munster – Tipperary, Limerick, Cork, Clare, Kerry and Waterford – hang from the ceiling. There, too, in the dressing room is the Munster banner with the stag and the three crowns representing Thomond, Desmond and Ormond. We fought for that flag and what it meant but, mostly, we fought for each other. All these years, our dressing room has been a special place.

Tonight, though, is different. Tonight I will leave this sanctuary, my studs clicking out a steady beat as I cross beneath the stand, and prepare to run out for my 202nd cap and become Munster's most-capped player ever. The players clap me, slap my back as I leave them behind. I think briefly of Axel, whose record I'm passing out tonight, and I think of the other Munster players whose names are legend, men like Gallimh and Claw. I wonder if my name will live on like theirs...

I can hear the murmur of the crowd just ahead, just a few yards away through the tunnel that leads out onto the pitch and into the centre of the home of the Brave and the Faithful, where anything is possible.

Forti et Fideli Nihil Difficile: The MacCarthy clan's motto sums up the deal between Munster players and The Red Army – we are brave and they are faithful. It's a pact that has served us all well.

But how much longer will I be on this side of the partnership? How much longer do I have as a player before I join everyone else, sitting in the stands wrapped up against the chill Autumn evenings in the west of Ireland talking, laughing and shouting about the action out on the pitch? Watching, not playing.

The thought dies away, replaced by anticipation as I enter the tunnel. My stomach tightens and the hairs on the back of my neck stand up, but there is no real need to feel nervous – these are our people, my people, and they will look after me tonight of all nights.

Their roars and their warmth embrace me as I run out onto the pitch of Thomond Park, the floodlights illuminating every blade of grass in this hallowed ground. I have had great nights here and, maybe, a few great nights still lie ahead of me. But it's strange to be out here on my own, taking the applause alone as my team-mates wait to run out behind me.

I have only a few seconds to savour this and, as I raise my hand and turn to salute the people, they rise to their feet to thank me for my years of service to Munster and to them.

But quietly, inwardly, I'm saying, Thank you.